Discard

Encyclopedia
of American
Government

Encyclopedia of American Government

Volume IV
School Law – Women in Politics
Index

Consulting Editor
Joseph M. Bessette
Claremont McKenna College

Project Editor
R. Kent Rasmussen

SALEM PRESS, INC.
PASADENA, CALIFORNIA   ENGLEWOOD CLIFFS, NEW JERSEY

Managing Editor: Christina J. Moose
Project Editor: R. Kent Rasmussen
Research Supervisor: Jeffry Jensen
Photograph Editor: Karrie Hyatt
Production Editor: Joyce I. Buchea
Bibliographical Research: Kevin J. Bochynski

Library of Congress Cataloging-in-Publication Data
Encyclopedia of American government / consulting editor Joseph M. Bessette ; project editor R. Kent Rasmussen.
  v. <1   > ; cm.
  Complete in 4 vols.
Includes bibliographical references and index.
  1. United States—Politics and government—Encyclopedias. I. Bessette, Joseph M. II. Rasmussen, R. Kent.
JK9.E52   1998
320.473'03—dc21   98-28986
ISBN 0-89356-117-7 (set)   CIP
ISBN 0-89356-121-5 (vol. 4)

First Printing

Table of Contents

School Law 637
Search and Seizure 639
Segregation 642
Separation of Powers 645
Sheriffs 648
Slavery 650
Social Security System 655
Spoils System 659
State Government 660
State Police 667
States' Rights 670
Supreme Court 672

Tariffs 680
Taxation 681
Technology and Government 685
Telecommunications Law 690
Term Limits 693
Terrorism 696
Town Meetings 701
Transportation Management 704
Treason 708
Treasury Department 710
Two-Party System 713

Urban Renewal and Housing 717

Veterans' Rights 721
Veto Power 724
Vigilantism 728
Voting Behavior 730
Voting Processes 734
Voting Rights 735

War Crimes 739
Watergate 741
Welfare 745
Wills 749
Woman Suffrage 750
Women in Politics 754

The Constitution of the United States
    of America 761
Glossary 775
Bibliography 795

List of Subjects by Category III
Index VII

Encyclopedia
of American
Government

S

School Law

Many laws and court rulings have been made to ensure equal educational opportunities for all students and to define the responsibilities of the public schools to society.

Issues relating to public education have historically been left to state governments. Some federal requirements have been set in place, yet within the boundaries of these federal guidelines, states are free to run public schools as they wish.

States have given local school boards authority over local school systems. These boards may institute policies, always in compliance with state and federal laws, which expand upon or interpret the laws for their particular needs. Individuals on these boards may not act alone, but only when meeting together officially as a board.

Compulsory Education. Compulsory education laws are basic to state governments. Laws pertaining to how early and how long children must attend school vary; however, it is recognized that states are responsible for ensuring that children receive basic skills and training in CITIZENSHIP. One of the first compulsory education laws was enacted in the early 1920's, when Oregon required all school-age children to attend public schools. After that law was successfully challenged in 1925, a compromise agreement allowed the state to require children to attend school, while leaving parents the right to make private schools an option.

In certain cases, the U.S. SUPREME COURT has granted exceptions to the compulsory-education requirement. For example, In *Wisconsin v. Yoder* (1972), Wisconsin's compulsory-education law was judged to violate Amish children's free exercise rights under the First Amendment.

Free Speech in Schools. Occasionally, the rights and responsibilities of students, parents, taxpayers, teachers, and staff clash with the rights of public schools. For example, in 1943 the Supreme Court overturned a law that required students to recite the Pledge of Allegiance and salute the flag. The Court sided with members of the Jehovah's Witnesses, who argued that the school requirement violated their religious beliefs and practices.

Students and teachers need not give up their constitutional right to free speech simply because they operate in a public school setting. In 1969 the Supreme Court ruled, in *Tinker v. Des Moines Independent Community School District* (1969), that although the schools have the right to set rules for order and student behavior, students need not "shed their constitutional rights to freedom of speech or expression at the schoolhouse gate." The case had developed when students wore black armbands to classes to protest the Vietnam War and were punished by suspension.

Discrimination and the Schools. Students in public schools are entitled to a free, appropriate, and equal education. In one case, *Plyler v. Doe* (1982), the Supreme Court required the state of Texas to educate students who were illegal immigrants, since they were subject to state laws because of their residency within the state's perimeter, legally or not.

Awareness of educational discrimination against students with disabilities began growing in the 1950's. Section 504 of the Rehabilitation Act of 1973 forbade discrimination based on disability in any program receiving federal dollars. Although public schools typically receive much more of their funding from the state and local community than from the federal government, they are subject to this regulation. All states have passed their own legislation expanding upon this general guideline for their own school systems.

In 1975 Congress passed the Education for all Handicapped Children Act, renamed the Individuals with Disabilities Education Act (IDEA) in 1990. It required that the same programs and services be made available to all students, regardless of disability. It required that students with disabilities be placed in regular classrooms with necessary supplemental services wherever possible.

Female students have also taken legal actions against public school systems to ensure that discriminatory practices are eliminated as much as possible. These actions culminated in

the passage of Title IX of the Education Amendments of 1972, which holds that any program receiving federal financial assistance cannot legally discriminate against any individual on the basis of gender. Most applications of Title IX requirements in secondary public schools have to do with ensuring that female students have an equal amount of access to appropriate sports and activities as do male students.

Other Educational Issues. Another issue in school law is the relationship between church and state. State institutions, including schools, are not to promote or restrict the exercise of any particular RELIGION. Many misunderstandings have arisen from this seemingly simple assertion, and applicable laws do differ from state to state. Students may pray in school silently and individually. In some states student-led services can be held on school grounds before or after school hours. Many states still

Once a familiar sight in public schools, school prayer is now legally restricted to private schools. (Don Franklin)

The September, 1997, meeting of the Hancock County School Board in Sneedville, Tennessee, attracted considerable public attention as board members debated the coming school year budget. (AP/Wide World Photos)

allow prayers at school functions such as graduation ceremonies.

Other laws and regulations involving public schools also vary from state to state. These address, for example, the use of corporal punishment, SEARCH AND SEIZURE matters, and how much freedom students have to express controversial views in school publications. Generally, the core issue involves the right of individual students to act as they wish, set against the need of the school institution to maintain an orderly and safe environment. The law typically sides with the school on these issues, with a view to promoting what is best for the student population as a whole.

Bibliography

Hentoff, Nat. *American Heroes: In and Out of School.* New York: Delacorte Press, 1987.

McCarthy, Martha M., Nelda H. Cambron-McCabe, and Stephen B. Thomas. *Public School Law: Teachers' and Students' Rights.* 4th ed. Boston: Allyn & Bacon, 1998.

Nolte, M. Chester. *Guide to School Law.* West Nyack, N.Y.: Parker, 1969.

Reutter, E. Edmund. *Schools and the Law.* 4th ed. Dobbs Ferry, N.Y.: Oceana Publications, 1980.

Ruffin G. Stirling

Search and Seizure

Search and seizure law provides a focal point for the collision of competing objectives within the American justice system. The Fourth Amendment requires an appropriate balance between criminal investigations and protection of people's privacy and possessions.

The power of members of POLICE agencies to search suspects and seize evidence is crucial to their ability to enforce criminal laws. However, the Fourth Amendment's prohibition on "unreasonable" searches and seizures was written to avoid granting too much power to police officials and to preserve the PRIVACY and liberty of all citizens.

The U.S. SUPREME COURT has regularly been presented with cases requiring the justices to interpret the Fourth Amendment in a way that satisfies the dual goals of protecting people's rights and simultaneously permitting police officers to conduct effective investigations. Because of their dissatisfaction with government abuses under British colonial rule, the Framers of the U.S. BILL OF RIGHTS wrote the Fourth Amendment to set explicit limits on government power to conduct searches and undertake seizures. The amendment guaranteed people security against "unreasonable searches and seizures" and required that government agents obtain warrants, justifying their need to conduct the searches, before undertaking searches.

Legal Doctrines. For most of American history, the Fourth Amendment had little impact on police searches because the Supreme Court paid little attention to such issues. Moreover, the amendment was initially applied only against federal law enforcement officials and not against state or local police. Some state judges interpreted their state constitutions to place limits on local enforcement activities, but police officers in many areas searched people and homes with impunity. Such searches were sometimes carried out for purposes of intimidation and harassment.

The Supreme Court's development and enforcement of strong search and seizure rules began with the case of *Weeks v. United States* in 1914. Here the Court invalidated federal officers' warrantless search of a home by creating the "exclusionary rule." The Court declared that if any federal searches violate the Fourth Amendment, no evidence discovered during those searches could be used against a defendant in court, even if it demonstrated a defendant's guilt. By making exclusion of evidence the remedy for improper searches and seizures, the Supreme Court effectively declared that it was more important to protect people's rights to privacy and liberty than to make sure that every criminal law was strictly enforced.

The Fourth Amendment

The right of the people to be secure in their persons, houses, papers, and effects, against unreasonable searches and seizures, shall not be violated, and no Warrants shall issue, but upon probable cause, supported by Oath or affirmation, and particularly describing the place to be searched, and the persons or things to be seized.

Incorporation of the Fourth Amendment. In 1949 the U.S. Supreme Court declared that the Fourth Amendment's protections are also applicable against state and local police, although the justices declined to apply the exclusionary rule to such officers. In 1961, however, the Court began to treat state and local police searches in the same manner as federal searches by applying the exclusionary rule to all law enforcement officers (*Mapp v. Ohio*). The Court's decision generated an outcry from local law enforcement officials, who claimed that the justices were preventing the police from catching guilty criminals.

One critic of the ruling was President Richard Nixon, who used his appointment powers to place on the Supreme Court new justices who believed that the search and seizure rules were too harsh on the police. One of his appointees, Chief Justice Warren Burger, wrote an opinion containing strident criticisms of the exclusionary rule and expressed the view that Fourth Amendment rights could be protected without excluding useful evidence found during improper searches. Eventually, the Supreme Court's composition changed to contain a majority of justices who shared Burger's view.

During the 1980's in particular, the Supreme Court issued many new decisions making it easier for law enforcement officers to conduct searches and seize evidence without obtaining proper warrants. The Court has identified a variety of situations in which po-

could be defeated if officers were always required to obtain a warrant before conducting a search.

A Difficult Balance. American search and seizure laws reflect changing decisions about the most appropriate balance between the need to investigate crimes and the Fourth Amendment's mandated goal of protecting people from governmental intrusions. During

Under Chief Justice Warren Burger (center front) the Supreme Court of the late 1960's gave law enforcement officers increased powers of search and seizure. (Harris and Ewing/Supreme Court of the United States, Office of the Curator)

lice officers can search and seize people or evidence without any warrant. Such situations include automobile searches, stopping and frisking suspicious persons on the street, searches incident to an arrest, and searches conducted in emergency circumstances. In each of these circumstances, society's need to enforce laws and preserve criminal evidence

the 1960's, when many Americans became keenly aware of the concept of constitutional rights and the existence of harsh and discriminatory law enforcement practices, the Supreme Court gave great emphasis to the protection of rights, even if it meant that some guilty offenders would go free. In the 1970's and 1980's, however, fear of crime became a growing concern for many Americans. The greater attention given to issues of law and order by the public and politicians was reflected in changes in the Supreme Court's composition and, eventually, in changes in legal doctrines affecting search and seizure. By the mid-1990's, the Supreme Court had relaxed many of the restrictions placed on police officers' search and seizure methods during the 1960's.

Although the rearrangement of priorities gave police officers a freer hand in conducting searches and using improperly obtained evidence, the changes did not represent an abandonment of the Fourth Amendment's restrictions on search and seizure. Even the justices who believed that greater emphasis should be placed on crime control still identified some circumstances in which police officers' search and seizure activities went beyond constitutional boundaries. For example, in 1993 the Court invalidated the seizure of cocaine from a man's pocket, asserting that police engaged in a warrantless stop-and-frisk search of a suspicious person on the street had erred in extending their inquiry beyond a search for a weapon.

Bibliography

Klein, Irving J. *Principles of the Law of Arrest, Search, Seizure, and Liability Issues.* South Miami, Fla.: Coral Gables, 1994.

LaFave, Wayne R. *Search and Seizure: A Treatise on the Fourth Amendment.* 3d ed. St. Paul, Minn.: West, 1996.

Whitebread, Charles, and Christopher Slobogin. *Criminal Procedure: An Analysis of Cases and Concepts.* 3d ed. Westbury, N.Y.: Foundation Press, 1993.

Wilson, Bradford. *Enforcing the Fourth Amendment: A Jurisprudential History.* New York: Garland Publishing, 1986.

Christopher E. Smith

Segregation

Segregation is the separating of people by their race, religion, gender, or social class. Though once sanctioned by social custom and law, it has come to be viewed as an unacceptable denial of civil rights and social justice.

Segregation is an enduring feature of American social history. It has been practiced against members of many different racial and ethnic groups; however, its best-known and most pervasive use was against African Americans. Before the Civil War, the segregation of African Americans was inherent in the institution of SLAVERY. The oppressive nature of the system served both to control slaves and intimidate free blacks.

After the Thirteenth Amendment ended slavery in 1865, American society was in flux. White leaders needed new ways to ensure continued segregation and white domination. Segregation was legally reinforced in the South and in some northern states through a

---

De Jure and de Facto Segregation

Racial segregation has traditionally been classified as either "de jure" or "de facto." De jure segregation, literally separation "by law," was mandated by law. Most widely practiced in southern states, de jure segregation has virtually disappeared from the United States since the CIVIL RIGHTS ACTS of the 1960's. De facto segregation, meaning literally separation "in fact," is segregation that exists naturally; however, it was often reinforced by the rule of law. De facto segregation has continued to exist throughout the United States, particularly in residential patterns. Residential segregation, whether enforced by law or not, has led to other forms of segregation, most notably in schools.

Brown v. Board of Education

On May 17, 1954, the U.S. Supreme Court handed down its landmark *Brown v. Board of Education* decision. The Court unanimously ruled that racial separation of pupils in public schools deprived members of minority groups of equal educational opportunities. The Court concluded that separate educational facilities were "inherently unequal."

Arguing this case on behalf of all African Americans was Thurgood Marshall, head of the NAACP Legal Defense and Education Fund. He sought to overturn the Supreme Court's infamous 1896 "separate but equal" ruling in *Plessy v. Ferguson.* The separate but equal doctrine had allowed states and local governments to maintain segregated facilities so long as they were considered "equal" in quality.

From its founding in 1909, the National Association for the Advancement of Colored People (NAACP) had fought against the *Plessy* decision. Instead of attacking the *Plessy* decision directly, however, the NAACP initially sought to ensure that African Americans received access to "equal" facilities, such as schools. In a series of Supreme Court cases in the 1930's and 1940's, the NAACP repeatedly demonstrated that schools for blacks were not equal to white schools in quality or resources. After numerous court victories, the civil rights organization moved to challenge the separate but equal policy directly. Five different challenges to segregated schools emerging in 1949 were eventually consolidated into the *Brown* case. The Supreme Court handed down its historic decision five years later. Separate but equal schools were out and unitary schools became the law of the land.

Actual implementation of this decision was neither immediate nor ever complete; however, the principles that it established laid the basis for dismantling all forms of legal segregation throughout the United States.

system of restrictions and prohibitions known as black codes and Jim Crow laws. These statutes mandated racial discrimination, requiring African Americans to live in separate neighborhoods, use separate public facilities, attend separate schools, eat in separate restaurants, and generally conduct their lives separately. It was not until the middle of the twentieth century that this network of de jure segregation laws came undone.

The constitutionality of legal segregation was upheld by the U.S. SUPREME COURT in its nearly unanimous *Plessy v. Ferguson* decision in 1896. The decision declared that a Louisiana law requring separate railroad cars for white and black passengers was permissible, so long as the separate facilities were "equal." The decision gave states the right to separate the races physically and established the "separate but equal" doctrine that would underlay legal segregation for more than a half century.

Brown v. Board of Education. This "separate but equal" doctrine was infrequently challenged in courts until after World War II. Only with the Supreme Court's unanimous decision in *Brown v. Board of Education* (1954) did the legal institutions of segregation begin to be dismantled. *Brown* specifically concerned public schools but spelled the beginning of the end for all forms of legally mandated segregation. Chief Justice Earl Warren reasoned that "separate educational facilities" for black Americans were "inherently unequal." Intangible inequalities of segregation denied African Americans the justice guaranteed in the equal protection clause of the Fourteenth Amendment to the U.S. Constitution.

De Facto Segregation. Despite the end of de jure, or legal, segregation, various forms of segregation remain facts of American life. De facto segregation, in which the physical separation of people is enforced by the dictates of social custom or circumstance, rather than law, has long been a feature of American civic culture. Before the Civil War, white-sponsored segregation policies regarding churches, entertainment, housing, schools, and transportation were partially defeated by successful black protests; segregated schools, however, were unanimously upheld by the Supreme Court in *Roberts v. City of Boston* (1850).

One way that northern blacks accommodated to segregation policies in the pre-Civil War period was to form their own churches, such as the African Methodist Church, founded in 1816. Largely Protestant, these churches and the "African" schools attached to them became sources for expression of black frustration with segregation. De facto segregation in the pre-Civil War South, fueled by the slave rebellions of Gabriel Prosser, Nat Turner, and Denmark Vesey, kept blacks from military service, professional and business life, public accommodations, and voting.

After the Civil War, de facto segregation continued in the North, maintained by social and spatial distance, and de jure segregation began to rule the South. Following World War I, there was a vast migration of African Americans from the rural South to the urban North; they settled primarily in black areas of large cities.

Civil Rights Legislation. After *Brown v. Board of Education*, school desegregation was resisted in many areas until the mid-1960's. Even after the passage of the sweeping CIVIL RIGHTS ACT of 1964 and the Voting Rights Act of 1965, de facto segregation, most notably by segregated residence patterns, continued. The so-called ghetto rebellions of the 1960's in Detroit, Los

Segregated seating was once commonplace in movie theaters and other public gathering places, with the least desirable seats almost always reserved for African Americans. (Library of Congress)

Angeles, and Newark focused American attention on the realities of urban segregation.

Many decades after the *Brown* decision, de facto segregation continues to be a fact of life in American schools and in the United States generally. Residential segregation may actually have increased since 1980. A 1993 study stated that 66 percent of black American children attended schools populated chiefly by minority students. The same study noted that the South, once the center of legally enforced segregation, was the region of the country with the second-largest percentage (39 percent) of black students attending predominantly white schools. The persistence of de facto segregation in American cities results from white out-migration from urban areas to suburbs.

Bibliography

Loevy, Robert D. *The Civil Rights Act of 1964: The Passage of the Law That Ended Racial Segregation.* Albany: State University of New York Press, 1997.

Peach, Ceri, Vaughan Robinson, and Susan Smith, eds. *Ethnic Segregation in Cities.* Athens: University of Georgia Press, 1981.

Rasmussen, R. Kent. *Farewell to Jim Crow: The Rise and Fall of Segregation in America.* New York: Facts on File, 1997.

Williamson, Joel, ed. *The Origins of Segregation.* Boston: D. C. Heath, 1968.

Woodward, C. Vann. *The Strange Career of Jim Crow.* 3d rev. ed. New York: Oxford University Press, 1974.

Malcolm B. Campbell

Separation of Powers

Separation of powers, or the division of the executive, legislative, and judicial functions, is manifested in presidential government in that the president is elected separately from the legislature.

Separation of powers, or the splitting of government functions into categories and institutions (the executive, legislative, and judicial), is a distinguishing characteristic of presidential governments. The people elect the president directly and separately from the legislature, unlike that which happens under the fusion of powers of a parliamentary government, in which the people elect a legislature that in turn elects the executive.

Philosophical Origins. The notion of separation of powers is associated with French political philosopher Montesquieu, who analyzed British parliamentary government in the eighteenth century—when monarchs still exercised real power. Montesquieu's observation that when legislative and executive powers are united in one person or body, "there can be no liberty," was quoted directly by James Madison, a principal Framer of the Constitution and author of the Federalist Papers.

The U.S. Constitution. The clearest exposition of the doctrine of separation of powers appears in the U.S. CONSTITUTION. Its first three articles describe the separate powers of the legislative, executive, and judicial branches of the federal government. The Framers wrote the Constitution for a representative, rather than direct, democracy. Their dislike of the British monarchy is reflected in the Constitution's measures to prevent excessive concentrations of power. At the same time the Framers wrote the Constitution to replace the Articles of Confederation, which they believed did not concentrate power enough for government to be effective. The Framers thus sought a balance—the creation of a central government that would be powerful but not too powerful. They provided it with substantial powers while including important limits.

Separation of powers has three elements. The first is division of government functions among executive, legislative, and judicial branches. The second element is the requirement that no individual hold office in more

When George Washington ignored a summons to appear before Congress, he set an important precedent for the presidency that helped to maintain the separation of powers among the branches of government. (Library of Congress)

which state legislatures rather than the people elected senators). Different election methods theoretically prevent any one political faction from taking over all three branches at the same time.

Voters directly elect members of the House of Representatives every two years but elect the president indirectly through the ELECTORAL COLLEGE. The president appoints federal judges and the Senate confirms them. The people elect senators to staggered six-year terms with no more than a third of the Senate being changed in any one election. A large and single-minded majority might elect a sympathetic majority in the House of Representatives and one of their number as president in a single presidential election year, but they would still not alter more than a third of the Senate. The fact that the Framers went to such lengths to prevent single-faction political dominance indicates that they understood the danger of simple majority rule.

Checks and Balances. As a further restraint against dictatorship, the Framers created an overlapping system of CHECKS AND BALANCES. Congress passes the laws, but the president may veto them. The VETO is in turn subject to a congressional override by a two-thirds vote in both houses. Neither house of CONGRESS can pass laws or override vetoes without the agreement of the other.

The SUPREME COURT may declare acts of Congress or the president unconstitutional. The justices, however, are appointed by the president, who in turn needs the consent of

than one branch at the same time. For example, one person cannot be a U.S. senator and a federal judge simultaneously. The third element is the intention to prevent any single group from controlling more than one branch. For this reason American voters select officials in the three federal branches differently. The methods of election were even more diverse under the original Constitution (in

the Senate to do so. The president may be removed by a process of IMPEACHMENT that requires action in both houses. The president and the executive bureaucracy administer the laws, but they can only do so with funds appropriated by Congress. There are even checks between the two legislative chambers, and their duties are not precisely identical. The Senate confirms some presidential appoint-

dent is exercising a legislative power when vetoing a bill. The president also uses the threat of a veto to persuade Congress to amend bills before passage. The president has the main executive power, but the Senate performs EXECUTIVE FUNCTIONS when it confirms or denies presidential appointments. The courts have the main judicial power, but the president acts as a judge when pardoning

President Bill Clinton delivering his state of the union address to members of both houses of Congress, the Supreme Court (left front), and his own cabinet (center front) in January, 1996. (Reuters/Mike Theiler/Archive Photos)

ments and ratifies treaties, while all revenue measures (taxes) must originate in the House. The House, the power most directly answerable to the people, controls the money.

Checks and balances keep the separation of powers from being entirely separate. Congress has the main legislative power, but the presi-

someone convicted of a federal crime. The Congress behaves as a court in cases of impeachment. The Supreme Court legislates when it interprets laws. The more checks there are, the less separation occurs.

Checks and balances create intermixing of power among the separated institutions, which diminishes the amount of separation. Still, separation of powers would not be effective without checks and balances, because the checks oblige the different branches of government to cooperate. The Framers of the Constitution also intended that the separately empowered institutions would have an interest or motivation in keeping other institutions from abusing their powers.

Separation of Powers and "Gridlock." Some people have called for abandoning the presidential system and its separation of powers because it is said to lead to gridlock. Gridlock, however, may simply be taken to mean that the American people have not fully made up their minds on an issue. Separation of powers was designed to block a narrow majority from imposing its will on others. Although it is disheartening to see important legislation stall while Congress and the president bicker, the operation of separation of powers continues to prevent simple majorities from deciding what will be the law for all.

It is the Supreme Court's power of JUDICIAL REVIEW that functions to police the boundaries between the separated powers. Other democratic systems, such as parliamentary governments, are able to operate without separation of powers or checks and balances, but it is not clear that they are superior for this reason.

Bibliography
Fisher, Louis. *Constitutional Conflicts Between Congress and the President.* 4th ed. Lawrence: University Press of Kansas, 1997.

Foley, Michael, and John E. Owens. *Congress and the Presidency: Institutional Politics in a Separated System.* New York: Manchester University Press, 1996.

Jones, Charles O. *The Presidency in a Separated System.* Washington, D.C.: Brookings Institution, 1994.

Korn, Jessica. *The Power of Separation: American Constitutionalism and the Myth of the Legislative Veto.* Princeton, N.J.: Princeton University Press, 1996.

Schroedel, Jean R. *Congress, the President, and Policymaking: A Historical Analysis.* Armonk, N.Y.: M. E. Sharpe, 1994.

Shane, Peter M., and Harold H. Bruff. *Separation of Powers Law: Cases and Materials.* Durham, N.C.: Carolina Academic Press, 1996.

Wilson, Bradford P., and Peter W. Schramm, eds. *Separation of Powers and Good Government.* Lanham, Md.: Rowman & Littlefield, 1994.

Richard L. Wilson

Sheriffs

As chief law enforcement officials in counties, sheriffs aid the criminal and civil courts by delivering writs, summoning juries, and executing judgments; maintaining county jails; and performing other duties.

The office of country sheriff orginated in England before the eleventh century Norman Conquest. After the English created their North American colonies, settlers called their first LAW ENFORCEMENT officials "constables," as they had responsibilities very similar to those of their English namesakes.

Sheriffs in America. It was not until after the AMERICAN REVOLUTION that sheriffs emerged as law enforcement agents of frontier JUSTICE in the American West. Pre-Civil War sheriffs, typically appointed to their positions, exercised wide-ranging powers. Among their many duties were collecting taxes, apprehending criminals, conducting elections, and maintaining local jails. Sheriffs often appointed deputies to assist them, especially with the apprehension of fleeing criminals. As western territories became states, sheriffs increasingly became locally elected officeholders.

By the early 1900's, many states had begun

The Origin of "Sheriff"

The office of sheriff originated in England some time before the Norman Conquest of 1066. Each shire, or county, was at that time administered by a representative of the king known as a reeve. Appointed reeves were usually barons who were allies of the king. These officials had nearly absolute power within their jurisdictions. Eventually the title "shire reeve" became "sheriff." Sheriffs collected taxes, commanded militias, delivered writs, and judged criminal and civil cases. After William the Conqueror reorganized England's government in the mid-eleventh century, the role of sheriffs was dramatically reduced. Under King Henry II in the late eleventh century, the position assumed an essentially law enforcement role. By the reign of Queen Elizabeth I in the late sixteenth century, most of the duties of the sheriff had been transferred to the newly created offices of constable and justice of the peace.

to create new law enforcement agencies that took work and duties from local sheriffs. The complexities of organized crime and other developments, including the automobile and the expanding highway system, necessitated the creation of highly trained and skilled state and federal POLICE agencies capable of meeting the challenges of modern criminal activity. Most sheriffs, generally popularly elected, did not have the training or professional qualifications to deal with the modern criminal who could move rapidly from one jurisdiction to another. Another often-heard complaint was that the sheriff in many communities was nothing more than the servant of the local elite.

Sheriff's Departments. The more than three thousand sheriff's departments operating throughout the United States are vital parts of national law enforcement. In many counties they still are responsible for local law enforcement and county jails and juvenile fa-

U.S. marshals and sheriffs responsible for law enforcement in Indian Territory (now part of Oklahoma) around 1900. (Western History Collections, University of Oklahoma Library)

cilities. Nearly a quarter of all law enforcment personnel in the United States serve in sheriff's departments. In the states that require the position by law, the duties and responsibilities of the office vary widely from state to state. In many rural and unincorporated areas of the United States, local sheriffs are often primary sources of law enforcement protection. Alaska and New Jersey are the only states that do not maintain the office of sheriff. Sheriffs are elected in all but two states.

Bibliography

Prassel, Frank R. *The Western Peace Officer: A Legacy of Law and Order.* Norman: University of Oklahoma Press, 1972.

Rosa, Joseph G. *The Gunfighter: Man or Myth?* Norman: University of Oklahoma Press, 1969.

Walker, Samuel. *The Police in America: An Introduction.* 2d ed. New York: McGraw-Hill, 1992.

Donald C. Simmons, Jr.

Slavery

From the 1840's to 1861, a principal American political issue was whether the institution of slavery should extend into the western territories. Conflict between northerners and southerners over African American slavery contributed to the outbreak of the Civil War in 1861.

Political conflict over the institution of slavery existed in the United States from the nation's beginnings to the end of the Civil War, when it was abolished. The most divisive issue in the history of American politics, it helped cause the Civil War. The North-South debate concerned not so much moral issues as it did slavery's impact on the political strength of the two sections.

In 1776 the Second Continental Congress deleted a mildly antislavery paragraph from the draft version of the DECLARATION OF INDEPENDENCE. In 1787 slavery-related issues nearly caused the breakup of the convention at which the U.S. CONSTITUTION was written. The Constitution was saved only by the Compromise of 1787, the first of several cross-sectional compromises that helped keep peace until 1861. Three-fifths of the slaves were to be counted in determining the apportionment of the House of Representatives; slave owners were allowed to cross state boundaries to recapture fugitive slaves; and Congress was prevented from interfering with the slave trade for twenty years.

Before 1800 many southerners were willing to discuss abolishing slavery because the institution then seemed to have a limited economic future. However, invention of the cotton gin in the 1790's revolutionized the southern economy by making the cultivation of cotton crops by slaves profitable. Afterward, southerner landowners refused to abandon slavery. Demand for cotton from the Industrial Revolution's expanding textile factories grew, making slavery ever more profitable.

The Missouri Compromise. Several events occurring between the 1810's and 1830's caused southerners to fear that northerners might force the federal government to injure slavery. They were alarmed by U.S. SUPREME COURT decisions that enlarged federal powers and by Congress's enactment of TARIFFS protecting northern industries at the expense of southern taxpayers. Above all, the South was alarmed by northern efforts to restrict Missouri's entry into the Union as a slave state. For their part, northerners feared that Missouri's admission as a slave state would destroy the balance between slave and free states. Some southerners threatened to secede from the Union if Missouri was not admitted. The crisis was ended by the Missouri Compromise of 1820. Its admission of Missouri as a slave state was counterbalanced by the admission of Maine as a free state.

Early colonial era slave sale advertisement. (Library of Congress)

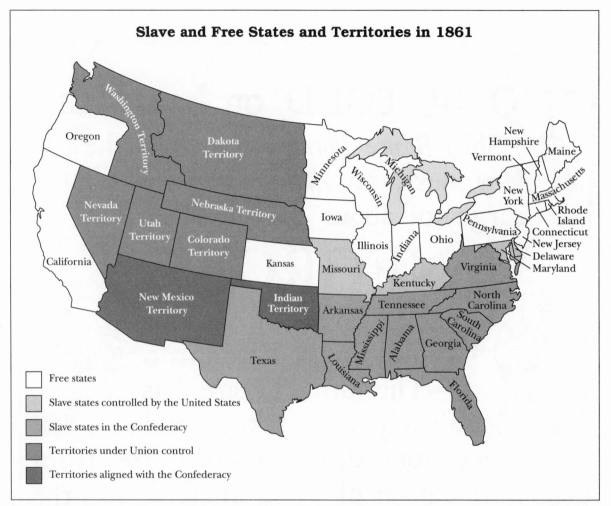

Slave and Free States and Territories in 1861

Free states

Slave states controlled by the United States

Slave states in the Confederacy

Territories under Union control

Territories aligned with the Confederacy

Source: Adapted from Eric Foner and John A. Garraty, eds., *The Reader's Companion to American History.* Boston: Houghton Mifflin, 1991.

To prevent future disputes over admitting new states, Congress established the Missouri Compromise line, which prohibited slavery north of the line. Though the immediate crisis was resolved, southerners soon began to insist that slavery was entirely a "domestic" institution subject to regulation only by state governments. Before the Civil War, most northerners conceded that slavery was primarily a local southern issue. By the 1830's, however, many northerners believed that some slavery issues could be legitimately regulated by the federal government. Encouraging this trend was the rise of the abolitionist movement during the 1830's. Centering its message on the moral wrong of slave ownership, the abolitionists supported a radical program of immediate emancipation and equal rights for AFRICAN AMERICANS.

Although only a small percentage of northerners favored abolition, antislavery agitation helped awaken northern sectionalism. Southerners tried to censor abolitionist mailings and to suppress the abolitionists' First Amendment right to petition Congress. These southern actions transformed the meaning of the slavery issue for northerners: It was no longer simply the unpopular issue of black bondage;

The Emancipation Proclamation

January 1, 1863

By the President of the United States of America

A Proclamation Whereas, on the twenty-second day of September, in the year of our Lord one thousand eight hundred and sixty-two, a proclamation was issued by the President of the United States, containing, among other things, the following, to wit:

That on the first day of January, in the year of our Lord one thousand eight hundred and sixty-three, all persons held as slaves within any State or designated part of a State, the people whereof shall then be in rebellion against the United States, shall be then, thenceforward, and forever free; and the Executive Government of the United States, including the military and naval authority thereof, will recognize and maintain the freedom of such persons, and will do no act or acts to repress such persons, or any of them, in any efforts they may make for their actual freedom.

That the Executive will, on the first day of January aforesaid, by proclamation, designate the States and parts of States, if any, in which the people thereof, respectively, shall then be in rebellion against the United States; and the fact that any State or the people thereof, shall on that day be, in good faith, represented in the Congress of the United States by members chosen thereto at elections wherein a majority of the qualified voters of such States shall have participated, shall, in the absence of strong countervailing testimony, be deemed conclusive evidence that such State, and the people thereof, are not then in rebellion against the United States.

Now, therefore, I, Abraham Lincoln, President of the United States, by virtue of the power in me vested as Commander-in-Chief, of the Army and Navy of the United States in time of actual armed rebellion against the authority and government of the United States, and as a fit and necessary war measure for suppressing said rebellion, do, on this first day of January, in the year of our Lord one thousand eight hundred and sixty-three, and in accordance with my purpose so to do, publicly proclaimed for the full period of one hundred days, from the day first above mentioned, order and designate as the States and parts of States wherein the people thereof, respectively, are this day in rebellion against the United States, the following, to wit:

Arkansas, Texas, Louisiana (except the parishes of St. Bernard, Plaquemines, Jefferson, St. John, St. Charles, St. James, Ascension, Assumption, Terrebonne, Lafourche, St. Mary, St. Martin, and Orleans, including the City of New Orleans), Mississippi, Alabama, Florida, Georgia, South Carolina, North Carolina, and Virginia (except the forty-eight counties designated as West Virginia, and also the counties of Berkeley, Accomac, Northampton, Elizabeth City, York, Princess Ann, and Norfolk, including the cities of Norfolk and Portsmouth); and which excepted parts are, for the present, left precisely as if this proclamation were not issued.

And by virtue of the power, and for the purpose aforesaid, I do order and declare that all persons held as slaves within said designated States, and parts of States, are, and henceforward shall be, free; and that the Executive government of the United States, including the military and naval authorities thereof, will recognize and maintain the freedom of said persons.

And I hereby enjoin upon the people so declared to be free to abstain from all violence, unless in necessary self-defense; and I recommend to them that, in all cases when allowed, they labor faithfully for reasonable wages.

And I further declare and make known, that such persons of suitable condition, will be received into the armed service of the United States to garrison forts, positions, stations, and other places, and to man vessels of all sorts in said service. And upon this act, sincerely believed to be an act of justice, warranted by the Constitution, upon military necessity, I invoke the considerate judgment of mankind, and the gracious favor of Almighty God.

In witness thereof, I have hereunto set my hand and caused the seal of the United States to be affixed.

Done at the City of Washington, this first day of January, in the year of our Lord one thousand eight hundred and sixty-three, and of the Independence of the United States of America the eighty-seventh.

ABRAHAM LINCOLN, By the President
WILLIAM H. SEWARD, Secretary of State

it was now also the highly popular issue of white CIVIL RIGHTS.

Political Parties and Slavery. During the 1830's-1840's, the two major political parties, the Democrats and Whigs, tried to keep the slavery issue out of national politics. Nevertheless, from the 1840's to 1861, the most significant issue in American politics was the question of whether slavery should be allowed to expand into the territories. After the Mexican-American War of 1846-1848, the most extreme northern position was that slavery should be entirely prohibited in territories that were not yet states. Many Americans supported a second position, popular sovereignty, which proposed allowing the residents of each territory to decide the fate of slavery in the territory. Some hoped to extend the Missouri Compromise line to the Pacific Ocean; this was a third position. The most extreme southern position was that no restrictions could be placed on the expansion of slavery into the territories and that the federal government should protect slavery.

Compromise of 1850. California's request for admission to the Union as a free state produced a serious crisis in 1849-1850. Southerners resisted actions by Congress to prohibit slavery in the new state, and southern militants threatened civil war. The California crisis was resolved by the Compromise of 1850. California was admitted as a free state, the popular sovereignty formula was applied to other new territories obtained during the Mexican-American War, and southerners received additional protection for their slave property through the passage of a more effective fugitive slave law.

Although small antislavery parties such as the Liberty Party and the Free Soil Party existed before 1854, most voters retained their allegiance to the Whigs and Democrats while sometimes crossing party lines to defend their sectional interests. As the slavery issue and sectionalism became paramount after 1854, a political realignment occurred in which voters joined new parties based on their sectional interests.

The Civil War. The politics of slavery and the rise of a new sectionally based party system prompted the outbreak of the Civil War and, ultimately, the abolition of slavery in the United States. Southerners, reading the results of the election of 1860, believed the American political system had become weighted against southern interests. The fact

Slaves were never content with their lot and often ran away or rebelled. This contemporary drawing illustrates Nat Turner, the leader of one of the greatest slave rebellions, being captured in South Carolina in 1831. (Library of Congress)

that Lincoln could win election with a small plurality of the vote because the Republicans controlled states that had a majority of the electoral vote suggested that the South had become a permanent minority within the United States. Fearing they could no longer protect slavery against a federal government controlled by northerners, seven southern states seceded from the Union and formed the Confederate States of America. Lincoln's efforts to enforce federal authority in the Confederate States led to the outbreak of the Civil War in April, 1861, and the secession of four more states.

Aftermath of the War. The politics of slavery continued to affect American government through the Civil War years and beyond. The withdrawal of southern states from the Union enabled the Republicans to win control of every branch of the federal government. Radicalized by the war, Republicans increasingly abandoned their earlier toleration of slavery and began to support complete abolition, a policy strongly opposed by the Democrats.

In 1863 President Lincoln issued the Emancipation Proclamation, declaring that slaves in the rebelling states were free. In 1865 slavery was abolished throughout the United States, including the defeated South, by the Thirteenth Amendment. The Civil War was followed by the period known as Reconstruction (1865-1877), in which Republicans and Democrats argued regarding which rights should be given to the former slaves.

Bibliography

Black, Daniel P. *Dismantling Black Manhood: An Historical and Literary Analysis of the Legacy of Slavery.* New York: Garland, 1997.

Cooper, William J., Jr. *The South and the Politics of Slavery, 1828-1856.* Baton Rouge: Louisiana State University Press, 1978.

Finkelman, Paul. *Slavery and the Founders: Race and Liberty in the Age of Jefferson.* Armonk, N.Y.: M. E. Sharpe, 1996.

Miller, Randall M., and John D. Smith, eds. *Dictionary of Afro-American Slavery.* Westport, Conn.: Praeger, 1997.

Wood, Betty. *The Origins of American Slavery: Freedom and Bondage in the English Colonies.* New York: Hill & Wang, 1997.

Harold D. Tallant

Social Security System

The Social Security system is a program of pensions, other transfer payments, and medical-expense subsidies for elderly, disabled, and unemployed persons, and certain low-income groups. The system taxes the wages of most American workers, provides cash benefits and medical-expense reimbursements for most Americans over sixty, and is the source of unemployment compensation and some welfare payments to low-income families.

The Great Depression which began in 1929 led to many political proposals for government subsidies to needy and unemployed persons. In 1935 the New Deal government of President Franklin D. Roosevelt created a vast system to provide pensions for the elderly, unemployment compensation for wage earners, and support for specified categories of public assistance when Congress passed the Social Security Act.

Old-Age and Disability Pensions. The Social Security Act of 1935 imposed a payroll tax, initially of 2 percent, half paid by the worker and half by the employer, in "covered" employment. A worker paying the tax could become eligible to receive a pension upon retirement at age sixty-five. Pension benefits came as a "right," earned by contributing to the system; no "means test" was imposed on the pensioners. A parallel separate program for railroad workers was created by the Railroad Retirement Act of 1937.

Because unemployment was severe in 1935,

a motive for the pension program was to encourage older workers to retire and make way for younger ones. The initial structure of the system, however, primarily involved tax collections, which began in 1937. Benefit payments were not scheduled to begin until 1940. This

paid out. The inflowing surplus was to constitute a trust fund "invested" in Treasury Department securities, and the interest paid on these would be added to the fund. Although the system imitated private insurance in many respects, not all workers paying tax would receive

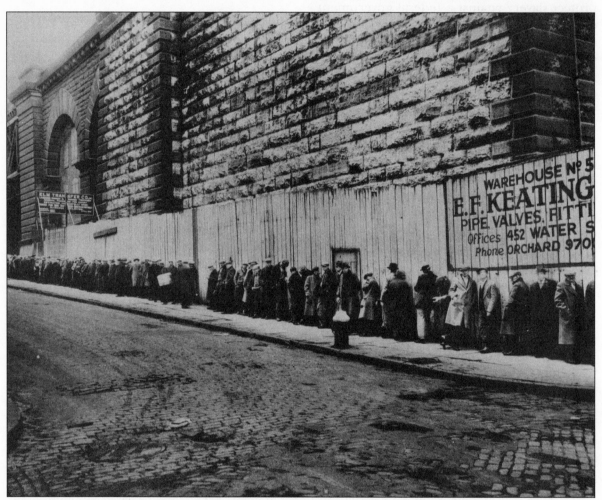

The Social Security Act was passed in 1935 in the hope it would prevent the repetition of scenes such as this breadline of out-of-work New Yorkers during the Great Depression of the 1930's. (Library of Congress)

was highly deflationary and contributed to the economic recession of 1937. As a result, the law was revised in 1939 to speed payment of benefits.

The tax and benefit levels were designed to make the system financially self-supporting and, in early years, to take in more money than was

benefits. Most were required to put in ten years of covered employment. Also, benefits were not proportional to contributions. Low-wage workers received pensions that represented a higher proportion of their former wage. Persons continuing to earn wages past age sixty-five would have their pension benefits reduced.

Raising Benefit Levels. In response to the inflation during the 1940's, Social Security benefit levels were repeatedly increased. To finance the increases, there were periodic increases in the payroll tax and in the maximum amount of wages subject to tax. By 1994 the tax was 7.65 percent on the worker and an equal amount on the employer. Initially about 60 percent of gainfully employed persons were covered, but extensions in 1950 increased coverage to about 90 percent. Persons were permitted to retire as early as age sixty-two on a reduced scale of benefits.

In 1956 Congress extended the pension program to cover persons unable to work for reason of disability. Unlike age, disability is a relatively arbitrary concept, and the program has run into problems determining whether a person is really unable to work or simply would prefer not to. The pension program is known by the acronym OASDI (Old Age, Survivors, and Disability Insurance).

Medicare. In 1965 the retirement program was given a major extension with the creation of the Medicare program to subsidize medical expenses incurred by persons receiving Social Security retirement pensions. Medicare benefits are similar to those under private medical insurance in that each beneficiary is free to go to a physician of choice for treatment. A portion of the resulting bill is paid by Social Security. One consequence of Medicare was greatly increased consumption of medical services by the elderly. The government's expenditures increased far more than had been predicted. A parallel program called Medicaid made grants to states to subsidize medical care for eligible low-income families.

Unemployment Compensation. A separate section of the Social Security Act of 1935 created a system of unemployment compensation. The individual states were encouraged to create their own systems. All states quickly developed programs. Workers who had been employed for some minimum period of time could receive unemployment benefits if they lost their jobs. Initially only about half the country's wage earners were covered, but the

This seventy-six-year-old Vermont woman was the first American to receive a Social Security check with increased benefits under a new law in 1950. The amount of her monthly check was $41.30—an increase of $18.75 a month over her previous benefits. (AP/Wide World Photos)

Average Monthly Social Security Benefits in 1990

Type of Beneficiary	Amount
Retired workers	$ 603
Retired worker and wife	1,027
Disabled workers	587
Wives and husbands	298
Children of retired workers	259
Children of deceased workers	406
Children of disabled workers	164
Widowed mothers	409
Widows and widowers, nondisabled	557
Parents	482
Special benefits	167

Source: U.S. Bureau of the Census, *Statistical Abstract of the United States: 1992*. Washington, D.C.: U.S. Government Printing Office, 1992.

coverage expanded as time passed. As with OASDI benefits, unemployment compensation was paid as a matter of right and was not subject to any means test.

Public Assistance. A third element of the Social Security Act of 1935 was a program to provide GRANTS-IN-AID to state governments to subsidize their programs of public assistance—that is, "welfare" programs paid only to persons eligible on the basis of low incomes and poverty. The law designated three categories: needy elderly persons, blind persons, and families with dependent children. Over time, the Aid to Families with Dependent Children (AFDC) program became the most controversial part of the "welfare" system. Women were often denied benefits if there was an able-bodied male in the household, and critics charged that the program encouraged marital breakups and child-bearing by unmarried women. By the 1990's the number of children in poverty had risen rapidly, many of them born to young women without the financial, educational, emotional, or physiological resources to care for them. AFDC was a major target of proposals for WELFARE reform. In

1994 about 4.6 million adults received AFDC payments, reflecting about 9 million children.

The public-assistance elements of Social Security underwent a major revision in 1972, when a transfer benefit called Supplemental Security Income (SSI) was created. Benefits are conditional on financial need, and the program absorbed persons receiving benefits in the previous elderly and blind categories. Persons with disabilities were also eligible. By the mid-1990's individuals were eligible for SSI only if they owned assets worth $2,000 or less ($3,000 for a couple), not counting their homes, automobiles, and certain other personal property. Maximum possible benefits were $458 for individuals and $687 for couples.

In the early 1990's, efforts to reduce the federal government's deficit focused attention on Medicare. Numerous proposals were advanced for health-care reform, with the aim of holding medical costs in check and slowing the rapid rise in federal spending. Other elements in Social Security were also under scrutiny as some projections showed the OASDI system losing its self-supporting character early in the twenty-first century.

One important economic benefit of the system has been the provision of a kind of fiscal "automatic stabilizer" for the economy. During a business recession, revenues from the wage taxes tend to decline, while unemployment benefits and retirement claims increase. Benefit payments raise people's disposable incomes and enable them to spend more, thus reducing the severity of the recession. Economic recovery reverses these tendencies.

Bibliography

Axinn, June, and Herman Levin. *Social Welfare: A History of the American Response to Need*. 3d ed. New York: Longman, 1992.

Carter, Marshall N., and William G. Shipman. *Promises to Keep: Saving Social Security's Dream*. Washington, D.C.: Regnery, 1996.

Kingson, Eric R., and James H. Schulz, eds. *Social Security in the Twenty-first Century.* New York: Oxford University Press, 1997.

Stephenson, Kevin, ed. *Social Security: Time for a Change.* Greenwich, Conn.: JAI Press, 1995.

Tynes, Sheryl R. *Turning Points in Social Security: From "Cruel Hoax" to "Sacred Entitlement."* Stanford, Calif.: Stanford University Press, 1996.

Paul B. Trescott

Spoils System

A spoils system is one in which victorious political candidates use their lawful powers of appointment to reward loyal political supporters with government offices.

The debate over the power of appointment and public policy has led to the establishment of a CIVIL SERVICE system that is designed to add continuity to public administration without impairing the abilities of new political leaders to carry out their policies

The constitutional basis of appointment appears in Article 2, section 2 of the U.S. CONSTITUTION, which authorizes the president of the United States to appoint diplomatic officers, Supreme Court justices, and other government officers. For presidents, or other executive leaders, to carry out their ideas and policies, they must have loyal associates who agree with their objectives and seek to implement their plans.

History. The election of Thomas Jefferson to the presidency in 1800 marked the first change of political parties. He made many changes when he came to office. President Andrew Jackson also did so some years later, and he was accused of instituting a "spoils system." During his first year in office he removed 919 out of 10,000 government employ-ees, and during the eight years he was in office he changed about 20 percent of government office holders.

Jackson was consistent to the ideas he believed in, however; the central idea of Jacksonian democracy was belief in self-government, in the broad sense of individuals and families governing their own affairs without governmental interference. Government, they believed, should be elected by, and respond to, the people. Jacksonians did not look to government for help, but they did fear that government could become a tyrant, or dictator. They therefore were against career bureaucrats; they wanted public officials changed with each new administration. They called this procedure "rotation in office." It was their political enemies who used the term "spoils system."

The debate continued throughout the

Andrew Jackson is credited with introducing the spoils system to American government after he became president in 1829. (Library of Congress)

The Constitution and Presidential Appointments

Article 2, section 2 of the Constitution gives the president of the United States broad powers to appoint government officials:

He shall have Power, by and with the Advice and Consent of the Senate, to make Treaties, provided two thirds of the Senators present concur; and he shall nominate, and by and with the Advice and Consent of the Senate, shall appoint Ambassadors, other public Ministers and Consuls, Judges of the supreme Court, and all other Officers of the United States, whose Appointments are not herein otherwise provided for, and which shall be established by Law: but the Congress may by Law vest the Appointment of such inferior officers, as they think proper, in the President alone, in the Courts of Law, or in the Heads of Departments.

nineteenth century until the establishment of the civil service later in the century. That system was well-known to the Progressive movement of the early twentieth century, but the federal government did not start growing to its present enormous size until the New Deal period of the 1930's. The major complaint soon was directed not toward a spoils system but to the inertia of the huge federal bureaucracy, which sometimes seems to lumber along unresponsively to either public opinion or public elections.

However, many government positions simply require clerical or administrative skills and do not establish public policy. If people holding such jobs lose their positions merely because they are members of a different political party, it is argued, the power of appointment is being abused. Opposing arguments include the points that public policy is affected by how vigorously it is enforced and that if lesser officials do not agree with policy objectives and "drag their feet," then the implementation of policy is impaired. In addition, the argument is made that people who work hard to get their political party elected to office deserve to get a reward. Further, fresh faces and new personnel can add a new dynamic to an organization.

Bibliography

Carson, Clarence B. *The Sections and the Civil War, 1826-1877.* Wadley, Ala.: American Textbook Committee, 1985.

Freedman, Anne. *Patronage: An American Tradition.* Chicago: Nelson-Hall, 1994.

Gross, Martin L. *The Political Racket: Deceit, Self-interest, and Corruption in American Politics.* New York: Ballantine Books, 1996.

Miller, Nathan. *Stealing from America: A History of Corruption from Jamestown to Reagan.* New York: Paragon House, 1992.

William H. Burnside

State Government

As semisovereign bodies within the federal system, state governments have structures similar to that of the national government and carry out many functions that affect the daily lives of Americans.

The political system of the United States of America consists of one national government and fifty state governments. Constitutions are the fundamental organizational device of state governments. They describe the structure, institutions, and processes of state governments. They also delineate powers and responsibilities, and place limits on the use of power, to protect citizens from unreasonable governmental action. No two states have identical constitutions, although a few have borrowed passages from other states in drafting their constitutions.

Historical Background. After the North American colonies declared their indepen-

New York's state capitol building in Albany is unusual in being one of the few state capitols without a dome. (AP/Wide World Photos)

Governor Steve Merrill opens the 1995 session of New Hampshire's state legislature, outlining priorities for the coming year. Similar scenes occur annually in all fifty states. (AP/Wide World Photos)

dence from Great Britain in 1776, they sought to organize their own political systems. The result was the formation of thirteen independent states, each constitutionally governed. When representatives gathered in Philadelphia some ten years later to frame a new constitution to govern all the states, they had to address the interests of the existing states, which did not want to be legislated out of existence. The solution to emerge was the creation of a federal political system that recognizes the authority of both state governments and the national government.

Federalism. The practice of FEDERALISM and the role of states in this partnership have changed over time. Four important periods can be identified. Initially, states and the na-

tional government acted independently of each other, exercising power in separate policy areas. During the nineteenth century the balance of power shifted toward the national government, giving rise to a period characterized by the increasing dominance of the national government in domestic affairs. This period gave way to a third stage in the middle part of the twentieth century, as states and the national government worked together to address complex social and economic problems. By the close of the century, however, observers noted a resurgence of the states, as the national government started shifting responsibilities back to states.

Federalism offers both federal and state governments advantages. For example, it helps decentralize decision making, as many significant policy decisions are made by state rather than national public officials. States have a far greater impact on their citizens' daily affairs than does the national government. Second, a federal approach promotes policy diversity among the states, as differences in public preferences are reflected in the actions of state governments. Finally, federalism is a mechanism for preventing the concentration of power in a single government. Much like the SEPARATION OF POWERS doctrine, federalism distributes power and therefore protects the citizenry against the abuse of governmental authority.

State Constitutions. Unlike the U.S. Constitution, which is noted for its simplicity and elegance, state constitutions are notoriously long, detailed, and frequently amended. State constitutions do share a number of common characteristics, making it possible to outline some general conclusions about the organization of state governments. Among the state constitutions, two important constitutional doctrines stand out: separation of powers, and checks and balances.

Separation of Powers. All state constitutions adhere to the principle of separation of

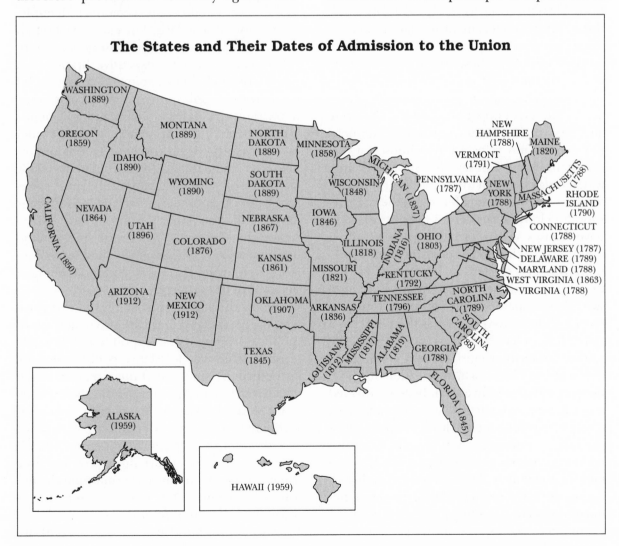

The States and Their Dates of Admission to the Union

WASHINGTON (1889)
OREGON (1859)
IDAHO (1890)
MONTANA (1889)
NORTH DAKOTA (1889)
MINNESOTA (1858)
WISCONSIN (1848)
MICHIGAN (1837)
NEW HAMPSHIRE (1788)
VERMONT (1791)
MAINE (1820)
MASSACHUSETTS (1788)
NEVADA (1864)
UTAH (1896)
WYOMING (1890)
SOUTH DAKOTA (1889)
IOWA (1846)
PENNSYLVANIA (1787)
NEW YORK (1788)
RHODE ISLAND (1790)
CALIFORNIA (1850)
COLORADO (1876)
NEBRASKA (1867)
ILLINOIS (1818)
INDIANA (1816)
OHIO (1803)
CONNECTICUT (1788)
NEW JERSEY (1787)
DELAWARE (1789)
MARYLAND (1788)
WEST VIRGINIA (1863)
VIRGINIA (1788)
KANSAS (1861)
MISSOURI (1821)
KENTUCKY (1792)
ARIZONA (1912)
NEW MEXICO (1912)
OKLAHOMA (1907)
ARKANSAS (1836)
TENNESSEE (1796)
NORTH CAROLINA (1789)
SOUTH CAROLINA (1788)
TEXAS (1845)
LOUISIANA (1812)
MISSISSIPPI (1817)
ALABAMA (1819)
GEORGIA (1788)
FLORIDA (1845)
ALASKA (1959)
HAWAII (1959)

powers, as does the U.S. Constitution. Separation of powers is a distribution of distinct governmental responsibilities among three branches of government: the legislative, the executive, and the judicial. Each branch serves a unique function, with officials selected by different procedures to ensure political independence. The centerpiece of state government is the legislative branch. State legislatures have the power to determine public policy through the enactment of laws. Fearful of tyrannical rule by a single chief executive, the states generally adopted a governmental model built around a strong elected legislature. This approach is designed to promote the interests of citizens in the lawmaking actions of government.

Legislative Branches. All states have bicameral legislatures, except Nebraska, which has a unicameral legislature. Bicameral legislatures are composed of upper chambers, called "senates" in virtually all states, and lower chambers, most commonly referred to as houses of representatives, or "houses" for short. Senates, which range between thirty and fifty members, tend to be much smaller than their corresponding lower chambers. A majority of states have houses with more than one hundred members each. Both senators and representatives are elected in legislative districts that are apportioned according to population size. State senators typically serve four-year terms, while a two-year term is the norm for a state's lower chamber. A few states restrict the number of terms a legislator may serve.

Except for Nebraska, the leadership positions in state legislative chambers are divided among political parties, with the majority group controlling the top leadership positions and the committee systems. Leaders are needed to oversee and conduct the daily affairs of a chamber. After a bill is introduced, committees are responsible for recommending or not recommending pending legislation. Committees correspond to the general func-

tional responsibilities of state government, ranging from taxation to education. It is within committees that most legislative work is undertaken. By serving on committees, legislators develop expertise in selected policy areas of state government. For a bill to become a law it usually must survive house and senate committees and then receive the support of a majority of members in both chambers. Most legislative proposals die in committee, though many states have procedures for dislodging bills.

Executive Branches. The executive branch has responsibility for ensuring that the will of the legislative branch is carried out. This is done through the enforcement and implementation of state laws. The executive branch is the administrative arm of state government. The structure of the executive branch is a hierarchical chain of command composed of numerous organizations and political leaders. How rigid the chain of command is depends on the state. Sitting at the top is a state's chief executive officer, the governor. Governors are expected to manage and coordinate the daily activities of state government. In most states governors are popularly elected for a four-year term, although some governors have a two-year term. Many states place restrictions on the number of terms a governor may serve consecutively, with the most common being a maximum of two terms.

Below the state governor on the executive chain of command there are two major sets of political leaders: those appointed by the governor (subject to legislative confirmation or approval in many instances), and those elected by voters. Appointed officials generally serve at the pleasure of the governor. Elected officials enjoy an independent source of power, voter support, making it more difficult for a governor to exert direct control over their actions. Most states have multiple elected officials, forming a pluralistic executive structure that is less hierarchical.

The number and type of elected and ap-

Like the federal government's chief executive, state governors play a central role in shaping government budgets. Here South Dakota governor Bill Janklow explains property tax trends during his 1995 budget speech to the state legislature. (AP/Wide World Photos)

pointed public officials vary considerably from one state to the next. Most but not all states have elected lieutenant governors. The lieutenant governor presides over the state senate in some states and may be empowered to vote in case of a tie. Candidates for lieutenant governor are permitted to run for office independently of the governor in several states and therefore may be a member of a different political party. Below the lieutenant governor are a number of important leadership positions corresponding to the many functional activities of government. These leadership po-

sitions represent the major administrative areas of state government, such as transportation, welfare, and health. The agencies that these leaders represent are entrusted to carry out the wishes of the legislative branch under the guidance of the governor.

Judicial Branches. The third branch of state government is the judiciary. State COURTS are responsible for the application and interpretation of laws. State courts are usually called upon to apply criminal and civil law, as enacted by the legislative branch and enforced by the executive branch, to regulate behavior and resolve conflicts. In some cases, state courts, especially the highest courts, are asked to interpret laws and evaluate the actions of government officials in terms of constitutional consistency. A state court may find an action to be inconsistent with either the state constitution or U.S. Constitution. This is the power of JUDICIAL REVIEW.

State court systems follow no single pattern. Historically, states adopted decentralized and fragmented court systems, establishing numerous lower courts, each having limited legal jurisdiction and covering a small geographical area. The result was an elaborate patchwork of courts, which persists in many states. In the twentieth century, selected states took steps to reform their court systems by creating more unified and consolidated structures.

All states employ a hierarchical court structure with most having a single court, usually called the supreme court, at the top. Below the supreme court there may be intermediate appeals courts, courts of general jurisdiction, and courts of limited jurisdiction. Cases generally flow in the opposite direction, starting in courts with limited jurisdiction and working their way up, on legal appeal, to higher courts. Lower courts are much more likely to engage in the application of law rather than the interpretation of law. In some states, depending on the type of court, judges are popularly elected for fixed terms. In others, judges are appointed for various durations. Yet other states combine the two approaches: Judges are initially appointed and then run for office in retention elections.

In virtually all states enforcement of traffic laws is the responsibility of state police outside the jurisdiction of cities. (AP/Wide World Photos)

Checks and Balances. A second constitutional doctrine influencing the organization of state government is that of checks and balances. While each branch is empowered to perform a unique function, powers are also granted to each to check or control the activities of the other branches. The legislative branch, for example, determines financial appropriations for the other two branches of government. How an entity is funded can greatly affect its performance. The executive branch exercises discretion in implementing laws and court decisions, possibly altering the original intentions of these decisions. Courts may find the activities of another branch unconstitutional and therefore invalid.

There are other checks and balances in the states, though implementation varies substantially from one state to the next. This includes such powers as legislative confirmation of judges, and executive removal of public officials. Most checks and balances are explicitly identified in state constitutions, while a few are not. The concept of a bicameral legislature, for example, is an implicit check because both chambers must work in tandem to pass legislation.

Veto power is a frequently mentioned example of a check because it offers a state governor direct control over actions of the legislature. In some states, governors can only veto entire bills. In other states, however, the governor may veto portions of bills; this is known as a line-item veto. The governor of North Carolina, on the other hand, has no veto power. Provisions to override vetoes are common. Most states require a large majority vote (either two-thirds or three-fifths) of legislators to override a governor's veto, while others call for a simple majority.

Both doctrines—separation of powers, and checks and balances—establish a governmental system in which power is overlapping and shared. This organizational arrangement is sometimes criticized for being slow and ineffi-cient. However, it prevents any one branch from completely dominating state government. This basic system, with variations, is reflected in all the states.

Bibliography

Adrian, Charles R., and Michael R. Fine. *State and Local Politics.* Chicago: Nelson-Hall, 1991.

Elazar, Daniel J. *American Federalism: A View from the States.* 3d ed. New York: Harper & Row, 1984.

Gray, Virginia, Herbert Jacob, and Robert Albritton, eds. *Politics in the American States: A Comparative Analysis.* 5th ed. Glenview, Ill.: Scott, Foresman, 1990.

Harrigan, John. *Politics and Policy in States and Communities.* 5th ed. New York: HarperCollins College Publishers, 1994.

Van Horn, Carl E., ed. *The State of the States.* 2d ed. Washington, D.C.: Congressional Quarterly Press, 1993.

William A. Taggart

State Police

Statewide police forces with jurisdiction over motor vehicle traffic laws, state police are law enforcement agencies with a growing range of criminal law responsibilities.

No two states have identical state police systems, but most have agencies with many similar functions. State highway patrol officers or "troopers" are the most visible state police, but many statewide criminal justice responsibilities fall to agents with special POLICE powers stemming from myriad laws and regulations relating to alcoholic beverages, narcotics, consumer affairs, corrections, gaming and racing, state parks and recreation, hunting and fishing, and fire investigations. In a generic sense, officers who have statewide policing authority are state police, whatever their official designation.

Background. The Texas Rangers, founded in 1835, several years before Texas gained statehood, were a territorial equivalent to a state police. They were a paramilitary force

them under its Department of Public Safety in the 1930's.

Massachusetts established its state police in 1865, primarily to control vice and bring hard-drinking Irish Catholic immigrants under control. Some became competent detectives and

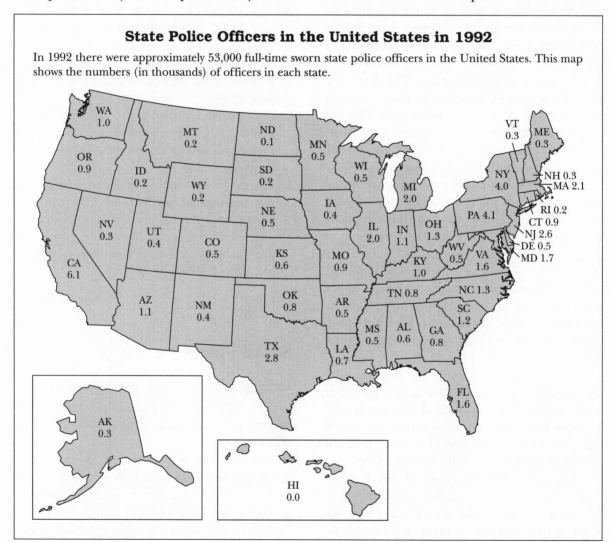

State Police Officers in the United States in 1992

In 1992 there were approximately 53,000 full-time sworn state police officers in the United States. This map shows the numbers (in thousands) of officers in each state.

Source: U.S. Bureau of the Census, *Statistical Abstract of the United States: 1997.* 117th ed. Washington, D.C.: U.S. Government Printing Office, 1997.

organized to protect settlers against Indians. Later, when Texas became a state, they were used for border patrol duties. They were a lawless lot, notorious for mistreatment of members of minorities until Texas brought

were kept on in rural communities after 1876, when Massachusetts, embarrassed by the bigotry within the force, officially disbanded the state police.

Civil unrest and crime arising from industrial expansion led to the creation of other state police. In particular, steel-mill and coal-mining areas were plagued with labor violence. In 1865 Pennsylvania's state legislature responded by creating the infamous Iron and Coal Police, who were little more than thugs used by mill and mine owners to terrorize striking workers.

By the beginning of the twentieth century, with worker unionization and a great tide of immigration, conditions had worsened. Spurred by the violent anthracite coal strike of 1902 and a federal commission's finger-pointing, Pennsylvania organized a state police modeled on the quasi-military constabularies of Ireland and the Philippines. Officers were army veterans with anti-insurrection training. By World War I, with notable impartiality, they had brought peace to the region.

Between 1908 and 1923, fourteen states created similar forces. Most were less impartial than Pennsylvania's state police, particularly in the West, where they were violently anti-union and probusiness. Their use soon declined, however, for in the economic boom era of the 1920's, new laws brought the immigration flood to a trickle and labor-organizing efforts to a standstill. State police thus needed another purpose for their continued existence.

Automobiles and Highways. The automobile provided a good purpose for state police. By 1920, it was rapidly becoming a necessity of middle-class families, not merely the toy of the rich. Once out of town and city jurisdiction, drivers were growing reckless and dangerous. Better roads also gave criminals ready access to and escape from cities and towns, making robberies a growing problem.

A few states responded by creating agencies

A Florida state highway patrolman stops a driver suspected of being an illegal immigrant. (Envision)

with authority over both traffic regulation and criminal investigation, but most limited their state police to highway patrols. Between 1920 and 1940, twenty-six states created new state police, but only ten of them had powers extending much beyond regulating traffic.

Dealing with criminals was another matter. Twenty-four states had centralized criminal-identification bureaus by 1934, but the most important advances came with new technologies such as the two-way radio and expanded telephone service, which made the coordinated pursuit of fugitives and roadblocks effective crime-fighting strategies.

The Refurbished Image. During the 1930's, state police were still being used in dubious ways—for example, to block entry into states by Dust Bowl refugees. By the eve of World War II, however, they enjoyed a much improved reputation. They had brought increased safety to the highways through patrolling and public education programs. They had also earned respect as courteous professionals, virtually free of political influence and class biases.

The postwar era at first brought few changes. There was less recruitment from the armed services but little rethinking of the structure and role of state police. In 1959 a new series of state initiatives began addressing the issue of police training. Syndicated CRIME also became a major focus because of its dramatic spread. To fight organized crime, including auto theft and drug trafficking, most states formed computer links with the National Crime Information Center, begun in 1967. Interstate cooperation was also instituted. For example, the New England State Police Compact provided for the pooling of crime-fighting resources. The Omnibus Crime Control and Safe Streets Act (1968) also helped, providing extensive federal funds for various state training and research programs and authorizing state control of coordinated anticrime planning.

Bibliography

Bechtel, H. Kenneth. *State Police in the United States: A Socio-Historical Analysis.* Westport, Conn.: Greenwood Press, 1995.

Maher, Marie Bartlett. *Trooper Down: Life and Death on the Highway Patrol.* Chapel Hill, N.C.: Algonquin Books, 1988.

Smith, Bruce. *The State Police: Organization and Administration.* Montclair, N.J.: Patterson Smith, 1969.

John W. Fiero

States' Rights

Going back to the founding of the United States, the doctrine of states' rights holds that individual states retain certain rights, liberties, and authority that the federal government cannot take from them.

The United States is governed under a system known as FEDERALISM, under which the national, or federal, and state governments share powers. Proponents of states' rights advocate giving more powers to the states and less to the federal government. The Tenth Amendment to the U.S. CONSTITUTION explicitly conceded to the states all powers that it did not specifically delegate to the federal government. The language of the amendment is clear, but it left open the question of where the federal government's constitutionally defined powers ended.

State Interposition. During the late 1790's Thomas Jefferson and James Madison both wrote resolutions declaring that when federal

---

The Tenth Amendment

The powers not delegated to the United States by the Constitution, nor prohibited by it to the States, are reserved to the States respectively, or to the people.

Fought principally over the issue of states' rights, the Civil War lifted Ulysses S. Grant from obscurity to national prominence, enabling him to be elected president after the war and to oversee postwar Reconstruction. (National Portrait Gallery, Smithsonian Institution)

federal infractions of the Constitution, the states have the right to interpose themselves as they choose.

Nullification. As the predominantly agricultural South lost control over national politics to New England and the Upper Midwest, southerners fought against northern-inspired federal legislation. In 1828 and 1829 southern spokesmen attacked federal protectionist tariffs and public lands legislation by proclaiming states' rights. Asserting the compact theory of the Constitution, the independence of the states, and the states' right to determine—free of federal judicial interference—when their liberties were infringed upon by the federal government, they deplored the "consolidation" of federal power and reiterated their right of interposition.

The idea of nullifying uncongenial federal legislation arose during the tariff controversies of 1828 and was elaborated upon in 1832 by leading political figures in South Carolina, Georgia, Mississippi, and Virginia, most notably by John C. Calhoun. Only President Andrew Jackson's threat to use federal force avoided the breakup of the Union.

Secession. The compact theory of the Constitution, interposition, and nullification all implied an independent state's right to secede to preserve its liberty and sovereignty. Such interpretations during the 1850's resulted in deepening sectional animosities, primarily over slavery issues. The election of President

government exercises powers not delegated to it, states have the right not to obey. One way states could do this was by "interposing" themselves between federal authority and their own people to check the "evil" flowing from unconstitutional federal legislation.

Southerners were not alone in holding such views. In 1815, for example, delegates from five New England states protested federal policies during the War of 1812. They asserted that when there are deliberate and dangerous

Abraham Lincoln and rise to power of the Republican Party precipitated secessionist movements during 1860. Thereafter, the sovereignty of the federal government and the indissolubility of the Union were settled on the battlefields of the Civil War.

The Union victory in the Civil War in 1865 established the superiority of the federal government over the states, but did not end all questions about the limits of states' rights. During the 1940's and 1950's the doctrine of states' rights reemerged vigorously. It represented a conservative southern protest against the growth of federal power and, of equal importance, an attempt to prevent federal authority from altering white southern resistance to the extension of full CIVIL RIGHTS to AFRICAN AMERICANS.

Dixiecrats and States' Rights. After the Civil War both state and especially federal powers expanded steadily. The range of congressional power has been vastly extended, for example, by broadened U.S. SUPREME COURT interpretations of the commerce clause and of the Fourteenth and Sixteenth Amendments. Into the 1990's, executive powers were magnified by war powers and expanded foreign policy powers, even more than were those of the Congress, leading many observers to speak of the emergence of an "imperial presidency" between the 1960's and 1980's.

General acquiescence to federal sovereignty did not quiet outcries in behalf of states' rights. Political protests, like those of the Dixiecrats, or States' Rights Party, erupted in the late 1940's and early 1950's. The resistance of some southern governors to the racial integration of public schools and extensions of civil rights affirmed deeply rooted local and sectional traditions hostile to federal policies regarding racial relations. Many other states' rights advocates reflected popular fear and disenchantment with the sheer power, pervasiveness, and cost of federal government that began with President Franklin Roosevelt's

New Deal programs (1933-1938). Characterized as "states' rights constitutionalism," such views embody apprehensions which first plagued drafters of the Constitution and are as old as the Republic.

Bibliography
Garson, Robert A. *The Democratic Party and the Politics of Sectionalism, 1941-1948.* Baton Rouge: Louisiana State University Press, 1974.
Goldwin, Robert A., ed. *A Nation of States.* Chicago: Rand McNally, 1974.

Mary E. Virginia

Supreme Court

The highest court in the federal court system, the Supreme Court interprets the Constitution, sets limits to the scope and power of the legislative and executive branches of government, and establishes policies that affect the daily lives of Americans.

The United States has a dual court system—one state, one federal. Within this system, the Supreme Court wields enormous power. Sitting at the top of the system of federal COURTS, it is the court of last resort—both for the federal courts and the state COURTS when federal questions are involved. The Supreme Court acts as the nation's conscience, determines the meaning of the Constitution, declares acts of both Congress and the president unconstitutional when they conflict with constitutional principles, and protects the rights and liberties of minorities from the tyranny of hostile majorities.

The Courts and the Constitution. Because of disagreements over how the federal courts should be organized and how much power they should have, the Framers of the U.S. CONSTITUTION left Article 3 of the Constitution, which established the judicial branch of

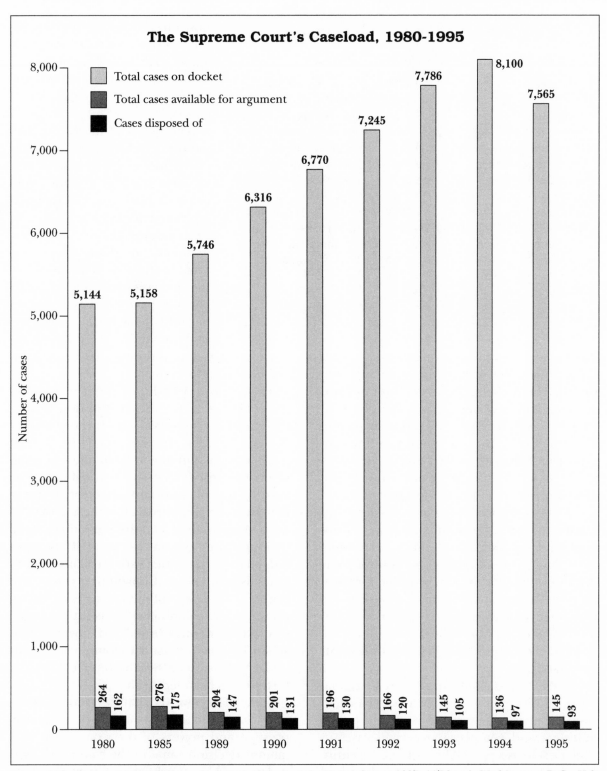

The Supreme Court's Caseload, 1980-1995

Total cases on docket
Total cases available for argument
Cases disposed of

Number of cases

Year	Total cases on docket	Total cases available for argument	Cases disposed of
1980	5,144	264	162
1985	5,158	276	175
1989	5,746	204	147
1990	6,316	201	131
1991	6,770	196	130
1992	7,245	166	120
1993	7,786	145	105
1994	8,100	136	97
1995	7,565	145	93

Source: U.S. Bureau of the Census, *Statistical Abstract of the United States: 1997.* 117th ed. Washington, D.C.: U.S. Government Printing Office, 1997.

Chief Justices of the United States

Chief Justice	Years Served	Appointed by
John Jay	1789-1795	George Washington
Oliver Ellsworth	1796-1800	George Washington
John Marshall	1801-1835	John Adams
Roger B. Taney	1836-1864	Andrew Jackson
Salmon P. Chase	1864-1873	Abraham Lincoln
Morrison R. Waite	1874-1888	Ulysses S. Grant
Melville W. Fuller	1888-1910	Grover Cleveland
Edward D. White	1910-1921	William Howard Taft
William Howard Taft	1921-1930	Warren G. Harding
Charles Evans Hughes	1930-1941	Herbert Hoover
Harlan Fiske Stone	1941-1946	Franklin D. Roosevelt
Fred M. Vinson	1946-1953	Harry S Truman
Earl Warren	1953-1969	Dwight D. Eisenhower
Warren E. Burger	1969-1986	Richard M. Nixon
William Rehnquist	1986-	Ronald Reagan

government, short and vague. The only court required by the Constitution is the Supreme Court. The establishment of lower federal courts is left to Congress, as is the power to alter the number of justices who sit on the Supreme Court. During the Court's first century of existence, it had from five to ten justices at a time. All the justices are appointed by the president, with consent of the Senate.

The Constitution's Framers also clearly intended the courts to be independent of Congress and the executive branch. To protect federal judges from retaliation for unpopular decisions, the Constitution provided for them to have lifetime appointments, as well as the guarantee that their salaries will not be reduced while they hold office. The only constitutional mechanism for their removal is IMPEACHMENT.

Article 3 also limits the Court's original jurisdiction, or authority to hear a case first, to cases involving AMBASSADORS, other public ministers and consuls, and certain cases in which a state is a party. Throughout the entire history of the Court, fewer than two hundred cases have arisen out of its original jurisdiction. Most cases that come before the Court each year are heard on appeal. The Court's appellate jurisdiction, or authority to hear cases on appeal from lower courts, is left to Congress.

The Power of the Court. The Supreme Court got off to a slow start. During its decade, it conducted little business and commanded little respect. When it convened for the first time in 1790, two justices did not bother to attend, and both resigned before the end of its first term. Later the first chief justice resigned to become envoy to Great Britain because he was not convinced that the Court would ever acquire the dignity and respect that he believed it should be afforded.

From 1790 to 1803 little happened to dispel the concerns of the first chief justice. During this period, Congress did pass the Judiciary Act of 1789, which established the federal court system, but the role of the Supreme Court was still ambiguous, particularly in regard to the all-important power of JUDICIAL REVIEW—the power to declare the acts of Congress, the president, and the legislatures of the various states unconstitutional if they are judged to be in conflict with the Constitution. On this matter, the Constitution was silent. Without the power of judicial review, the Supreme Court could never realistically be considered a coequal branch of government. When Thomas Jefferson appointed John Marshall chief justice in 1801, however, the Court's fortune was destined to change.

Judicial Review. Marshall devoted his thirty-four years as chief justice to enhancing the prestige and powers of the Court. His most famous decision came in the case of *Marbury v. Madison* (1803), when the Court, speaking through him, declared part of the Judiciary

Act unconstitutional because it conflicted with limitations placed by the Constitution on the original jurisdiction of the Supreme Court. By striking down a minor provision of a congressional law, the Court established its right of judicial review over the legislative branch of government. Subsequent cases extended the power of judicial review to presidential acts and to the actions of state legislatures.

Effects of Supreme Court Decisions. The impact of Supreme Court decisions often reaches far beyond the particulars of a given case and creates public policy as far-reaching as any produced by Congress or the president of the United States. For example, in 1954, when the Court ruled against SEGREGATION in public schools in *Brown v. Board of Education*, it signaled the end of legally created segregation of the races in the United States. The *Brown* case stands as testimony to the depth and breadth of the Court's policy-making power.

More than a half century earlier, in *Plessy v. Ferguson* (1896), the Court had upheld a Louisiana statute requiring segregation of railroad cars. In so doing the Court had reinforced the right of states to segregate the races in all forms of transportation, public accommodations, and facilities. Though the *Plessy* decision was later considered both immoral and ill conceived, the Court's decision had, for decades, made segregation constitutional.

Checks and Balances. The power of the Supreme Court does not, however, go unchecked. Since the Court has no police or army force of its own, it depends on the executive branch to enforce its decisions. Occasionally, such help is not forthcoming. A classic example was President Andrew Jackson's refusal to return land that the state of Georgia had seized from the Cherokee Nation between 1827 and 1830. Jackson defied the Court's *Cherokee Nation v. Georgia* (1831) decision because public opinion weighed heavily in his favor and against the Native Americans.

The Court's powers are also restrained by the other branches of government and the states. The fact that justices are appointed by the president with the consent of the Senate ensures the other two branches of government a major role in determining the composition of the Court and, indirectly, the character of the Court's decisions. Finally, Congress and the states can undo a Court decision interpreting the U.S. Constitution by changing that document through the amendment process.

Types of U.S. Supreme Court Opinions	
per curiam	brief and unsigned opinions
unanimous	accepted by all justices
majority	accepted by majority of justices when the Court is divided
concurring	issued by justices who agree with a ruling, but for different reasons that they wish to explain
dissenting	written by justices on the losing side

The Justices. Typical Supreme Court justices are white male Protestants from relatively well-to-do families. By the late 1990's only two AFRICAN AMERICANS (Thurgood Marshall and Clarence Thomas) and two women (Sandra Day O'Connor and Ruth Bader Ginsburg) had served on the Court.

Selection of Justices. Most justices have previous judicial experience. The criteria for selecting them are highly political. As a general rule, presidents appoint persons from their own political parties. However, once justices are appointed to the Supreme Court, predictions about their future decisions often prove extremely unreliable, as President Dwight D. Eisenhower learned after his selection of Earl

Warren as chief justice. To a large extent, Eisenhower chose Warren because of his solid conservative record as governor of California; however, as chief justice Warren led the way toward some of the most liberal decisions in the Court's history.

When vacancies on the Court occur, the president assembles names of possible nominees from a wide variety of sources, including the attorney general, members of the legal community, party leaders, and INTEREST GROUPS. The JUSTICE DEPARTMENT then helps the president screen potential nominees and subjects serious contenders to background checks by the Federal Bureau of Investigation.

After nominees are chosen, the president submits their names to the Senate Judiciary Committee. Nominations must be confirmed by majority vote of the full Senate. By custom, presidents are allowed considerable discretion in judicial appointments. By the mid-1990's the Senate had refused to confirm only 29 of 138 presidential nominees to the Court. Only 7 nominations were rejected in the twentieth century.

Chief Justices of the United States. Chief justices have relatively meager formal powers. They decide which petitions for hearings should be considered by the full Court. They also preside over the Court in oral argument and in conference and assign most of the writing of opinions.

Administration of Justice. In the late twentieth century, the caseload of the Supreme Court increased dramatically, from fewer than nine hundred cases in 1930 to more than six thousand a year in the 1990's. Of the thousands of cases that find their way to the Court's calendar

each year, fewer than two hundred are selected by the justices for consideration. For the vast majority that are denied review, the decisions of the lower courts are left standing. The method for deciding which cases warrant oral arguments and full consideration by the Court is the informal "rule of four." By tradition, when four or more justices agree that a case should be heard, the Court issues a writ of *certiorari,* or order to the lower court to prepare a record of the case and to send it up to the Supreme Court for review.

Although he was president of the United States from 1909 to 1913, William Howard Taft's main ambition was to be chief justice—a goal he achieved when fellow Republican Warren Harding appointed him to that position in 1921. (Supreme Court of the United States, Office of the Curator)

Not only are the odds against cases ever receiving full consideration by the Supreme Court, but the costs can be extremely high. Unlike litigants in most European countries, parties in the United States must pay their own way. This is referred to as the "American rule." The Court's filing fee is three hundred dollars; another one hundred dollars is added if a case is granted oral argument. While other fees may be encountered, the direct costs to a litigant are well under a thousand dollars. Nevertheless, before the case reaches the Supreme Court, the costs of bringing a case through the trial and appeal process can cost millions of dollars.

Hearing Cases. Once the Court agrees to review a case, the lawyers for each side submit a brief that summarizes the lower court's opinion, presents their arguments, and discusses past cases on which the Court has ruled that are relevant to the legal issues in question. Sometimes other written briefs, called *amicus curiae* (friend of the court) briefs, may be submitted by individuals, organizations, or government agencies that have an interest in the case. After these briefs are circulated among the justices, a date is set for the attorneys to present their oral arguments. During oral arguments, the justices often interrupt to ask questions or to request additional information. At times, the justices may even try to help attorneys if they are having a difficult time.

After hearing oral arguments, the justices meet in a conference room where no outsiders

Members of the U.S. Supreme Court in 1993; seated (from left to right): Sandra Day O'Connor, Harry Blackmun, Chief Justice William H. Rehnquist, John Paul Stevens, and Antonin Scalia; standing: Clarence Thomas, Anthony Kennedy, David Souter, and Ruth Bader Ginsburg. (AP/Wide World Photos)

are allowed. There, in complete secrecy, they debate the cases before them. The chief justice summarizes the facts and legal issues involved in each case and makes suggestions for their disposal. Then, in order of seniority, the justices present their views or conclusions. Cases are decided on the base of majority rule. In the event of a tie (when even numbers of justices are sitting), the ruling of the lower court is left standing. However, the conference vote is not binding.

Writing Opinions. After the conference vote, an opinion must be written. This is the most difficult and time-consuming task of a Supreme Court justice. Writing an opinion for

a major case can take months. Once an opinion is drafted, it is circulated among the other justices for review and comment. Frequently, an opinion has to be redrafted and recirculated several times before a majority can be reached. The goal of the author is always to achieve the largest majority possible. This frequently entails considerable political negotiating and bargaining among the justices.

Decisive majorities are important because the legal system is based upon the principle of stare decisis (let the decision stand) or precedent, which means that the principles of law established in earlier cases should be accepted as authoritative in similar cases. The greater the majority, the clearer the message.

Judicial Activism. The Supreme Court has always generated political controversy. However, the more activist role of the Court in recent times has brought the issue of judicial power to the forefront of the political debate. Supporters of judicial activism argue that the Court corrects injustices that the White House, Congress, state legislatures, and city councils fail to address, such as racial discrimination. Such corrections, they argue, are vital for a democratic society.

Critics of judicial activism advocate judicial restraint. From their perspective, no matter how desirable Court-declared rights and principles might be, when the justices depart from their appropriate roles as interpreters of the Constitution to undertake broad and sweeping policy initiatives, they become nonelected sovereigns in black robes usurping the legitimate authority of Congress and state legislatures.

Other Court observers believe that both those who support judicial

Sandra Day O'Connor and Chief Justice Warren Burger shortly before O'Connor was sworn in as the first woman justice on the Supreme Court in 1981. (AP/Wide World Photos)

activism and those who advocate judicial restraint fail to grasp the complexity of the issues that come before the Court. According to this group, the Court should take an activist role whenever legislation restricts the democratic process by which decisions are made or whenever legislation interferes with the rights of minorities. In all other instances, they contend, established political process should be allowed to work without interference from the Court. Given the power of the Court in the American political system, it is little wonder that questions over its proper role fuel one of the perennial debates of American politics.

Bibliography

Biskupic, Joan, and Elder Witt. *Guide to the U.S. Supreme Court.* 3d ed. Washington, D.C.: Congressional Quarterly, 1997.

_____. *The Supreme Court at Work.* 2d ed. Washington, D.C.: Congressional Quarterly, 1997.

Greenberg, Ellen. *The Supreme Court Explained.* New York: W. W. Norton, 1997.

Paddock, Lisa, and Paul M. Barrett. *Facts About the Supreme Court of the United States.* New York: H. W. Wilson, 1996.

Sunderland, Lane V. *Popular Government and the Supreme Court: Securing the Public Good and Private Rights.* Lawrence: University Press of Kansas, 1996.

Wilson, Bradford P., and Ken Masugi. *The Supreme Court and American Constitutionalism.* Lanham, Md.: Rowman & Littlefield, 1997.

Thomas J. Mortillaro

T

Tariffs

Government taxes on products imported from other countries, tariffs have been a major source of government revenue.

An important motivation for forming the U.S. government in 1787 was to remove tariffs on goods moving among the states. Prior to the Civil War, tariffs on foreign imports were the principal source of funding for the federal government. Only with the coming of the federal income tax since 1913 has tariff revenue lost its significance.

Reasons for Tariffs. Political pressure for high tariffs comes from industries feeling the pressure of competition from imported products. Tariffs are termed "protective" when they are used to influence buyers to spend less on imports and more on substitute domestic products. Such tariffs are defended as saving American jobs. In practice, however, they often support relatively inefficient firms. Money spent to buy imports are in turn used overseas to buy American export products, and the exporting industries are likely to be those which make more efficient use of the nation's resources. Reduced import barriers

After the Senate overwhelmingly passed legislation supporting the General Agreement on Tariffs and Trade's plan to cut tariffs in December, 1994, President Bill Clinton addressed top leaders of Congress outside the White House. (AP/Wide World Photos)

benefit consumers by keeping prices down and encouraging competition—as American automobile buyers began discovering in the 1960's. Some industries, however, believe that import competition is unjust, since the countries of origin often pay much lower wages.

Historical Changes. Historically, low tariffs were favored by farmers producing products for export, such as cotton and grain. Bitter controversies have centered on tariff policy, with the 1994 dispute over the North American Free Trade Agreement (NAFTA) being simply one example. Increases in tariff rates by the United States tend to injure the economies of the countries supplying it with imports. This situation has been known to provoke retaliation, which can make all countries worse off.

As the world economy slid into deep depression after 1929, many countries raised tariffs and other import barriers to try to stem flows of funds to other countries. The Smoot-Hawley tariff in the United States (1930) was a notorious example. In the mid-1930's, Secretary of State Cordell Hull instituted a new policy of negotiating with other countries for mutual tariff reductions. In the period after World War II, emphasis shifted to multilateral negotiations of trade concessions. These centered on the General Agreement on Tariffs and Trade (GATT), set up in 1947.

After the 1940's the general level of U.S. import tariffs declined. In 1993 about 40 percent of U.S. imports entered duty-free, and customs collections averaged only about 5 percent of dutiable imports. Other types of import restrictions, however, such as quotas, have often been used. Efforts by low-income countries to achieve economic development have been impeded by the unwillingness of the developed countries to accept more imports from the developing areas.

Bibliography

Dudley, William. *Trade: Opposing Viewpoints.* San Diego, Calif.: Greenhaven Press, 1991.

Jackson, John H. *Restructuring the GATT System.* New York: Council on Foreign Relations Press, 1990.

Lawrence, Robert Z., and Charles L. Schultze, eds. *An American Trade Strategy: Options for the 1990's.* Washington, D.C.: Brookings Institution, 1990.

Paul B. Trescott

Taxation

Acquiring funds through taxation and appropriating those funds to purposes deemed to be public priorities are fundamental powers of legislative bodies in representative governments.

Growth of government and the importance of economic activities has made taxation and the appropriation of the monies raised through taxation crucial government functions. In representative governments, this "power of the purse" generally has been restricted to elected delegates serving in legislative bodies.

Background. At the time of the AMERICAN REVOLUTION, Great Britain lacked a fully developed system of national budgeting. As a result, there was no defined structure for the Framers of the U.S. CONSTITUTION to emulate. The general welfare clause of the Constitution gives Congress broad power of the purse by granting it authority to collect taxes. Two other powers granted through the Constitution, the war power and the power to regulate interstate and foreign commerce, further extend congressional appropriation authority.

The Constitution required that all new government undertakings must be approved twice. A program is authorized by Congress through an authorization bill, while its financing is provided separately through an appropriations bill. The two-step process tends to restrain spending, as evidenced by the fre-

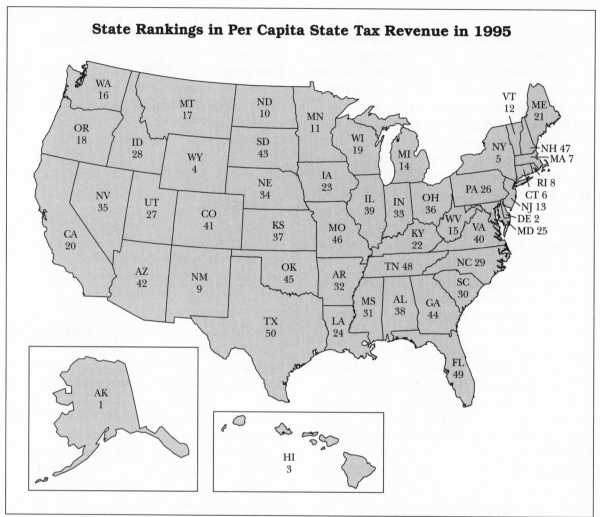

State Rankings in Per Capita State Tax Revenue in 1995

Source: U.S. Bureau of the Census, *Statistical Abstract of the United States: 1997.* 117th ed. Washington, D.C.: U.S. Government Printing Office, 1997.

quently lower amounts of program finance that are usually approved in appropriations bills.

The power balance between Congress and the president has always been delicate. Although it was commonly accepted that Congress has the exclusive power of appropriation, the emphasis prior to the late 1700's was on Alexander Hamilton's concept of "executive discretion." Under this doctrine, general lump-sum appropriations were first made by Congress, then allocated to more specific purposes by the president. In opposition to Ham-

ilton, the Jeffersonians began promoting the concept of "legislative restraint," or limitation of executive discretion through the enactment and oversight of specific appropriations.

With the election of Thomas Jefferson as president in 1800 and the demise of the Hamiltonian approach of executive discretion, Congress assumed the dominant role in fiscal matters in the United States. The president was obliged to follow the spending directives of Congress, departing from those only in cases of national emergency. In theory, budget formulation was Congress's role, while the president was relegated to execution without discretion. In practice, presidents have historically found many ways to achieve discretionary powers. Periodic efforts by Congress to enforce their specific appropriations often ended in failure.

Modern U.S. Taxation. Passage of the Budget and Accounting Act of 1921 established the basic framework for the modern budget system in the United States. The act made the executive branch responsible for transmitting a NATIONAL BUDGET to Congress. In addition, the General Accounting Office was established as an arm of Congress, to monitor executive compliance with congressional intent and the limits of appropriations. These changes to the budget system made the U.S. process of national budgeting similar to Great Britain's in structure, though not in terms of the implicit balance of power between the president and the Congress. In the United States, once the Congress receives the president's budget, it has the authority to change any expenditures or revenues. It is not unusual for the final congressional budget to differ markedly from that of the president.

In 1974 Congress' enactment of the Congressional Budget and Impoundment Control Act further strengthened congressional power of the purse and completed the framework for the modern U.S. budget system by establishing the Congressional Budget Office.

The power of the purse granted under the general welfare clause appears to give the U.S. Congress unlimited spending power. Whether Congress can raise and spend money for whatever may contribute to the general welfare or only to the extent specified elsewhere in the Constitution (such as through the war powers granted or the commerce clause), however, has long been a source of controversy.

Congress's Expanding Power of the Purse. The growth of federal government spending and the state and local spending increases that the federal government has encouraged re-

veals a permissive interpretation of the constitutional power of the purse. In addition to its own direct expenditures, the national government has used the power of the purse to compel desired activities at the state and local levels. For example, although the national government cannot directly regulate EDUCATION or AGRICULTURE through its provision of GRANTS-IN-AID, Congress can influence state and local conduct in those policy areas. The power of the purse also has been used to discourage undesirable practices. For example, Congress can stipulate that federal funding will be withheld from a program if any person connected with the program is denied benefits on the basis of race, national origin, or gender.

Federal Debt and Deficits. Although the United States devotes less of its national product to government than most other developed nations, its huge federal budget deficit caused many citizens to begin questioning the scope of government activity and its costs. In 1972 President Richard Nixon tried unsuccessfully to force Congress to adopt a $250 billion spending ceiling. His insistence that the U.S. Congress enact a spending ceiling that year and the ensuing battle between the executive and legislative branches of government foreshadowed a continuing spotlight on the appropriate extent of legislative power of the purse.

In the early 1980's, in the face of continuing growth of the FEDERAL DEBT, President Ronald Reagan argued for two specific changes to the Constitution to compel Congress to contain the nation's fiscal affairs. The first constitutional amendment that Reagan advocated would have mandated a balanced federal budget. Under such a provision, Congress would have been constitutionally prohibited from spending in excess of available revenues. Reagan's second revision would have given the president a line-item veto. With this change, presidents would be able to veto some parts of bills while approving others. This would have ended the practice of requiring presidents to accept or reject entire appropriations bills, which often means refusing to appropriate funds for favored purposes in order to prevent other expenditures.

Balanced-Budget Proposals. Of Reagan's two proposals, the balanced budget concept enjoyed the most national support. Supporters of a constitutional amendment argued that only a constitutional provision would force lasting change in federal spending because Congress can change laws at will. By 1984 the legislatures of thirty-two states had called for a constitutional convention to draft a balanced-

budget amendment. Congress was responding to the mounting pressure by acting on its own amendments, but it consistently failed to garner enough support. Enactment in 1985, however, of the Balanced Budget and Emergency Deficit Control Act, better known as "Gramm-Rudman-Hollings" (after its sponsors, senators Phil Gramm, Warren Rudman, and Ernest Hollings), came close to requiring Congress to align spending and taxes.

Gramm-Rudman-Hollings established a series of declining deficit targets fashioned to bring the federal budget into balance by 1991. A controversial provision of the law would have required the president to initiate uni-

After President George Bush reneged on his campaign pledge not to raise taxes in 1990, members of Americans Against Tax Hikes demonstrated near the White House to register their displeasure. (AP/Wide World Photos)

Texas senator Phil Gramm, a leading advocate of reducing government spending, holds a new conference on the budget in mid-1993, as fellow Republican senators look on. (AP/Wide World Photos)

form reductions in spending called "sequestrations" if Congress failed to reach specified deficit targets. This provision was voided by a Supreme Court ruling that sequestrations were unconstitutional.

The Gramm-Rudman-Hollings act was acknowledged by many to be too extreme because of its stringent targets and explicit challenges to legislative power of the purse. Focus on deficit reduction continued through the late 1990's before the deficit was appreciably reduced.

Bibliography

Boskin, Michael J. *Frontiers of Tax Reform.* Stanford, Calif.: Hoover Institution Press, 1996.

Brown, Karen B., and Mary L. Fellows. *Taxing America.* New York: New York University Press, 1996.

Brownlee, W. Elliot. *Federal Taxation in America: A Short History.* Washington, D.C.: Woodrow Wilson Center Press, 1996.

Morgan, Iwan W. *Deficit Government: Taxing and Spending in Modern America.* Chicago: Ivan R. Dee, 1995.

Pollack, Sheldon D. *The Failure of U.S. Tax Policy: Revenue and Politics.* University Park: Pennsylvania State University Press, 1996.

Josephine M. LaPlante

Technology and Government

Modern technology helps citizens cut through barriers that hamper their participation in political processes, while at the same time conferring on political elites even greater power to manipulate public opinion and behavior.

Internal Revenue Service worker checks tax forms scanned into computers. In the late 1990's the IRS was struggling to upgrade the agency's increasingly antiquated computer systems. (AP/Wide World Photos)

In the summer of 1787, when the Framers of the U.S. CONSTITUTION defined the American federal system, the physical distances separating the original thirteen states presented a technological challenge. As in ancient Rome, horseback riders and crude signal systems were still the fastest practical means for long-distance land communications, and sailing ships were the fastest means of sea communications. The new federal system provided a means for citizens to participate in running a national government whose officials might convene as much as a thousand miles from their homes.

Federalism. The federal system described in the Constitution reflected the technology of its time. For example, the ELECTORAL COLLEGE met on the same day in separate state capitals, making it difficult, if not impossible, for mem-

bers to scheme together to elect a tyrant. Because it took time to count, certify, and report the results of the popular election of representatives, and because winter travel was difficult in many areas of the country, a Congress elected in the autumn of even-numbered years did not convene until the following March.

While indirect election of senators and the president stemmed partially from the Framers' fears of the excesses of democracy, it also stemmed from the difficulty of citizens gaining firsthand knowledge of the men who aspired to these positions. It thus seemed wiser to have representatives to the state legislatures choose the senators and presidential electors.

Modern Industrial Society. In contrast to the slow-paced life of the late eighteenth century, modern industrial societies have motorized vehicles, railroad trains, and airplanes, and engine-driven vessels have replaced sailing ships. Where printed media provided the principal means of mass communication two centuries ago, modern societies have electronic media, including radio, telegraph, telephone, television, motion pictures, audio and video recordings, and computer networks.

Where farmers, craftsmen, and small businessmen once dominated the economy, great corporations now employ millions of workers.

businesses were once locally owned and managed, the ownership of great firms has separated from their management, and many enterprises have grown roots and branches throughout the entire world.

Local militias of citizen soldiers are no longer a match for massive national ARMED FORCES. Technological advances have made it possible for aggressors to strike decisive blows in less time than it would take to mobilize

A large proportion of the money invested by the federal government in technology and research has gone into the development of more advanced weapons. (U.S. Department of Defense)

Where small independent firms and individual entrepreneurs contracted with one another locally for supplies and services, modern corporations have expanded horizontally and vertically to take over competitive enterprises and to absorb sources of supply, distribution, and marketing. Where individual American

civilian militias for defense. As a consequence, modern nations find it necessary to protect themselves by maintaining substantial armed forces that are in constant states of readiness.

Technology and Government Institutions. Despite the great differences between the lifestyles of the late eighteenth and late twentieth centuries, formal changes in governmental institutions incorporate only a few of the technological advances. Americans now elect their senators directly and convene new congresses in January. Technology influenced this belated recognition that modern modes of travel and mass communication have brought information about current political events quickly to many previously isolated communities and have permitted safer travel in winter. Nevertheless, technology has not fundamentally altered governmental institutions.

Aside from the size to which government institutions have grown, the Framers would have little trouble recognizing the institutions that the original Constitution created. What technology has drastically changed is the *informal* patterns of politics. These include the ways that provincial, state, and local governments throughout the world relate to their national governments, how legislative and executive branches of government relate to each other, how citizens monitor governmental activities, and how governmental elites attempt to monitor and influence citizens' attitudes and behaviors.

The Media. One might expect that in a free society the mass MEDIA would act as a fourth estate, monitoring government and acting to redress imbalances among its various branches. As the people rarely speak with one voice, however, legislative politics tends to be complicated, messy, and difficult for news reporters to cover. While the politics of the executive branch can also be complicated and messy, much of its give and take occurs behind closed doors. In the end, the chief executive can usually speak for the administration without fear of contradiction from within the executive branch.

News reporters often find it convenient to simplify national politics by allowing the chief executives to define political issues, while looking to opposition spokespersons for reactions. Meanwhile, the detailed work of the legisla-

ture gets relatively little coverage. The fact that television has become the dominant medium through which people get political news has reinforced this trend. Portraying politics as a struggle between chief executives and opposition leaders on television is easier and visually more satisfying than presenting politics as a complicated struggle involving interactions among legislative committees, bureaucratic agencies, interest groups, and political parties.

To accommodate television, election campaign themes usually focus on personalities and broad symbolic issues. Citizens learn about the candidates' public records or stances regarding public policy through simplistic campaign advertisements. Technology is employed primarily to project positive images of candidates, or, more often, negative images of opponents. U.S. election campaigns have become very expensive as saturation advertising on television has become the norm. Indeed, for most major political contests, candidates conduct capital-intensive campaigns using professional consultants and managers, and emphasizing television, targeted mailing, and other centrally directed communications. Labor-intensive campaigns using local party workers are no longer the norm.

Computer Networks. For legislatures to redress the power balance with executive branches, for regional governments to operate more independently of the national government, and for individual citizens to become more active participants in public policy formation, enhanced methods of communication hold out the promise of new opportunities. Growing public access to computer-based information systems has presented such opportunities in the 1990's. Computer-based networks allow citizens and their representatives to inquire about information available and to delve as deeply into subjects as they desire. Moreover, such networks also operate as decentralized communication systems. In practical terms this means that citizens possess the

Computer technology entered New York supreme court justice Lewis Friedman's courtroom in late 1997, beginning a two-year trial during which it was to be used to permit videotaped testimony, documents, and other evidence to be viewed on computer screens during trials. (AP/Wide World Photos)

power to send informed messages about questions of public policy directly to representatives and others.

The preponderance of control over modern information technology has resided within the executive branch of government and within established institutional elites, such as private corporations. They have attempted to use this control to ensure that political opinions expressed in the mass media reflect their institutional voices, not those of independent analysts, resource-poor groups, ordinary citizens, or most of their elected representatives. Modern communications technologies, such as those of computer communication, provide a means for overcoming this control. By lowering the organizational costs for forming new groups, new political parties,

or dissenting factions within established groups or parties, they can revitalize traditional mechanisms of democratic control. If citizens do not take advantage of independent sources from which to access information about matters of public concern, their opinions become even more susceptible to manipulation by the established elites who already control much of the information that is reported in the mass media.

Public opinion, properly conceived, is the collective expression of groups of citizens, not the aggregate expression of individuals who respond to PUBLIC OPINION POLLS. Such opinion can be articulated by leaders or spokespersons in an orderly fashion, or it can be demonstrated through direct, and sometimes disorderly, actions of groups themselves.

Either way, the accumulated opinions of individuals who have developed their ideas in splendid isolation—even those who have used the information bases of the Internet to inform themselves—do not correspond to this conception of public opinion.

At its core, democratic politics involves collective decision making about problems of public concern. Similarly, public opinion involves the collective expression of citizens' considerations about public problems, where those considerations take place within democratic political forums, such as public meetings or sessions of democratically elected legislatures. Political actions by a multiplicity of interest groups, well informed through data acquired via computer networks, may actuate democratic control of modern government.

Bibliography

Grossman, Lawrence K. *The Electronic Republic: Reshaping Democracy in the Information Age.* New York: Viking Press, 1995.

Notess, Greg R. *Government Information on the Internet.* Lanham, Md.: Bernan Press, 1997.

Rheingold, Howard. *The Virtual Community.* Reading, Mass.: Addison-Wesley, 1993.

Selnow, Gary W. *High-tech Campaigns: Computer Technology in Political Communication.* Westport, Conn.: Praeger, 1994.

Trend, David. *Cultural Democracy: Politics, Media, New Technology.* Albany: State University of New York Press, 1997.

Michael Margolis

Telecommunications Law

Laws and regulations governing electronic communications have always lagged behind technology, thereby generating controversies over whether, and how, various forms of electronic communication should be regulated.

Telecommunications began in the nineteenth century with the invention of the telegraph and telephone and then expanded dramatically in the twentieth century with the addition of radio, television, cable television, satellite, and computer communications. Telecommunications law covers aspects of these technologies ranging from assigning frequencies and issuing licenses to broadcasters to regulating the content of various media—from television to the Internet.

Communications Act of 1934. Commercial broadcasting began in 1920, and the first permanent radio network, the National Broadcasting Company (NBC), was established in 1926. It soon became apparent that a coherent national policy was required in order to regulate broadcasting. Regulation began in earnest with passage of the Communications Act of 1934, which established both the Federal Communications Commission (FCC) and a philosophy for governing use of the airwaves. Telecommunications law long consisted primarily of this legislation and its amendments. The broadcast media, the act stated, are different from the print media: The airwaves are a public trust, and frequencies should be licensed to private users who will act according to public interest. No one can own a broadcast frequency.

This approach was largely a result of a belief that usable broadcasting frequencies were "scarce." It was the FCC's job to allocate them for various private, governmental, and commercial uses. Although frequencies ultimately turned out to be less scarce than had been thought, the broadcasting industry has had to operate within a context of regulation unknown to the print medium. Whereas the print media have virtually unlimited freedom of speech, the FCC has the power to regulate broadcast content. It can fine broadcasters or revoke or simply not renew licenses of stations broadcasting objectionable programming.

The FCC also promulgated the "fairness

doctrine," requiring stations to provide equal time for the presentation of opposing views regarding any controversial opinions presented. This doctrine was part of the FCC's broader mission to require radio and television stations to be socially responsible.

stations they carried. Major cable legislation has included the 1984 Cable Communications Policy Act, which substantially deregulated the industry.

Another new communications technology began when the first communications satellites

An American couple watches the first live television signal broadcast from Europe via the first telecommunications satellite in 1962. (Library of Congress)

Expanding Technologies. In 1949, during a freeze on the issuing of new television licenses, a few small companies began to transmit television programming via cable. The FCC at first decided that it would not regulate cable operations, but it changed its mind in 1965—it first regulated microwave-fed cable systems, then all cable television. It placed numerous restrictions and requirements on cable television operators, one of which was that they carry local stations and limit the number of distant

began operating in 1962. The Communications Satellite Act of 1962 amended the Communications Act and created the Communications Satellite Corporation (COMSAT), a private corporation, to help provide effective international satellite communication.

Through the decades, the FCC adopted new policies and regulations piecemeal as technology advanced, telecommunication practices changed, and the Communications Act was amended. By 1976 the face of telecommunications had changed so much that Congress considered significant changes in legislation.

New Calls for Change. By the late 1980's the telecommunications field was again undergoing revolutionary changes with the proliferation of computers, computer networks, and individual users equipped with modems. By the mid-1990's millions of individuals, as well as businesses and institutions, were communicating via electronic mail and newsgroups through services giving them access to the Internet. There were other changes as well. Major long-distance carriers were operating in competition with American Telephone and Telegraph (AT&T), and they wanted to be allowed to expand into new areas that technology would now support, such as carrying television signals and competing with the cable companies.

In turn, cable companies, which had grown greatly, wanted to be freed of what they viewed as outdated restrictions. Somewhat contradictory currents were also at work in Washington, D.C., where there were simultaneous calls for continuing economic deregulation and for increasing regulation of the content of radio, television, and the Internet.

In 1995 Congress passed new telecommunication bills that contained sweeping changes. The final form of the bill was enacted into law in 1996, and its essence was significant deregulation. Among the major changes were allowing long-distance telephone carriers, local telephone companies, and cable television operators to enter one another's markets, loosening restrictions on the number of stations a broadcaster can own, and deregulating charges for premium cable services.

Included in the act was a provision requiring the installation of electronic chips (the "V-chip") in new television sets to allow parents to restrict programs their children view. Also part of the act was a prohibition on the broadcasting of "indecent" material over computer networks unless steps are taken to restrict children's access to the material. This last provision, the subject of considerable controversy, pitted advocates of unregulated free speech on the Internet against those fearful of, among other things,

Telephones, Televisions, and Radios in the United States and Selected Countries in 1995

Country	Telephone main lines per 100 people	Television receivers per 1,000 people	Radio receivers per 1,000 people
United States	63	776	2,122
Argentina	16	347	673
Brazil	7	278	393
Canada	59	647	1,051
China	3	250	184
Cuba	3	200	347
Egypt	5	126	307
France	56	579	891
Germany	49	550	935
Ghana	0	(na)	229
India	1	61	81
Italy	43	436	802
Japan	49	619	912
Mexico	10	192	256
Philippines	2	121	144
Puerto Rico	33	322	713
Russia	17	379	339
South Africa	9	101	314
Spain	39	490	312
Sweden	68	476	879
Taiwan	43	317	(na)
United Kingdom	50	612	1,429

Source: U.S. Bureau of the Census, *Statistical Abstract of the United States: 1997.* 117th ed. Washington, D.C.: U.S. Government Printing Office, 1997.

exposing children to obscenity.

The possible effects of the 1996 act were heatedly debated before it was passed. Consumer advocates were certain that higher cable television rates would result from deregulation; supporters of deregulation countered that increased competition should ultimately lower rates for all telecommunications services affected. It was acknowledged that concentration of ownership of broadcasting facilities would increase significantly, but there was uncertainty regarding how important that was, as increasing satellite and telephone-line transmission of television signals made such concentration seem less ominous.

Bibliography

Emeritz, Robert E., ed. *The Telecommunications Act of 1996: Law and Legislative History*. Bethesda, Md.: Pike & Fischer, 1996.

Grossman, Lawrence K. *The Electronic Republic: Reshaping Democracy in the Information Age*. New York: Viking Press, 1995.

Kennedy, Charles H. *An Introduction to U.S. Telecommunications Law*. Boston: Artech House, 1994.

Sullivan, Thomas F. P., ed. *Official Telecommunications Dictionary: Legal and Regulatory Definitions*. Rockville, Md.: Government Institutes, 1997.

Teske, Paul E., ed. *American Regulatory Federalism and Telecommunications Infrastructure*. Hillsdale, N.J.: Lawrence Erlbaum Associates, 1995.

Matthew Fisher

Term Limits

Term limits are formal or informal restrictions on how long elected officials may stay in office. Supporters of the concept argue that they will restore more competitive elections; opponents argue that they will unconstitutionally restrict voters' choices.

Delegates to the Constitutional Convention in 1787 did not regard term limits as sufficiently important to be included within the new national government's rules. The Convention unanimously rejected presidential, judicial, and congressional term limits. Nevertheless, many state political leaders expected that voluntary rotation in office would be the custom and that substantial turnover would occur in the U.S. House of Representatives.

Term Limits in Early U.S. History. Early members of Congress rarely served more than two terms, and it was not uncommon during the first century of congressional elections for 40 percent or more of the members to be first-term "freshmen." Rotation in office was a reality in the first part of the 1800's. President George Washington's decision not to seek a third term set a precedent of voluntary two-term limits in the office of president. State constitutions often limited the terms of their governors, a legacy of the colonial experience.

Things began to change as members of Congress, state legislators, governors, and even council members made serving in office more of a full-time job and a career. Since 1950 the percentage of officeholders winning reelection has surpassed 70 percent. Term limits would increase membership turnover in those elected offices, bringing an influx of new members and, perhaps, new ideas. Term limits are needed in an institution such as Congress, say their supporters, because the practice of voluntary rotation has long been absent from Congress.

Modern Interest in Term Limits. In the late 1980's voters in many parts of the United States began to enact laws that limited the length of time elected officials could stay in office. Popular support for these legal or constitutional restrictions surprised political observers. Nationally, PUBLIC OPINION POLLS have indicated that as many as 65 to 75 percent of Americans approve of term limits.

In the 1990 and 1992 elections, term limits

Key Terms

INITIATIVE: process by which citizens enact their own laws or constitutional amendments by placing them on the ballot to be approved or rejected by popular vote

PROFESSIONAL POLITICIAN: elected official who makes a lengthy or even lifetime career out of public service

RETROACTIVE TERM LIMITS: limits on political service that apply to the time a person held office prior to the time the law was enacted

ROTATION: voluntary form of term limits in which elected officials leave public office after brief periods of service

TURNOVER RATE: proportion of officeholders who are replaced by newcomers in an election

TWENTY-SECOND AMENDMENT: 1951 amendment to the U.S. Constitution that limits presidents to two full terms in office

on state legislators, executives, and federal legislators passed in sixteen states. It is unlikely that lawmakers in any state will choose to limit their own terms in office. Therefore, political ACTIVISTS and interest groups in these sixteen states worked to obtain enough signatures on petitions to place INITIATIVES on their ballots for voters to approve or reject. An initiative, a feature of direct democracy at the state and local levels of government, allows citizens to place specific issues such as term limits on the ballot for voters to decide. Only states that have adopted the initiative have passed congressional and state legislative term limits. Twenty-four states have an initiative process; the remaining twenty-six states and the federal government do not.

The first ballot initiative that limited the number of consecutive terms or total years in office for state legislators passed in Oklahoma on September 18, 1990. This ballot measure limited state legislators to a total of twelve years in either house of the state legislature. In 1990

California voters approved an initiative limiting state assembly members to six years of service and state senators and other statewide officials to eight years. These are lifetime limits, and the years served in office need not be consecutive.

Colorado's Amendment 5 was the first in the nation to limit the terms of its members of Congress, as well as state legislative and executive officials. Of the three 1990 measures, Colorado's had the greatest electoral support, with 71 percent voting for it. Colorado limits state lawmakers to eight years: four consecutive two-year terms in the House or two consecutive four-year terms in the Senate. Congressional term limits are set at twelve years: six consecutive two-year terms in the U.S. House of Representatives or two consecutive six-year terms in the Senate. Limitations do not affect present officeholders in Congress until the year 2002.

The idea of limiting the terms of delegates to Congress was part of the Articles of Confederation, by which state delegates were limited to a total of three years in a six-year time period. Limiting terms for Congress and the president was debated during the Constitutional Convention in Philadelphia in 1787, but overwhelmingly rejected.

Voters in fourteen more states—Arizona, Arkansas, California, Florida, Michigan, Missouri, Montana, Nebraska, North Dakota, Ohio, Oregon, South Dakota, Washington, and Wyoming—approved term limits on members of Congress in 1992.

Twelve states in 1992 had initiatives limiting state legislators' terms in office. In 1993 Maine voters passed a term limits initiative. Term limits vary with the different states. For example, Florida limits members of Congress to eight consecutive years, while Michigan limits members of the House to three two-year terms in a twelve-year period and senators to two six-year terms in twenty-four years. Maine and Arizona limit state legislators to four consecutive two-year terms in the House and Senate, while Wyoming limits a state legislator's terms to three consecutive two-year terms in the House in a twelve-year period and three consecutive four-year terms in a twenty-four-year time period in the state senate.

Present in the debate over term limits is the question of whether the state legislature or voters in a state through an initiative have the constitutional authority to limit the terms of members of Congress. A federal court ruled that Washington State's term limit was an unconstitutional addition to the age, residency, and citizenship qualifications for Congress found in the U.S. Constitution. Thus, limits on congressional service in office may have to be achieved by formally amending the U.S. Constitution. Arkansas's supreme court ruled in

favor of state legislative term limits but struck down, as an impermissible qualification, ballot access provisions for members of Congress. The U.S. Supreme Court will be called upon to resolve these legal disputes.

Supporters and opponents of term limits have debated the concept's strengths and weaknesses. Supporters believe that term limits would increase turnover in elected office and bring new faces and fresh policy ideas into government. Citizen-legislators, serving fewer years but staying in touch with citizens, would once again dominate the halls of a legislature. The number of women, minorities, and younger people serving as elected officials should increase as limits begin to phase out white, male representatives. Term limits are essential, say their advocates, in order to give

Members of the 102d Congress were collectively sworn into office by Speaker Thomas S. Foley in 1991. Since then, the implementation of term limits in a growing number of states has ensured that increasing numbers of congresspersons each term are newcomers. (AP/Wide World Photos)

The Twenty-second Amendment

The accumulation of presidential power during Franklin D. Roosevelt's four-term administration persuaded congressional Republicans to work for a constitutional amendment limiting presidents to two terms. Democrats generally opposed such a restriction and considered the two-term limit a personal attack on a deceased president and his party, as well as a restraint on the right of voters to choose presidents freely. The vote in both houses of Congress reflected the partisan struggle over the proposed amendment. No Republican in either the House or the Senate voted against a two-term limit. A minority of Democrats in each chamber joined a united Republican majority to provide the two-thirds vote necessary to send a constitutional amendment to the states. Ratification by the required three-fourths of the states came in February, 1951. Thus, the Twenty-second Amendment, limiting the number of terms a president can serve in office, was added to the Constitution.

talented citizens a chance to serve their communities, and enable elected officials to devote more time to governing and making policy and less time to reelection activities.

Opponents of term limits concede that reelection rates among present officeholders are high, but argue that when turnover is measured over a decade or so, it is also high. In the 1988 election in California, 92 percent of state legislators who chose to run again were reelected. On the other hand, between 1979 and 1989 the turnover of members in the legislature averaged 70 percent. Incumbents are reelected, but they also step down from office in large numbers. Critics charge that term limits interfere with voters' basic right to choose whom they wish for public office and for as many times as they wish. Opponents of term limits also argue that replacing legislators frequently will result in transferring political power to the administrators and legislative staff to whom freshman legislators would turn for advice.

Term Limits in City Governments. Term limits are in place in one-third of the largest cities in the United States, but only in about 11 percent of other local governments. The average limit is eight years, and it applies to both mayors and council members. Term limits are more likely to occur in western cities that have the initiative device, and in council-manager cities.

The United States has had almost a half-century of experience with term limits on its chief executive. Presidents were limited to two terms in office by the Twenty-second Amendment to the U.S. Constitution. Furthermore, thirty-six states limit the terms of their governors.

Bibliography

Carey, John M. *Term Limits and Legislative Representation.* New York: Cambridge University Press, 1996.

Crane, Edward H., and Roger Pilon, eds. *The Politics and Law of Term Limits.* Washington, D.C.: Cato Institute, 1994.

Grofman, Bernard, ed. *Legislative Term Limits: Public Choice Perspectives.* Boston: Kluwer Academic Publishers, 1996.

Zeller, Laurie Hirschfeld, and John Calhoon. *Term Limitations for Local Officials: A Citizens' Guide to Constructive Dialogue.* Denver, Colo.: National Civic League Press, 1992.

Steve J. Mazurana

Terrorism

Terrorism is violence, or the threat of violence, usually directed against innocent civilians, in pursuit of political objectives. Americans have been leading targets of international terrorism, but domestic terrorism has been comparatively rare.

Oklahoma City's Alfred P. Murrah federal building shortly after it was destroyed by a terrorist bomb, which killed 168 persons, in April, 1995. (AP/Wide World Photos)

Often called a weapon of the weak, terrorism is used by those who have political objectives but lack power to influence governments or to engage in conventional warfare. Terrorists have a variety of political motives. Some of the most infamous groups are those seeking independence or autonomy for a national or ethnic group. Some are inspired by vague revolutionary ideologies.

In many cases, terrorist violence is used to attract world attention to a political cause or to protest the policies of governments. This explains why terrorist acts are often designed to attract maximum media coverage. Terror-ism may also represent an attempt specifically to incite a government to react violently, thereby alienating citizens and creating sympathy for the group resorting to the terrorist acts. Victims of terrorism may include people working for the governments or organizations that the terrorists oppose, such as policemen and soldiers. They may be citizens of countries against which the terrorists are protesting or citizens of countries viewed as assisting those whom terrorists are fighting.

Defining Terrorism. Terrorists often commit many of the same acts committed by common, or nonpolitical, criminals. Either may

Terrorist Incidents in the United States, 1982-1992

Type and Target	Number
Total incidents	**165**
Type of incident	
Bombing attacks	130
Malicious destruction of property	4
Acts of sabotage	2
Hostile takeover	4
Arson	8
Kidnapping; assaults; alleged assassinations; assassinations	11
Robbery; attempted robbery	5
Hijacking	1
Type of target	
Private residence/vehicle	18
Military personnel/establishments	33
Educational establishments	6
Commercial establishments	60
State and United States government buildings/property	31
Diplomatic establishments	17

Source: U.S. Department of Justice, Bureau of Justice Statistics, *Sourcebook of Criminal Justice Statistics—1993.* Washington, D.C.: U.S. Government Printing Office, 1994.

threaten or use violence and may commit criminal acts such as theft, kidnapping, or murder. Sometimes alliances are formed between groups of common criminals and terrorist groups. The difference between common CRIME and terrorism lies largely in the motives of perpetrators. Terrorism is crime which has a political objective, while common crime is undertaken for private motives such as profit or revenge. Common criminals have been known to allege that they have political motives in attempts to elicit sympathy from juries.

Domestic and International Terrorism. It can be difficult to distinguish between domestic and international terrorism. During the Vietnam War, terrorist acts such as bombing the offices of university faculty members, making bomb threats, and destroying government property were undertaken by Americans, especially of draft age. They were sometimes accused of having been inspired by foreign communists. Sometimes domestic terrorists appear to emulate the tactics of foreign terrorists whom they read about or see on television. The necessity of combating both varieties of terrorism creates some bureaucratic confusion, because the FEDERAL BUREAU OF INVESTIGATION (FBI) is in charge of gathering information about and capturing terrorists in the United States, while the Central Intelligence Agency (CIA) investigates overseas sources of terrorism.

State Sponsorship of Terrorism. Some governments believe it is in their interest to assist terrorist groups. In some cases, terrorist groups are actually created by governments to carry out violent acts on their behalf. From time to time, the regime of Libya's Muammar Qadhafi has employed agents to murder Libyan dissidents residing overseas, and the regime of Iraq's Saddam Hussein was accused of trying to assassinate former U.S. president George Bush on the occasion of his trip to Kuwait in 1993.

It is more common, however, for states to provide arms, safe haven, and other facilities to terrorists whom they hope to use for their own purposes. In some instances, diplomats take advantage of their legal immunity from search and arrest to carry weapons or store weapons for terrorists whom they sponsor. Such incidents as the 1983 suicide bombing of the U.S. Marine barracks in Beirut, Lebanon; the 1986 bombing of a West German discotheque frequented by U.S. soldiers; and the 1988 bombing of a Pan American airliner over Scotland were almost certainly sponsored by governments that wanted to harm American interests without showing their hand.

The Tactics of Terrorists. Terrorists use a

variety of tactics to intimidate or harm their adversaries. In the 1970's skyjackings, involving demands in return for the release of hostages, were common and provided perpetrators and their causes with widespread publicity. Skyjacking declined, however, as airport and airplane security improved. The bombing of planes continues, however, especially by groups that seek to avenge themselves against foes.

Some groups make extensive use of kidnapping to publicize their causes or to obtain funds. Some resort to suicide bombing—a tactic difficult to deter—while others plant bombs in public buildings. Some groups create terror by resorting to indiscriminate grenade or machine gun attacks. Another tactic is the assassination of public figures who serve as symbols of an enemy.

Weapons of Mass Destruction. Perhaps the greatest threat of terrorism in the future involves the possibility that terrorists may acquire weapons of mass destruction, such as nuclear or chemical weapons. Concern has long existed that a terrorist group might steal a nuclear device from a U.S. base or try to sabotage a nuclear power plant. The prospect of nuclear terrorism increased dramatically after the break-up of the Soviet Union because of the growing power of organized crime in Russia, and the economic difficulties confronting Russia, Ukraine, and other Soviet successor states. More worrisome has been the possibility that chemical or biological weapons, which are more widely distributed than nuclear weapons, might fall into the hands of terrorists.

Americans as Terrorist Targets. International terrorist incidents soared during the late 1960's and early 1970's. They remained relatively constant until the early 1990's, when they began to decline. Terrorist incidents have been especially prevalent in the Middle East, Western Europe, and Latin America, but U.S. citizens and property have been the most fre-

quent targets of such attacks. There are a number of reasons why U.S. interests are selected for attack by terrorists. Americans and American property are relatively vulnerable because they are to be found throughout the world. In addition, the United States is viewed as the world's leading capitalist society and as an ally of nations, such as Israel and Egypt, that terrorists have targeted. Finally, attacks on the interests of the United States are certain to receive considerable publicity.

The seizure of the U.S. embassy in Teheran, Iran, along with sixty-six hostages, by Revolutionary Guards in 1979 and the subsequent kidnapping of Western hostages, including a number of Americans, by Iranian sympathizers in Lebanon galvanized U.S. antiterrorist efforts. American revulsion at terrorism increased greatly with the highly publicized hijacking of a Trans World Airlines plane en

Casualties Resulting from International Terrorism Involving U.S. Citizens, 1981-1993

	Total	Dead	Wounded
Total	**2,197**	**586**	**1,611**
1981	47	7	40
1982	19	8	11
1983	386	271	115
1984	42	11	31
1985	195	38	157
1986	112	12	100
1987	54	7	47
1988	232	192	40
1989	34	15	19
1990	44	10	34
1991	21	7	14
1992	3	2	1
1993	1,008	6	1,002

Source: U.S. Department of Justice, Bureau of Justice Statistics, *Sourcebook of Criminal Justice Statistics—1993.* Washington, D.C.: U.S. Government Printing Office, 1994.

route to Athens in 1985 and destruction of a Pan American jumbo jet over Lockerbie, Scotland, in 1988.

Responses to Terrorism. To the public, the most evident response to terrorism is the screening of passengers at airports to prevent smuggling of bombs or other weapons. Growing concern about suicide bombings of the sort that took the lives of several hundred American Marines in Beirut, Lebanon, in 1983 has led to the proliferation of concrete barricades around public buildings in the United States. In addition, the establishment of the Special Operations and Research Unit and the Terrorist Research and Analytical Center within the FBI has increased the capacity of that agency to cope with domestic terrorist threats.

Beyond passive actions, it has proved difficult for U.S. officials to institute effective measures against terrorism. When the Reagan administration came to office in 1981, Secretary of State Alexander Haig made it clear that combating terrorism was a high government priority, declaring that international terrorism was the "ultimate abuse of human rights." In 1986, using bases in Great Britain, the United States bombed Libya in retaliation for what Washington said was Libyan involvement in a bombing in Europe that took the lives of American servicemen. U.S. officials have publicly refused to negotiate with terrorists but they have done so privately. The U.S. Army has trained special antiterrorist units, and many U.S. cities have created special police teams to deal with terrorist acts; such approaches have had some success.

International Cooperation. No one country, however powerful, can cope alone with international terrorism. Any effective strategy against terrorism must involve cooperation among many states. In the 1990's cooperation began to increase. For example, after Libya refused to surrender those accused of having plotted the destruction of the Pan American airliner over Scotland, the United Nations, at American and French insistence, imposed economic sanctions on the Libyans.

The intelligence services of the major Western democracies routinely exchange intelligence information with one another and with Interpol regarding the movement and activities of suspected terrorists. Perhaps the most important successes in the fight against terrorism in recent years followed the end of the Cold War and the collapse of communism in Eastern Europe and

On February 26, 1993, a bomb exploding in the subterranean garage of New York City's World Trade Center killed 6 people, injured 650, and caused another 1,000 to be treated for smoke inhalation, forcing the shutdown of the 110-story tall twin towers—one of the world's largest office complexes. (AP/Wide World Photos)

the former Soviet Union. As a consequence, terrorists were deprived of safe havens they had formerly enjoyed, and considerable useful intelligence information was made available to Western antiterrorist experts. Ultimately, all countries have an interest in cooperating with those who are the victims of terrorism lest they also become victims.

Domestic Terrorism. The relative freedom from terrorist attacks in the United States came to an abrupt end with the 1993 World Trade Center bombing. Secretary of State Warren Christopher spoke of how terrorist attacks "have brought home the ruthless persistence of evil, cowardice and intolerance in the world—and the frightening ease with which terrorists can obtain destructive technology." The discovery that Islamic militants were planning to set off car bombs in the highway tunnels under New York's Hudson River indicated the vulnerability of urban America to terrorist attacks.

Americans' sense of vulnerability to terrorism increased dramatically with the car bombing of a federal office building in Oklahoma City on April 19, 1995, with the loss of hundreds of lives, including numerous children. Suspicion initially fell upon foreign extremists, but the investigation instead led to the arrest of two young Americans, Timothy James McVeigh and Terry Lynn Nichols. Moreover, the explosive used was not a sophisticated bomb but a common and easily acquired fertilizer, ammonium nitrate, soaked in fuel oil.

Other events in 1995 highlighted the vulnerability of modern society to the acts of determined terrorists. In mid-1995 a threat to plant a bomb aboard an airplane by someone claiming to be the mysterious Unabomber spread fear among passengers and prompted an increase in airport security efforts. Between 1978 and 1996 the so-called Unabomber used the mail to send packaged bombs in sixteen attacks on scientists or others somehow involved with technology. Such incidents showed that despite efforts to increase security modern society cannot prevent determined terrorists from striking.

Bibliography

McGuckin, Frank, ed. *Terrorism in the United States.* New York: H. W. Wilson, 1997.

Mullins, Wayman C. *A Sourcebook on Domestic and International Terrorism: An Analysis of Issues, Organizations, Tactics, and Responses.* 2d ed. Springfield, Ill.: C. C. Thomas, 1997.

Riley, Kevin J., and Bruce Hoffman. *Domestic Terrorism: A National Assessment of State and Local Preparedness.* Santa Monica, Calif.: Rand Corp., 1995.

Simon, Jeffrey D. *The Terrorist Trap: America's Experience with Terrorism.* Bloomington: Indiana University Press, 1994.

Smith, Brent L. *Terrorism in America: Pipe Bombs and Pipe Dreams.* Albany: State University of New York Press, 1994.

Richard W. Mansbach

Town Meetings

The classic mode of small-town government in New England, town meetings are the modern version of the ancient Greek participatory democracy in which all citizens could participate in discussion and vote on issues.

The town meeting was the form of local government devised by the earliest European settlers in New England. It was a response to the need for some form of local decision making in the initial settlements. Because the earliest settlers were all of equal importance, they decided to provide for local government by meetings of all inhabitants at regular intervals. One of the earliest written documents in the colonies was the Mayflower Compact, signed by all the Pilgrims agreeing to work together to determine local issues that affected them all.

Origins. Town meetings as a system of local government were first developed in Massachusetts, as the first permanent European settlements in New England were located there. Both Connecticut and Rhode Island were settled by individuals who, for varied reasons, could not fit into culturally monolithic Massachusetts towns. They received separate charters from the Crown in the 1660's, but these provided for the same conditions of self-government as prevailed in Massachusetts. Maine was part of Massachusetts until 1820, when, following petition by the residents, the Massachusetts legislature agreed to allow it to separate. On separation, Maine retained the traditional system of local self-government through town meetings. New Hampshire became a royal province in 1679, but copied the governing structure of neighboring Massachusetts. Vermont became a separate entity during the AMERICAN REVOLUTION, but likewise adopted the prevailing form of local government.

Challenges to Town Meeting Government. While the system of local self-government through town meetings worked well during the colonial era, when the European settlements were overwhelmingly agricultural and communities tended to be like-minded, developments in the nineteenth century made the system unworkable in many places. Rapid population growth and increasing ethnic complexity, particularly in the industrial cities, required adaptation of the system to meet the new realities. Boston was the first to recognize that large population centers could not be governed in the old way. After petitioning the legislature, Boston was reauthorized as a city in 1822.

Communities that became cities abandoned town meetings as their legislatures and adopted various forms of the mayor-council system of government, in which the voters elect representatives to councils. This system, used throughout the rest of the United States, has not been overwhelmingly popular in New

---

Key Terms

ANNUAL TOWN MEETING: basic town meeting that votes on financial issues before the town

BOARD OF SELECTMEN: three to nine persons elected to provide continuous authority in a town and prepare the warrant for the town meeting

CONSTABLE: local official whose task it is to publicize the calling of a town meeting and to preserve order during the meeting

FREEMEN: town proprietors to whom participation in the earliest town meetings was restricted

GENERAL COURT: the legislative body of the colony, then of the province; this term is still used for the legislature of Massachusetts

OPEN TOWN MEETING: town meeting in which all citizens can participate

REPRESENTATIVE TOWN MEETING: body elected by the citizenry to deliberate and vote on town issues; used in towns where population growth has made open town meetings impractical

SPECIAL TOWN MEETING: town meetings other than the annual town meeting, called by selectmen to deal with nonfinancial issues

WARRANT: agenda of every town meeting, prepared by the board of selectmen

---

England, so that many communities, although their size would justify it, have chosen not to become cities.

An alternative to becoming a city, for local government purposes, that developed during the twentieth century was the representative town meeting. The representative town meeting, like the city council, is composed of individuals elected by the voters; they have the authority to vote on any issues on the town warrant, though individual voters continue to have the right to speak. Representative town meetings, in contrast to town councils, tend to be large bodies; the most common number in

Massachusetts is 240, the same as the number of legislators in the lower house of the General Court.

Modern Town Meetings. Before the 1950's communities in New England that wanted to change their local government from the traditional town meeting form had to apply to the state legislature for a special act applying only to their particular town. All such acts required subsequent approval by the local voters. In order to reduce the burden on the legislatures—there are more than one thousand communities in the New England states, each with its own local government—all the New England state legislatures enacted "home rule" statutes during the latter half of the twentieth century.

Under "home rule," communities may elect charter commissions with the mission of proposing an alternative charter. This must then go before the voters in a referendum, and many reform charters have been turned down by the voters. In matters of local government, New Englanders have remained conservative; this conservatism has kept town meetings in place as the legislature in most of the smaller communities of the region.

Democracy and Town Meetings. As a classic example of participatory democracy, the town meeting has certain great advantages. It gives the citizenry an opportunity to express their opinions on a proposed governmental measure before it goes into effect. To the extent that all effective government depends to some degree on acceptance by the governed, it reduces the amount of direct enforcement that is needed. It was originally adopted because no other enforcement mechanism, except the force of public opinion, was available in the colonial towns.

Residents of Elmore, Vermont, gather for their weekly Tuesday night town meeting in early 1998. (AP/Wide World Photos)

Time has also revealed some of the weaknesses of the town meeting form of local government. The complexity of many issues that must be dealt with by local officials, interconnected as they often are with state and federal systems, makes it difficult for ordinary voters to understand what is at stake. Because participation is voluntary, it tends to be low, although in the case of representative town meetings, those who put themselves up for election generally have a greater measure of commitment to the process. Where open town meeting still prevails, it is sometimes difficult to find a hall large enough to accommodate all voters. Too often, local issues are decided for personal reasons, rather than sound public policy.

Because participation is voluntary, town meetings can be dominated by committed special-interest groups. Because the constitutions guarantee every citizen the right to participate, groups such as municipal employees, who will be voting on the budgets of their agencies, often play a disproportionate role in the decision making.

In the late twentieth century, there has been a renewed emphasis on participatory democracy. National politicians have found a publicity advantage in holding "town meetings" on major policy issues, and although such meetings usually involve a carefully selected membership, they give the impression that the ordinary citizen has a voice in government. Despite major, worldwide commitment to democracy as a form of government, making it work has never been easy. Where appropriate, in small, relatively homogeneous communities, town meeting has been one of democracy's most successful mechanisms.

Bibliography

Christensen, Terry. *Local Politics: Governing at the Grassroots.* Belmont, Calif.: Wadsworth, 1995.

Johnson, Richard B. *Town Meeting Time: A Handbook of Parliamentary Law.* 2d ed. Malabar, Fla.: R. E. Krieger, 1984.

Zimmerman, Joseph F. *The Massachusetts Town Meeting: A Tenacious Institution.* Albany: Graduate School of Public Affairs, State University of New York, 1967.

Nancy M. Gordon

Transportation Management

Regulation of national transportation is an extensive and complex function of government. The nature of transportation makes it one of the most significant contributors to the nation's economy and social environment.

The primary modes of transportation within the United States include railroads, highways, water, oil pipeline, and air transport. The nation depends on transportation for economic, social, recreational, educational, cultural, political, and other purposes. Transportation services are continually challenged and beset by financial, operating, technological, political, and other problems. These challenges are an unending concern and high priority for governmental units at the local, state, and national levels.

Railroads. Railroads have played a particularly significant role in the development and creation of transportation systems in the United States. As early as 1830, they were established in the eastern states, including New York, Pennsylvania, and New England. As the nation expanded west, the railroads played a key role. In 1869 the first transcontinental railroad services began. By 1916 a quarter of a million miles of railroad tracks crisscrossed the United States. Railroad mileage totaled 184,000 miles in 1979.

Although initial railroad development was bitterly opposed by water canal and turnpike interests, government generally aided the railroads by granting them the power of eminent domain, allowing them to incorporate privately without state legislation, and by providing various types of financial aid from local, state, and federal governments.

Trucking. Highway freight transportation has also played a significant role in the development and creation of transportation systems in the United States. Although the railroad industry had earlier beginnings and thus greater market hold, the highway freight industry has experienced phenomenal growth and expansion. In 1916 only 250,000, trucks were registered in the United States; most were small vehicles engaged in local delivery service. The growth of intercity truck transportation was aided by such changes as improved pneumatic tires, expanding intercity use of automobiles—which increased public demand for better roadways—and better service capabilities than railroads could offer.

The number of non-government-owned trucks registered in the country reached 34 million in 1980. In 1980 there were approximately 17,000 interstate for-hire trucking companies regulated by the INTERSTATE COMMERCE COMMISSION (ICC).

Water Transportation. Water transportation served an important role for colonial America, making use of the ocean and navigable rivers. It has expanded to include ocean coasts (coastal) and between coasts (intercoastal), the Great Lakes, rivers, canals, and between the mainland United States and territories. Invention of the steamboat in 1807 greatly expanded the growth of water transportation on the Mississippi and Ohio Rivers. By 1880, however,

Air traffic control is a direct responsibility of the federal government. (AP/Wide World Photos)

steamboats had all but given way to the railroads. During the early nineteenth century, canals were built as state government enterprises throughout the country. Like the steamboat, however, canal transportation became a victim of railroad competition.

After both world wars the federal government provided funding for various programs to improve inland waterway systems and initiated a tow-boat-barge system for commodity shipping. By 1980 river transportation was again an important part of the nation's intercity freight transportation system, with emphasis on transporting bulk commodities.

Oil Pipelines. The first oil pipeline transportation system was built in 1865. By 1900 some 6,800 miles of interstate pipelines carried crude oil. Total pipeline mileage in the United States nearly tripled between 1915 and 1931, amounting to more than 115,000 miles in 1931. Because of increased demand for oil products during World War II, the federal government financed two major oil pipeline projects.

Highway Mileage in the United States

In 1995 the U.S. Federal Highway Administration reported that there were 3,912,226 miles of highways of all types throughout the country. This map shows the total highway mileage in each state (rounded off to the nearest 10 miles).

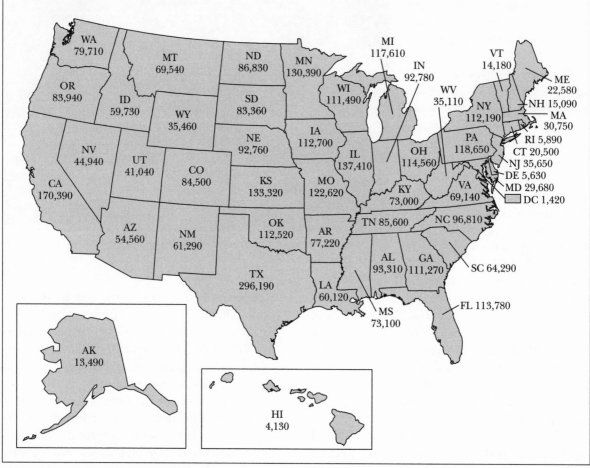

Source: U.S. Bureau of the Census, *Statistical Abstract of the United States: 1997.* 117th ed. Washington, D.C.: U.S. Government Printing Office, 1997.

Since 1950 demand for petroleum products has accelerated and the development of new oil fields in North Dakota, Montana, Utah, Arizona, Colorado, Alaska, and off-shore areas has greatly expanded the need for oil pipeline transportation. By 1977 there were over 67,000 miles of crude-oil gathering lines, 77,000 miles of crude oil trunk lines, and 81,000 miles of product lines in the United States.

Airlines. In 1925 the federal Kelly Act authorized the U.S. Post Office Department to contract with private air carriers to carry mail and provide limited passenger transportation facilities. Not until after World War II, however, was aircraft technology greatly accelerated. In the late 1950's and early 1960's the first pure jet passenger planes were developed; and in 1969 the first wide-bodied or jumbo jets were introduced. Meanwhile, airlines gradually dominated the for-hire intercity transportation of passengers.

Air freight service also began to expand,

but to a lesser degree. In 1939 for-hire air transportation carried 800 million passenger-miles, or only 2.3 percent of all for-hire intercity passenger miles carried. By 1980 for-hire air transportation carried 202 billion passenger miles, or 82.7 percent of all for-hire intercity passenger miles carried. Although air freight continued to expand, air carriers still handled only two-tenths of one percent of all intercity freight ton-mileage in 1980. Also in 1980 there were more than 208,000 general aviation aircraft and over 2,500 airline aircraft flying from approximately 620 airports in the United States with scheduled airline service.

Federal Regulation. The federal government has been actively involved with national transportation policy since the late 1800's. The Interstate Commerce Act of 1887 was an initial effort to dictate economic regulation on transportation carriers caused primarily by unfair price discrimination and destructive competition in the railroad industry. Eventually, federal legislation proved restrictive and somewhat punitive in nature, and it tended to promote pattern-setting influences that could negate future planning for changing circumstances and conditions. National transportation policy has followed fragmented, special-interest, crisis-reaction orientations. The nature of governmentally imposed economic

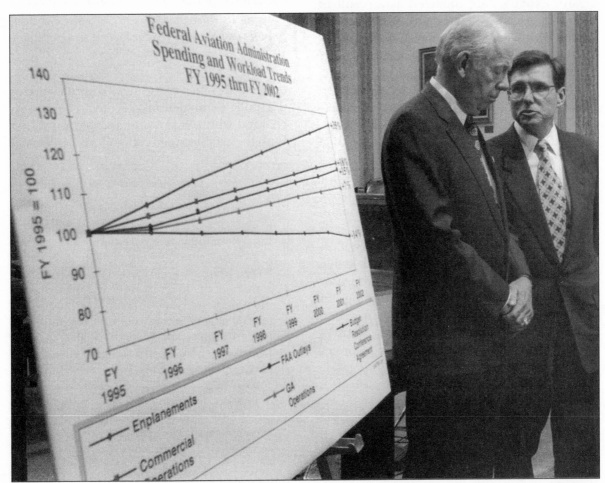

Officers of the Transportation Department announcing plans to reform the Federal Aviation Administration (FAA) in 1995. (AP/Wide World Photos)

regulation has resulted in both negative and positive effects on carriers as well as users.

Carriers have discovered the extreme restrictiveness of regulation. Economic regulation reduces the freedom of any regulated carrier to add or subtract services, to change prices, and to make other changes that unregulated industries do regularly. Another problem evolves from the nature of delays in decision making. Because of methodical bureaucratic process and approval delays, it is difficult for regulated carriers to react quickly to changes in the competitive marketplace. Regulated carriers often find their operational expenses are higher than they should be. Excessive expenses are incurred as a result of delays in decision making and inefficiencies forced on the carriers by regulation, such as those created by route, point, and commodity restrictions. Users are often subjected to inflexibility in transportation services. A related drawback for users is a reduction in transportation alternatives as regulation tends to reduce the number of carriers and available services between any two points.

Positive effects of economic regulation for both carriers and users include an avoidance of destructive competition. Service is maintained at acceptable levels and turnover is reduced in the transportation industry. Economic regulation has also produced a stable environment for carrier operations and user dependence on availability and pricing. In addition, economic regulation has eliminated unfair and discriminatory treatment of users in the form of unjust discrimination in prices and service and exorbitant prices.

Bibliography

Dempsey, Paul, and Andrew Goetz. *Airline Deregulation and Laissez-Faire Mythology.* Westport, Conn.: Quorum Books, 1992.

Kozolchyk, Boris, Gary T. Doyle, and Martin G. Olea Amaya. *Transportation Law and Practice in North America.* Tucson, Ariz.: National Law Center for Inter-American Free Trade, 1996.

Miller, James C., III, ed. *Perspectives on Federal Transportation Policy.* Washington, D.C.: American Enterprise Institute for Public Policy Research, 1975.

United States. *Compilation of Selected Surface Transportation Laws.* Washington: U.S. Government Printing Office, 1997.

John L. Farbo

Treason

The betrayal of one's nation through activities jeopardizing its interests or security, treason has traditionally been regarded as the highest crime known to society.

In some societies, persons who even criticized the policies or actions of their rulers were charged with treason and severely punished. With the establishment of modern democratic

The Rosenbergs

Among the most sensational treason cases in American history was that of Julius and Ethel Rosenberg, who were charged with conspiracy to transmit secret atomic data to the Soviet Union. In 1951 a federal court jury convicted them of treason and sentenced them to die for what Judge Irving Kaufman termed a "loathsome" offense. Despite prolonged appeals from many quarters, the Rosenbergs were electrocuted in 1953. They have remained the only Americans ever executed for ESPIONAGE during peacetime. Their dramatic trial, combined with widespread public fear of atomic weapons in the hands of communist nations, inspired a new wave of congressional treason hunting, which had an impact on American life for several years thereafter.

nations, however, the meaning of treason changed. The Framers of the U.S. CONSTITUTION defined treason restrictively to protect the rights of citizens to oppose the actions of their government in reasonable ways.

Constitutional Definitions. Article 3, section 3 of the U.S. Constitution defines treason as "levying War against them [the United States] or in adhering to their Enemies, giving them Aid and Comfort." Generally, levying war consists of being part of a group of armed persons actually moving against the government. Charges of giving aid and comfort to enemies of the United States require evidence of deliberate promotion of the cause of a recognized enemy.

The U.S. Constitution also states that no persons can be convicted of treason on the basis of circumstantial evidence alone. The accused must make an open confession in open court, or there must exist two witnesses to an overt act of treason. Obtaining convictions in court can be difficult because treasonous acts are usually committed covertly (through ESPIONAGE), and traitors are not prone to incriminating themselves.

Another special problem in obtaining treason convictions is the practice of foreign nations granting political asylum to people accused of treason in their native countries. Ironically, although treason may be regarded by the offended country as the worst kind of CRIME, it is not subject to extradition because it is ultimately regarded as political in nature.

In the United States, Congress alone holds the constitutional power to determine and declare what penalties shall be meted out for treason. CAPITAL PUNISHMENT and life in

After performing heroic service by leading the project that developed the atomic bomb during World War II, physicist J. Robert Oppenheimer was accused of disloyalty, and even treason, by some during the 1950's, when he expressed reservations about developing an even more powerful hydrogen bomb. (AP/Wide World Photos)

prison are the usual penalties. Persons convicted of treason are branded traitors.

Famous Treason Cases. Perhaps the most notorious early traitor in American history was Benedict Arnold, whose very name has become synonymous with disloyalty. A revered patriot holding a high position in the Continental Army during the AMERICAN REVOLUTION, Arnold offered to hand over the West Point fortifications to the British for money. After his plot was discovered, he escaped to England, where he was pensioned as a British officer until his death.

Important in legal history was the case of Aaron Burr, Thomas Jefferson's first vice president. He was charged with treason for conspiring to take over western territories of the United States. Public opinion was against Burr. However, his trial judge, John Marshall, was a strong Federalist who insisted upon a narrow constitutional definition of treason. He refused to allow testimony regarding Burr's supposed intentions and demanded two witnesses to testify on each overt act of treason. Burr's jury eventually decided he not been proved guilty according to constitutional requirements. This trial left a strong legal heritage, protecting the rights of all future Americans. If Marshall had allowed circumstantial evidence to be used in Burr's case, it would have made it easier for later governmental leaders to use conspiracy charges to silence legitimate political opposition.

Bibliography

Chaitkin, Anton. *Treason in America: From Aaron Burr to Averell Harriman*. New York: New Benjamin Franklin House, 1984.

Chapin, Bradley. *The American Law of Treason: Revolutionary and Early National Origins*. Seattle: University of Washington Press, 1964.

Pincher, Chapman. *Traitors*. New York: St. Martin's Press, 1987.

Sarbin, Theodore R., Ralph M. Carney, and Carson Eoyang, eds. *Citizen Espionage: Studies in Trust and Betrayal*. Westport, Conn.: Praeger, 1994.

Andrew C. Skinner

Treasury Department

The Department of the Treasury advises Congress and the president on tax policy, acts as financial agent for the federal government, manufactures currency, and enforces tax laws.

Two government agencies carry the primary responsibility of advising the U.S. government on economic policy and enacting that policy. The Federal Reserve System and its board of governors help set monetary policy (the government's actions in controlling such economic factors as the supply of money, interest rates, and inflation). The Department of the Treasury advises on and, in part, administers fiscal policy, which encompasses all matters of taxation and government expenditures. The secretary of the treasury heads the department and is appointed by the president.

The Treasury Department is empowered by Congress to make fundamental policy decisions concerning the management of government accounts and of the public debt. Although officials of the Treasury Department advise the president and Congress on policy matters, the department is expected to conduct its operations in accordance with established policies and in cooperation with the Federal Reserve System, an agency independent of political control.

The Federal Reserve System and its board of governors were granted independence from the political process to avoid the risk that the nation's monetary system would be manipulated for political advantage. The Federal Reserve System is entrusted with the power of being the government's bank—in which the Treasury Department keeps the government's accounts—and with implementing monetary policy. The Treasury Department is limited in its role regarding monetary policy; it reacts to the actions of the Federal Reserve System and prints money as required.

Law Enforcement. A major role of the Treasury Department lies in its criminal justice responsibilities. The department regulates wire transfers, investigates tax abuses, and prevents money laundering and the circulation of counterfeit currency. For most U.S. citizens, the most familiar part of the department is its INTERNAL REVENUE SERVICE (IRS). The department also includes the Bureau of Alcohol, Tobacco, and Firearms (ATF), the U.S. Customs Service, and the Secret Service, among other agencies.

The Internal Revenue Service. The Internal Revenue Service (IRS) is responsible for administering and enforcing internal revenue laws and related statutes, except those related to alcohol, tobacco, firearms, and explosives, which are regulated by the Treasury Department's Bureau of Alcohol, Tobacco, and Firearms. The IRS is charged with collecting the proper amount of income tax revenue at the least cost to the public and in a manner that warrants public confidence in the agency's integrity, efficiency, and fairness.

The IRS encourages voluntary compliance with tax laws, and it determines the extent and causes of noncompliance. It does this in part through selective auditing of tax returns. In a tax audit, a tax examiner checks the information on a tax return against records provided by the tax filer. Tax evasion is recognized as a significant problem of tax collection. Most often, filers fail to report income or provide false information regarding their rights to deductions. Improved data collection methods have made the job of the IRS easier. Employers and financial institutions must provide information directly to the IRS to be checked against tax returns.

Money Laundering. For a long time, fund transfers between banks were made primarily over international and domestic telegraph and telex networks. These forms of communication required a large staff of handlers and

Federal Reserve Board chairperson Alan Greenspan (left) and Federal Deposit Insurance Corporation chairperson William Seidman await a meeting of the Senate Banking Committee on the Treasury Department's regulation of the depository institutions in early 1991. (AP/Wide World Photos)

Officers of the Treasury Department's ATF with some of the weapons they confiscated from a Chinese arms dealer in 1996. (AP/Wide World Photos)

were vulnerable to fraud. Rapid technological advances have increased the speed and efficiency of wire transfers so that errors have been greatly reduced.

The efficiency of the system has not gone unnoticed by those who illicitly accumulate and distribute large amounts of cash. Up to 75 percent of all drug trafficking proceeds are "laundered" through wire transfers. Money laundering is the process of disguising the source of funds so that they appear to have been acquired through legal means. Although money laundering is generally associated with drug trafficking, it is also employed to disguise money earned from illegal gambling, extortion, bribery, prostitution, and loan-sharking.

The Treasury Department regulates bank operations through the comptroller of the currency, who supervises and periodically examines national banks. Individual states are responsible for banks operating under state charters. Money laundering can occur through banks by layering funds within accounts and transferring those funds electronically. When laundered funds are returned to the legitimate economy, they appear to have been derived from legal sources such as real estate deals, loans from front companies, and import and export invoicing. To identify a money laundering operation, the Treasury Department must associate funds with some illegal activity. The Internal Revenue Service often becomes involved in the uncovering of money laundering schemes because such schemes can be used to evade income taxes.

The Bank Secrecy Act. The core statutes governing currency transaction reporting and recordkeeping are found within the provisions of the Bank Secrecy Act, administered by the Department of the Treasury. These provisions are designed to assist in the detection and prosecution of illegal fund transfers. Agencies involved in this effort include the U.S. Customs Service, Internal Revenue Service, Office of Financial Enforcement, and Office of Financial Crime Enforcement Network (FINCEN).

The Bank Secrecy Act was enacted in 1970 but was virtually unenforced until the 1980's. The act was designed to help deter white-collar crimes such as income tax evasion by furnishing law enforcement officials with greater evidence of illegal financial transactions. Bank Secrecy Act regulations authorize the secretary of the treasury to target transactions with certain foreign institutions and transactions of domestic financial institutions that take place in certain geographic regions of the United States. These regulations provide the secretary with broad discretion in channeling resources to particular institutions and regions that might be prone to abuses and illicit manipulation.

Bibliography

Cooke, David C. *Your Treasury Department.* New York: W. W. Norton, 1964.

Katz, Bernard S., and C. Daniel Vencill. *Biographical Dictionary of the United States Secretaries of the Treasury, 1789-1995.* Westport, Conn.: Greenwood Press, 1996.

Luebke, Thomas E., ed. *Department of the Treasury.* U.S. Government Printing Office, 1986.

Sam R. Hakim

Two-Party System

Two-party systems provide voters within democratic systems the simplest possible electoral choices. They also increase the likelihood that a party that wins an election will have a majority in government.

Party systems are generally broken down into three types: multiparty systems, two-party systems, and single-party systems. Two-party systems give voters simple choices between parties in and out of power. Once elections are over and the elected officials assume office, a two-party system produces the party in power

---

> **Key Terms**
>
> MAJORITY PARTY: party that has a majority of the seats within the legislature
>
> MINORITY PARTY: party or parties that have fewer seats in the legislature than the majority party
>
> PARTY LEADER: the most powerful party official within the legislature
>
> PARTY WHIPS: group of high-ranking party officials who keep track of party members' voting behavior, to help implement party strategy

(majority party) and the opposition party (minority party). As in all other party systems, it is the role of political parties in a two-party system to win elections and then to organize government in a manner consistent with the principles the party espoused during the campaign.

Parties failing to receive majorities in legislatures become the opposition parties. The opposition, or minority, party assumes the role of criticizing the majority party and offering alternative policies to those advanced by the majority.

Third Parties. Two-party systems are rarely purely *two*-party systems. Third-party movements are not uncommon in any two-party system, and large interest groups can divide a party. Even the most secure two-party systems are not static systems. In the United States, for example, the two political parties that make up its two-party system have changed over the years. The two parties that make up the American party system have been, over the years, the Federalists and the Republicans, Democrats and Whigs, and the Republicans and Democrats. During transitional periods of the American party system there have always been a number of partisan groups hoping they would emerge as one of the two major parties.

Even during periods of relative party stability, there have been third-party movements

Thomas Nast's 1882 cartoon lampoons the ugly competition between the Democratic and Republican Parties to keep Chinese immigrants out of the United States. (Asian American Studies Library, University of California at Berkeley)

that have challenged one or both of the major parties. A classic example of such a third-party challenge occurred in the early twentieth century when the Progressive Party challenged the two major parties in America. The two major parties were able to withstand this challenge by incorporating progressive policies into their own party platforms. A number of third-party movements have ended with one or both of the major parties' incorporating key third-party policy proposals into their own party platform.

Flexibility of Parties. A hallmark of two-party systems has been the willingness of the major parties to accommodate popular policy proposal. It is their openness to new initiatives and their ability to recruit new leadership that keeps major parties strong. The Labour Party of Great Britain and the Whig Party of America are two examples of major parties that lost their dominant position when a third-party challenger proved more willing and able to adjust to changing political times.

The most enduring two-party systems are found in Great Britain and the United States. Parties in both countries evolved independently of their constitutional systems. Political parties usually begin as informal associations of people who share a common set of concerns or principles. The informality or spontaneity of party origins sometimes makes early party history difficult to establish. There are numerous political coalitions forged among legislators and candidates for public office. Some of these are quite transient and have no lasting impact beyond a single issue; other coalitions may be reestablished over a series of

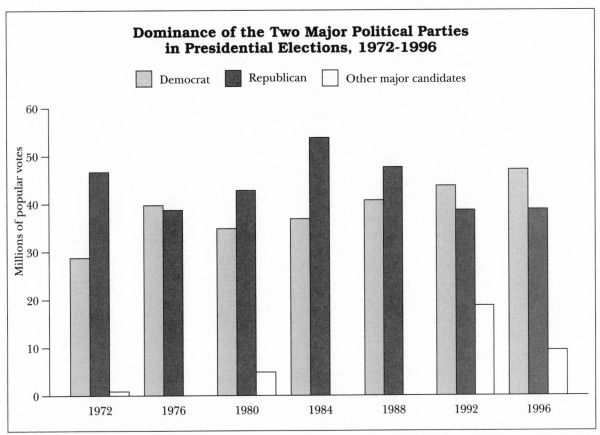

Dominance of the Two Major Political Parties in Presidential Elections, 1972-1996

Democrat   Republican   Other major candidates

Source: U.S. Bureau of the Census, *Statistical Abstract of the United States: 1997.* 117th ed. Washington, D.C.: U.S. Government Printing Office, 1997.

similar issues and, in time, become a fairly permanent group that has a high degree of cohesion over a wide range of policy issues. In the latter case, the group of politicians may even attempt to spell out some clear set of political principles that will guide their future political behavior. It is at this point that they may legitimately be considered an organized political party.

Two-party systems tend to develop in countries that have single-member electoral districts that utilize a winner-takes-all selection process. Election laws could very well be the most important variable in determining the kind of party system that develops in any given political system.

The presidential system in the United States has produced and sustained a very decentral-

ized party system. SEPARATION OF POWERS, which is the defining characteristic of a presidential system, seems to work against a strongly unified party system. In contrast, the parliamentary system in Great Britain clearly encourages a centralized party system. The principle of parliamentary sovereignty makes it easy for parliamentary parties to maintain control at the top levels of their organization.

As different as these two systems are, they provide the most stable and enduring two-party systems the world has witnessed. This fact has led some political observers to conclude that two-party systems require a fairly sophisticated electorate and a stable political environment. Two-party systems are, no doubt, enhanced by a political system that recognizes the importance of coalition building and political compromise. Narrowly defined, ideological parties have not enjoyed much political success in two-party systems. Both presidential and parliamentary systems have witnessed their greatest political unrest when there was not a dominant majority party at the helms of their governments.

Two-party Government in U.S. History.
Like most party systems the American system developed in stages. The first truly national party structure in the United States was organized in the House of Representatives in the early 1790's. Congressman James Madison organized House members to block the economic proposals of Alexander Hamilton, the first U.S. secretary of the treasury. While Madison's efforts met with only limited success, the party structure he created became a lasting part of the American political scene.

The congressional party system was so strong that by 1800 congressional caucuses were utilized by the parties to nominate candidates for the presidency. These congressional caucuses controlled the presidential nominating process until the 1820's. By 1832 a number of political parties had organized national presidential nominating conventions to select their presidential candidate. It was at this point that national parties in America developed as something more than merely congressional parties.

Bibliography

Ranney, Austin. *The Doctrine of Responsible Party Government: Its Origins and Present State.* Westport, Conn.: Greenwood Press, 1982.

Reynolds, David. *Democracy Unbound: Progressive Challenges to the Two Party System.* Boston: South End Press, 1997.

Rosenstone, Steven J., Roy L. Behr, and Edward Lazarus. *Third Parties in America: Citizen Response to Major Party Failure.* 2d ed. Princeton, N.J.: Princeton University Press, 1996.

Weatherman, Donald. *Endangered Guardians: Party Reform Within a Constitutional System.* Totowa, N.J.: Rowman & Littlefield, 1994.

Donald V. Weatherman

U

Urban Renewal and Housing

Government undertakes housing and urban renewal programs to help citizens obtain adequate shelter and to direct development toward land uses that contribute to the livability of urban areas. Programs have ranged from slum clearance to attempts to eliminate homelessness.

Housing and urban renewal were concerns of the U.S. government long before they were formally recognized as government functions. During the twentieth century federal involvement in these activities changed with altering social, political, and economic conditions in the country. The philosophies of the various presidential administrations also caused changes in the level of government involvement in these activities. Some presidents have placed great importance on direct involvement by the federal government, while others have advocated decentralization, which gives more control to the localities in which the programs are carried out.

Governmental programs in housing and urban renewal have been diverse, ranging from slum clearance during the Great Depression, to mortgage lending programs, to assisting local governments to lure upscale department stores to inner cities in the late twentieth century.

Urban Renewal in U.S. History. The original goal of urban renewal programs was to improve the social and economic conditions of the urban setting so that the middle-and upper-class populations would return from the suburbs to which they had fled, partly in response to the deterioration of the inner city. Their return, it was hoped, would result in an increase in property taxes collected and a reversal of the decline and decay of the central city.

Between 1892 and 1908 studies of slum conditions led to recommendations to condemn unsanitary housing and for the government purchase and improvement of substandard housing. Urban problems such as overcrowding, deterioration of housing, and racial strife were thought to be best dealt with by state and local authorities, not by the federal government.

The primary government objectives during the Great Depression of the 1930's were to provide employment and stimulate economic recovery. During this period, the federal government attempted to eliminate slums by acquiring buildings through powers of eminent domain. Slums that were cleared in this manner often were replaced with towering concrete housing projects such as are found in New York City and Chicago.

In 1935, when the government attempted to use eminent domain to eliminate slums in Louisville, Kentucky, a legal challenge was made. It was determined that providing housing to a relatively few people could not be considered to be in the national interest and did not justify the government's actions. After this decision, the government began to grant funds to localities to carry out the same purposes.

Housing Programs. During the Depression era, the federal government also became involved in home ownership programs when presidents Herbert Hoover and Franklin D. Roosevelt initiated mortgage lending systems to help people buy homes. These programs had a dual purpose: to rescue the banks that had survived the Depression, but which held loans on mortgages that people were unable to repay under the original terms; and to stimulate the construction industry and provide jobs.

The Federal Home Loan Bank Act of 1932 began a system to enable people to purchase homes on credit when there was a reasonable expectation that the loans could be repaid. The Federal Housing Administration (FHA), created in 1934, insured the loans, and enabled people to buy houses on credit by making a down payment that was small relative to the cost of the home. Construction of these homes was financed by loans to builders, who were required to pay only 15 percent of the costs if they satisfied the FHA requirements that they correctly judge the housing market and the value of the home, and that they build according to certain codes.

Post-World War II Housing Policies. Following the close of World War II, the Veterans Administration (VA) began approving mortgage loans to returning servicemen, with low down payments and twenty-five-year repayment terms. During this period, decent, affordable housing in cities was in short supply. VA loans enabled people to buy new homes in the suburbs for monthly payments often lower than their rent would have been for the substandard housing then available in the cities. This resulted in the rapid and sustained exodus of people from the cities to the suburbs, where land was plentiful and inexpen-

Detroit mayor Dennis W. Archer set urban renewal as a top priority for the decaying industrial city in 1994. (AP/Wide World Photos)

sive. As people left the inner cities to live in the suburbs, their tax dollars went with them, and the deterioration of the cities accelerated.

The Housing Act of 1949 was intended to eliminate residential blight, and established a federal program for central city redevelopment. Part of this legislation was captioned "Slum Clearance and Community Development and Redevelopment." The act's purpose was to provide a decent home and a suitable living environment for every American family.

It focused primarily on physically deteriorated areas, which were eligible for federal funds to be used for clearance and redevelopment. After a local government applied to the federal authority and was granted approval, it could acquire, through purchase or condemnation, property in the area to be renewed. Thus, middle-income housing construction was favored, and that the residents of these cleared areas—people of lower-middle and lower income—were displaced without help in relocating.

The Housing Act of 1954 changed the focus of governmental programs from redevelop-

Secret Service officer removing a banner protesting the Clinton administration's cuts in Housing and Urban Development programs that was hung on a White House gate in early 1995. (AP/Wide World Photos)

residential areas that met the standards for deterioration could be cleared and redeveloped for commercial, industrial, or any other use.

Under this program, the federal government provided grants of up to two-thirds of the project's costs. The act required that any federally funded urban redevelopment program follow a general plan for the entire community, which was the first time a community plan had been required. Critics claimed that ment to urban renewal, and aimed to clear the slums, prevent the development of new slums, and conserve housing that had not yet deteriorated. Congress specifically required that urban renewal projects be part of a workable program for community improvement. Each city seeking federal funding needed to provide a comprehensive plan for community development.

Urban Renewal. Government urban renewal entered the area of business renewal in

1959 and allowed for 20 percent of federal monies to be allocated for nonresidential purposes. Business renewal was intended to preserve the healthy commercial and business districts of the central city and encourage further development there.

As federal involvement in housing programs and urban renewal increased, it became necessary to coordinate the many programs related to these concerns more efficiently. In 1965 President Lyndon B. Johnson signed legislation creating the Department of Housing and Urban Development (HUD). Giving these activities cabinet-level status acknowledged their growing importance.

Housing and urban renewal are complex, multifaceted concerns of the U.S. government that affect all Americans both directly and indirectly. Providing housing and directing rational urban development are ongoing activities of government, and are affected by the country's changing social, economic, and political conditions.

Relieving one problem often causes other problems to worsen. For example, as central city neighborhoods are improved by new business development or by the rehabilitation of old buildings, former occupants who might have been able to make a living or afford the rents of the buildings in their previous, perhaps dilapidated, condition, are forced to relocate to areas that might be less desirable or affordable for them. By eliminating what might have been considered slum conditions, areas are "gentrified" to house upper-income residents, displacing the previous tenants.

The reality of limited tax dollars forces federal, state, and local governments to prioritize spending. Other programs and problems that are funded at a higher level than housing and urban renewal programs may still affect housing and the urban environment. For example, when buildings are demolished to make way for a federally funded transit project such as light rail construction, the inhabitants of those buildings are forced to relocate. As long as citizens require housing and cities continue to change and deteriorate, housing and urban renewal issues will be part of the government agenda.

Bibliography

Keating, W. Dennis, Norman Krumholz, and Philip Star, eds. *Revitalizing Urban Neighborhoods.* Lawrence: University Press of Kansas, 1996.

Moe, Richard. *Changing Places: Rebuilding Community in the Age of Sprawl.* New York: Henry Holt, 1997.

Pagano, Michael A., and Ann O. Pagano. *Cityscapes and Capital: The Politics of Urban Development.* Baltimore: Johns Hopkins University Press, 1995.

Van Vliet, Willem. *Affordable Housing and Urban Redevelopment in the United States.* Thousand Oaks, Calif.: Sage Publications, 1997.

Debbie Schiedel

V

Veterans' Rights

The federal, state, and local governments have given veterans preferential treatment in employment and have provided a broad range of benefits ranging from home loans and medical care to educational benefits.

After most American wars, federal, state, and local governments have passed legislation establishing special preferences and benefits for military veterans. The promises of benefits are generally viewed as "rights," and, as a consequence, veterans' rights usually have a very broad interpretation.

Background. The extension of benefits to veterans has followed a clear pattern. In the decades following the AMERICAN REVOLUTION, "fitness of character" was the principal criterion upon which government hiring decisions were based, and former military officers enjoyed considerable preference in hiring. The preference was based on the veterans' proven loyalty to the government and the likelihood that they were from the upper classes.

Following the Civil War, veterans were given land in the West to encourage development, as well as to reward service and to reduce unemployment. Some medical benefits were

The Vietnam Memorial in the Washington Mall, which commemorates members of the armed forces who lost their lives in the Vietnam War, is a powerful emotional symbol to military veterans. (R. Kent Rasmussen)

extended to veterans with disabilities after both the Civil and Spanish American Wars. For example, an 1865 federal act gave veterans with disabilities preference for appointments to public jobs. A number of states passed similar legislation during the late 1800's; World War I veterans were added in 1919.

During the 1930's the U.S. Civil Service Commission gave special examinations to veterans with disabilities and, if they passed, moved them to the top of hiring lists. Veterans' preference in public employment, however, did not expand significantly until passage of the Veterans Preference Act of 1944.

Preference in Employment. Preference in employment is perhaps the most familiar veterans' benefit. While preference legislation has primarily focused on protecting the reemployment rights of veterans returning to civilian life after active duty, veterans' preference means much more. The federal government and many state and local governments typically add points to civil service examination scores of veterans. Some state and local governments automatically move qualified veterans to the top of the register. Some governments extend the benefits to the families of veterans with disabilities. The extra points often elevate veterans to the top of hiring lists or registers and increase their prospects of being hired.

After veterans are hired, they have also enjoyed greater protection from dismissal. The Veterans' Preference Act of 1944 gave the Civil Service Commission authority to reinstate veterans removed from their positions, while the commission could only review and make recommendations concerning removals of nonveterans. When the federal civil service was reformed in 1978, President Jimmy Carter proposed changes in veterans' preference, because it was seen as a violation of the principle that hiring should be on merit or job qualifications, but Congress intervened to protect and expand the provisions.

Veterans are also offered some protection

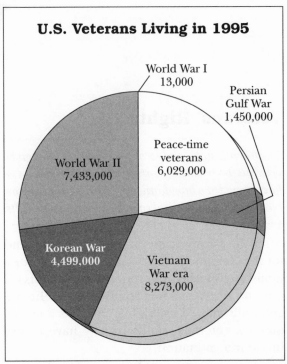

U.S. Veterans Living in 1995

World War I
13,000

Persian Gulf War
1,450,000

Peace-time veterans
6,029,000

World War II
7,433,000

Korean War
4,499,000

Vietnam War era
8,273,000

Source: U.S. Bureau of the Census, *Statistical Abstract of the United States: 1997.* 117th ed. Washington, D.C.: U.S. Government Printing Office, 1997.

in reductions-in-force or layoffs. When veterans' positions are eliminated, they can find other positions at an equal or lower rank and "bump" nonveteran occupants out of their jobs. In some state and local governments, veterans are also given preference in promotions and other personnel actions.

Challenges to Preference. On the whole, veterans' preference reduces flexibility in hiring, rewarding, disciplining, and laying off public workers and violates the merit principle. Indeed, veterans' preference has had a significant impact on the composition of the federal civil service, particularly at the senior level, in terms of reducing opportunities for women. Also, because the preference is not merit-based, it may have had a negative impact on the overall quality of the senior civil service. While there has been growing criticism of veterans' preference because it violates merit principles, there has been less criticism of programs to employ veterans with disabilities. The Vietnam Era Veterans' Readjustment Assistance Act of 1974 was passed to facilitate the employment of veterans and disabled veterans who can reasonably be expected to benefit from vocational rehabilitation services.

Challenges to veterans' preference in employment have not been successful. In 1976, for example, the U.S. SUPREME COURT reaffirmed that personnel practices are acceptable if there is no intent to discriminate. Three years after that the Court upheld the "absolute preference" for veterans in Massachusetts because there was no intent to discriminate against women, and women veterans were provided the same benefit. In fact, the Equal Employment Opportunity Act of 1972 prohibits discrimination in employment, with the specific exception of veterans' preferences. Notwithstanding the unsuccessful challenges to veterans' preference, some limits are increasingly being placed on "double dipping," or using military service credit to qualify for additional civilian pension benefits.

Other Benefits. Other veterans' benefits have included educational and medical assistance. The G.I. Bill educational benefits, which were originally extended to veterans returning home after World War II and the Korean War and to Vietnam War-era veterans without requiring them to contribute directly, became a voluntary contribution program (with the federal government matching the veterans' contributions) in the 1970's. The Department of

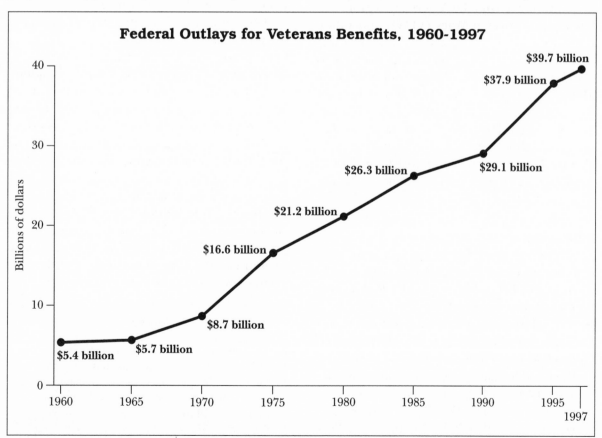

Source: U.S. Bureau of the Census, *Statistical Abstract of the United States: 1997.* 117th ed. Washington, D.C.: U.S. Government Printing Office, 1997.

Note: 1997 figure is estimated.

Veterans' Affairs Home Loan Guaranty Program was created to stimulate home buying after World War II by permitting veterans to purchase homes without a down payment and by underwriting the loans. The Veterans Administration, now Veterans' Affairs, hospital system still provides health care for disabled, aged, and indigent veterans, although budget cuts during the 1970's and 1980's forced cutbacks in care. Veterans are also provided with burial benefits, although space in veterans' cemeteries is becoming scarce.

Public support for veterans' rights and programs is diminishing because of the smaller percentage of the population who have served in the military, including the declining number of members of Congress who are veterans. Support from the American Legion, the Veterans of Foreign Wars (VFW), and other veterans' groups remains strong; however, fewer younger veterans are joining the American Legion and VFW because of a lack of identification with World War II and Korean War vets and political differences with the national organizations. The strength of the veterans' lobby, however, is evident in the elevation of the Veterans Administration to the cabinet-level Department of Veterans' Affairs in the 1980's.

Bibliography

Addlestone, David F., Susan Hewman, and Frederic Gross. *The Rights of Veterans: The Basic ACLU Guide to a Veteran's Rights.* New York: Avon Books, 1978.

Cayer, N. Joseph. "Merit System Reform in the States," in *Public Personnel Administration: Problems and Prospects,* edited by Steven W. Hays and Richard C. Kearney. 3d ed. Englewood Cliffs, N.J.: Prentice Hall, 1995.

Nigro, Lloyd G. *The New Public Personnel Administration.* 4th ed. Itasca, Ill.: F. E. Peacock, 1994.

William L. Waugh, Jr.

Veto Power

Veto power is the constitutional authority that the president of the United States uses to prevent congressional enactments from becoming law.

Delegates to the U.S. Constitutional Convention of 1787 wanted to prevent any of the three principal branches of the proposed new federal government from encroaching on the independence and powers of the others. The Constitution's granting of veto power to the president establishes the single most important limit on the exercise of power by the U.S. Congress. The primary purpose of the veto was to help maintain the independence of the executive branch from Congress.

The Constitution explicitly prevents Congress from avoiding or evading the president's veto power. The "presentment clause" requires that bills be presented to the president, as well as "every order, resolution or vote to which the concurrence of the Senate and House of Representatives may be necessary (except on a question of adjournment)." The president is constitutionally empowered to consider and pass on any congressional measure that has the potential to become law.

How the Veto Works. The actual operation of the veto power is simple. If the president approves a bill or resolution that has been presented, the president signs it and it becomes law. If the president disapproves of the

"Veto"

"Veto" is a Latin word that means "I forbid." The earliest known formal governmental use of this power occurring in the ancient Roman Empire, in which the tribunes of the people could nullify decrees of the senate or the proceedings of the magistrates by simply saying "Veto."

This contemporary cartoon celebrates President Andrew Jackson's veto of an unpopular bill to recharter the national bank in 1832. (Library of Congress)

measure, it may be returned to the house of Congress in which it was initiated, with a separate veto message setting forth the president's objections to the bill. Congress may then reconsider it, and if both houses pass it again by a two-thirds majority it becomes law. In this case, the president's veto is said to be overridden. If the president does not act on a measure within ten days, Sundays excepted, the measure becomes a law without a signature. If, however, Congress has adjourned in the interim, the measure does not become a law. When that happens, the bill is said to be "pocket vetoed."

Presidents and the Veto Power. The Constitutional Convention expected that Congress would be the dominant branch of the government. As the representative or popularly elected branch, Congress was supposed to reflect the public's political will better than the other two branches. Consequently, there was some doubt in the early years of the republic whether the veto power should be used unless the president believed a bill to be unconstitutional. This issue was fought out during George Washington's presidency. Although Washington established the precedent that a bill could be vetoed for political reasons alone, vetoes were infrequent until the administration of President Andrew Jackson.

The first six presidents vetoed six bills altogether. Jackson vetoed twelve, strengthening his administration's political influence with Congress. His most celebrated veto was that of the bill to recharter the Second Bank of the United States in 1832. This veto, together with the withdrawal of federal funds the following year, effectively brought the bank down. His free use of the veto established it as a powerful tool of presidential leadership. Later presidents followed Jackson's example. Often the mere threat of a presidential veto can influence policy.

Overriding Vetoes. The most important reason for the veto's political potency is that Congress can rarely muster the two-thirds majority required in each chamber to override a veto. Franklin D. Roosevelt, president from 1933 to 1945, vetoed 635 bills—more than any other president. Only nine of his vetoes were overturned by Congress, in part because he was very popular and always had Democratic majorities in both the Senate and House of Representatives.

Even a less popular president such as Richard Nixon was able to make his veto stick most of the time. During his five and a half years in office, Nixon vetoed forty-three bills. He was only overridden seven times, despite facing opposition party control of both houses and, after the unveiling of the Watergate scandal, growing unpopularity and distrust. President George Bush, a Republican, was able to sustain

forty-four of his forty-five vetoes, again despite Democratic control of both houses during all four years of his administration. Presidents John F. Kennedy and Lyndon B. Johnson issued fifty-one vetoes between them; not one was overridden.

Some political scientists argue that the veto is actually a sign of presidential weakness, not strength. The power is only used when Congress has refused to accept a president's views on an issue. For example, the frequency with which President Gerald Ford used the veto from 1974 to 1976 was a strong indication that Congress did not accept Ford's leadership. Ford vetoed sixty-six bills and was overridden twelve times.

Another important limitation on the veto power is its relative uselessness on fiscal and budgetary issues. Congress normally passes a single comprehensive appropriations bill and a few supplemental appropriations bills for each fiscal year. The president is unlikely to veto an entire bill simply because of dislike for one part of it. This weakness of the veto is all the more galling to presidents when Congress attaches irrelevant "riders" to appropriations bills. For example, after President Jimmy Carter vetoed a bill providing for increased salaries for Public Health Service physicians, Congress added the pay raise to mental health services legislation, a pet project of First Lady Rosalyn Carter. The president then signed the bill.

The Line-Item Veto. For these reasons, presidents as early as Ulysses S. Grant argued for a line-item veto—the power to strike out particular parts of congressional bills. To

Although the Democratic Party controlled both houses of Congress throughout Republican president George Bush's four years in office, he sustained all of his vetoes. (AP/Wide World Photos)

expedite the passage and signing of legislation, many members of Congress began supporting this idea during the early 1990's. Some argued, however, that granting the president line-item veto power might require a constitutional amendment because the Constitution gave Congress itself sole power to legislate. Some legislators, however, believed it was constitutionally possible for Congress to make most federal spending discretionary for the president, rather than mandatory.

In 1997 this theory was tested when Congress passed a law granting the president line-item veto power over certain specified portions of tax and appropriation bills. In April of that year a federal judge struck down the new law because the "dynamic of lawmaking is fundamentally altered." Despite this ruling President Bill Clinton tested the new presidential line-item veto authority the following September, when he vetoed several provisions of a bill sent to him. In June, 1998, the U.S. Supreme Court ended this experiment when it ruled the Line Item Veto Act of 1997 unconstitutional.

The Veto and Checks and Balances. The veto power is one of the essential balances that maintain the system of separation of powers in the United States. This incomplete check on legislative power has served to prevent most congressional encroachment on the executive, although its negative nature has prevented presidents from dictating the content of the laws to Congress. Thus, maintenance of the executive's independence from legislative domination has been the great success of the veto power

In the political sense, however, presidents face an uphill battle in dealing with Congress. Their two formal powers—recommending legislation to Congress and vetoing bills—help set the legislature's agenda and prevent some of what presidents oppose from passing, but Congress's law-making power is so formidable that the president's prerogatives are only mar-

---

Presidential Restraint

Seven U.S. presidents never exercised their veto power:

John Adams (1797-1801)
Thomas Jefferson (1801-1809)
John Quincy Adams (1825-1829)
William Henry Harrison (1841)
Zachary Taylor (1849-1850)
Millard Fillmore (1850-1853)
James Garfield (1881)

Three presidents exercised the veto but not a pocket veto:

George Washington (1789-1797)
James Monroe (1817-1825)
Franklin Pierce (1853-1857)

One president exercised the pocket veto not a regular veto:

Martin Van Buren (1837-1841)

---

ginally useful. Conflict between the two political branches of the government is inherent, because of the overlapping powers and differing constituencies of the two institutions. Presidents can influence Congress but can rarely dominate it. The power they need most—a lever to persuade Congress to pass the bills that support their program—does not exist except in the most unusual political situations. It was the emergency of the Great Depression that gave Franklin Roosevelt his initial mastery of Congress. In normal times, the public wish for dramatically successful political leadership from the president seems bound to be unfulfilled.

Bibliography

Edwards, George C., III, and Stephen J. Wayne. *Presidential Leadership: Politics and Policy Making.* 3d ed. New York: St. Martin's Press, 1994.

Korn, Jessica. *The Power of Separation: American Constitutionalism and the Myth of the Legisla-*

tive Veto. Princeton, N.J.: Princeton University Press, 1996.

Spitzer, Robert J. *The Presidential Veto: Touchstone of the American Presidency.* Albany: State University of New York Press, 1988.

Watson, Richard A. *Presidential Vetoes and Public Policy.* Lawrence: University of Kansas Press, 1993.

Robert Jacobs

Vigilantism

Unofficial and illegal pursuit of justice, vigilantism occurs when people dismiss formal procedures for administering justice as inadequate and take the law into their own hands.

Vigilantism can occur only when a formal justice system is in place that vigilantes circumvent. Some experts also view group activity as a defining characteristic of vigilantism; according to this view, the lone self-appointed upholder of justice would not be seen as a true vigilante. Vigilante groups believe that the government is not protecting the lives, well-being, or property of its citizens and feel that they must act—even though they are acting outside the law—to ensure that justice is being done.

Vigilantism in American History. Vigilantism has a fabled place in American, and especially western, history. The peak years of vigilante activity in the United States were roughly between 1850 and 1900. Early vigilante groups, which were given names such as "regulators" and "committees of public safety," sometimes carried out periodic round-ups and punishment of suspected criminals because of the absence of reliable local law enforcement officials. Especially well-known groups are the San Francisco vigilantes of the 1850's, vigilantes in the Montana Territory, and the violent vigilante groups of the Southwest in the latter half of the nineteenth century.

After the Reconstruction era, the American South also saw considerable activity that could be considered vigilantism, in the form of lynchings and harassment of AFRICAN AMERICANS deemed guilty of wrongdoing, although in truth these vicious activities represented a combination of vigilantism and terrorism designed to keep African Americans subservient to whites.

Punishments meted out by vigilante groups included whipping, tar and feathering, torture, mutilation, and murder. The term "lynching" first arose to describe whippings carried out by eighteenth century American vigilantes led by a Virginian named Charles Lynch. As the extent of vigilante violence grew in the nineteenth century, lynching became identified with the execution of "undesirables" by any vigilante group, but particularly of blacks by whites in the South.

Vigilantism in Old San Francisco

During the 1850's San Francisco was a wild boom town prospering in the wake of the 1848 California gold rush. In 1851 merchants who considered the town overly crime-ridden and out of control, formed a "committee of vigilance." Though active only a month, it hanged one man and drove twenty-eight others out of San Francisco. The committee's main targets were Australians, who were popularly suspected to be criminals because many of Australia's first European settlers were criminals expelled from Great Britain. San Francisco's second vigilante committee, formed in 1856, had more than six thousand members. This body hanged at least four people and forced another thirty out of town. The committee also took on the city's political machine. Some have argued that from the committee's beginning, its real purpose was to wrest political power from the largely Irish Catholic Democrats who controlled the city government through violence and intimidation.

After New York commuter Bernhard Goetz shot four youths who accosted him in a subway in December, 1984, he was popularly dubbed the "Subway Vigilante." (AP/Wide World Photos)

Vigilante Organization. Some vigilantes formed well-organized voluntary vigilance committees aimed at combating perceived threats to the group or community—threats which may have been real, exaggerated, or totally imaginary. In many instances the leadership of a vigilante group was drawn from the elite members of the community. Although vigilante activities have always been illegal, members of vigilante groups saw themselves as upholding and enforcing the law, not as violating it.

Modern Definitions. A distinction should be drawn between vigilante groups and other types of groups with whom they are sometimes considered. The essential element of a vigilante group is that it wishes to administer justice—as the group itself defines it—and punish wrongdoers whom the law is unwilling or unable to punish. A number of other types of modern groups that are sometimes grouped with vigilantes—hate groups, terrorist groups, survivalists—do not have this goal.

Quasi-vigilante Groups. Fear of crime in city streets and in mass transit systems has spawned groups that are sometimes, though generally inaccurately, deemed vigilante groups. These organizations range from the local neighborhood watch groups who seek to keep down crime in neighborhoods to transit and subway patrols such as New York's Guardian Angels. None of these "defensive" groups is truly definable as a vigilante movement, because few of their members have any wish to take the law into their own hands. They most often act as watchdogs, as deterrents to crime, and as eyes and ears for law enforcement agencies, although undoubtedly some members of these groups have occasionally pushed the limits of acceptable behavior when carrying out citizen's arrests.

Bibliography

Culberson, William C. *Vigilantism: Political History of Private Power in America.* New York: Greenwood Press, 1990.

Ingalls, Robert P. *Urban Vigilantes in the New South: Tampa, 1882-1936.* Gainesville: University Press of Florida, 1993.

Madison, Arnold. *Vigilantism in America.* New York: Seabury Press, 1973.

Moses, Norton H. *Lynching and Vigilantism in the United States: An Annotated Bibliography.* Westport, Conn.: Greenwood Press, 1997.

Sanford S. Singer

Voting Behavior

The most fundamental political activity in democratic systems, voting is the process by which citizens select representatives and make policy choices to govern themselves. How voters behave reflects public attitudes toward government.

Voting serves several purposes, not the least of which is to provide for peaceful transfer of power among political elites. Voting is often seen as the expression of a mandate for governing according to a political platform or agenda; however, it is also a measure of political strength among competing political groups. Voting confers legitimacy upon governing elites. It also strengthens the legitimacy of the constitutional order within which political competitions occur. Finally, voting is the single most important peaceful mechanism by which the people as a whole can exercise their self-determination.

Education, Income, and Voting Behavior. While political attitudes of voters and nonvoters within societies do not appear to differ greatly, several other characteristics distin-

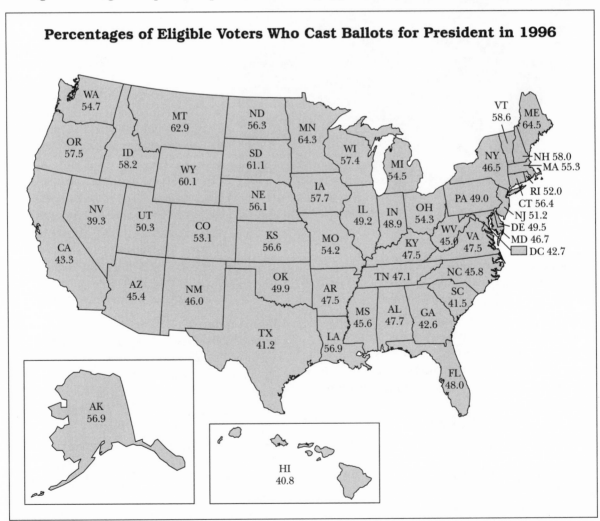

Percentages of Eligible Voters Who Cast Ballots for President in 1996

Source: U.S. Bureau of the Census, *Statistical Abstract of the United States: 1997.* 117th ed. Washington, D.C.: U.S. Government Printing Office, 1997.

Race and ethnicity have continued to play major roles in voting behavior. Here South Carolina congressional candidate Jim Clyburn greets fellow African Americans after voting in the 1992 general election. (AP/Wide World Photos)

guish voters from nonvoters in the American electorate. For example, individuals with higher levels of education vote at higher rates than do those with lower levels of education. In theory, at least, education allows a person to overcome certain systemic barriers to voting, and it improves a person's ability to deal with complex and conflicting campaign discourse. Furthermore, while individuals with high income levels are more likely to vote than those with low income levels—owing to the wealthy's greater economic stake in the political system—some of the impact of income is diminished by educational differences.

Older Americans tend to vote at higher rates than younger Americans—particularly voters under twenty-five years of age. This may be because younger voters have yet to appreciate their own stake in the political system. The same argument may partially explain the impact of race and ethnic background on voting behavior. White voter turnout is generally higher than that among AFRICAN AMERICANS and LATINOS. This may be attributable to a sense of apathy among nonwhites who doubt that their voices will be heard. More important, black voter turnout has yet to overcome the latent effects of past discrimination in civil and voting rights, especially in the South, where the stigma of discrimination is greater and African American voter turnout is lower than in other regions of the country. At the same time, nonwhite turnout is affected by lower levels of socioeconomic status.

Regional Variations in Voting Behavior. Voter turnout generally tends to be lower in the South than in other parts of the country. Among the factors that play a role are the generally lower educational and income levels of southerners and the history of more restrictive registration requirements, particularly those affecting African Americans and poor whites. In addition, the traditional paternalism of southern culture has tended to discourage the involvement of women in the electorate.

The Gender Gap. The 1980's and 1990's have provided some evidence of a gender gap in voter turnout nationwide. During this period women were slightly more likely to vote than were men. This trend is partly explained by increasing levels of education and income among women, by the heightened interest in feminist issues, and by the increasing success of women in winning elective offices and influencing policy decisions.

Political Party Affiliation. Party identification appears to have an impact on voter turnout. Citizens who decline to register with any party are the least likely to vote, followed by Democratic identifiers and then Republicans. Whatever advantages the Democratic Party is perceived to enjoy because of its status as the largest party within the electorate are partially nullified by the fact that its partisans are less likely to vote in presidential elections than Republicans are.

While PUBLIC OPINION POLLS indicate that the American electorate has grown less partisan since 1952, party identification still plays a strong role in the voting decisions of those voters who identify with a political party. Those who identify with, or lean toward, either the Democratic or the Republican Party tend to vote for their preferred party's candidates. Republican voters exhibit greater loyalty to party candidates than do Democrats, while the partisan preferences of independent voters fluctuate over time.

Other Factors. Despite the impact of long-term forces, it is clear that other forces of short-term duration also play important roles in determining American voter choices. Among these short-term forces are voters' perceptions of individual candidates and important issues. Several studies of voter attitudes from the 1950's point to an increase in candidate-centered voting, particularly in the 1980's. Republicans have dominated most

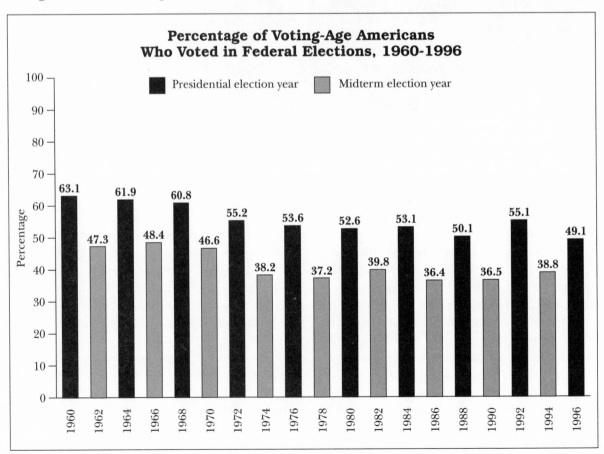

Source: Borgna Brunner, ed., *The Time Almanac 1998.* Boston: Information Please LLC, 1997.

presidential elections since the 1950's largely because of positive popular perceptions of their candidates, not because of increasing Republican identification in the electorate or widening acceptance of Republican policy agendas.

Issues vs. Candidates. While democratic theory focuses upon the importance of voters making decisions on the basis of issues, the reality is that issues are generally less important to predicting the choices of American voters than are either party identification or perceptions of the candidates. Issues cannot affect the vote unless voters are aware of them and regard them as relevant to their own interests.

However, the content of American POLITICAL CAMPAIGNS is increasingly focused on personality issues rather than policy debates. While the increased education of the American electorate makes it more capable of dealing with complex issues, the reality is that most citizens obtain news about political campaigns primarily through television and other electronic media, whose campaign coverage emphasizes "newsworthy," rather than substantive, issues.

Finally, changes in the partisan loyalty of certain groups give some clues as to the impact of other variables on voter choices. Much, for example, has been written about the coalitions of groups that have made up the Democratic and Republican Parties since the 1930's. Generally, the "New Deal" coalition of the Democratic Party has combined voters with low incomes, African Americans, union members, Roman Catholics and Jews, southerners, and residents of central cities. By contrast, Republican Party supporters are mostly voters not defined by these characteristics.

Trends in Voter Behavior. Voter participation is at the heart of democratic theory. Limits on voting, whether legal or cultural, are seen as damaging to the health of a democracy. While the electorate in America has expanded and become less selective, voter turnout has recently dropped. Average voter turnout in American presidential elections dropped from 63 percent in 1960 to about 50 percent in 1988.

There are those who argue that comparatively low or declining voter turnout is a sign that democracy in America is in critical condition. On the other hand, there is a line of argument that high voter turnout is a sign of political conflict and instability. If this is true, low turnout would be a sign that people are generally satisfied with the status quo. It is hard, however, to reconcile democratic theory and its goal of widespread self-determination with the notion that it may be healthier for democracy if people do not vote.

Bibliography

Barone, Michael, William Lilley, and Laurence J. DeFranco. *State Legislative Elections: Voting Patterns and Demographics.* Washington, D.C.: Congressional Quarterly, 1998.

Flanigan, William H., and Nancy H. Zingale. *Political Behavior of the American Electorate.* 8th ed. Washington, D.C.: Congressional Quarterly, 1994.

Guinier, Lani. *The Tyranny of the Majority: Fundamental Fairness in Representative Democracy.* New York: Free Press, 1994.

Niemi, Richard G., and Herbert F. Weisberg. *Controversies in Voting Behavior.* 3d ed. Washington, D.C.: Congressional Quarterly Press, 1993.

Piven, Frances Fox, and Richard A. Cloward. *Why Americans Don't Vote.* New York: Pantheon Books, 1988.

Rosenstone, Steven J., and John Mark Hansen. *Mobilization, Participation, and Democracy in America.* New York: Macmillan, 1993.

Seltzer, Richard, Jody Newman, and Melissa V. Leighton. *Sex as a Political Variable: Women as Candidates and Voters in U.S. Elections.* Boulder, Colo.: Lynne Rienner, 1997.

Michael Kurt Corbello

Voting Processes

The processes through which citizens exercise their right to vote must meet certain conditions for the government system to be considered fully democratic.

Voting is one of the many forms of political participation by which citizens in a democracy can attempt to influence public policy. The emphasis on citizen participation is the distinguishing characteristic of a democratic society, and the extent to which a society's population participates in its political arena is one method of evaluating how democratic it is. A truly democratic political system will place few barriers between its citizens and the process of voting. All democracies, however, have some restrictions that limit access to suffrage.

Conditions of Democratic Elections. To have truly democratic elections, it is generally agreed that several crucial conditions must be satisfied. Substantially the entire adult population must have the right to vote for candidates for office and elections must take place within prescribed time limits. No substantial group in the adult population may be prevented from forming a party or putting up candidates. All seats in the legislative chamber may be contested, and normally are.

POLITICAL CAMPAIGNS must be conducted fairly, and neither candidates nor voters may be prevented from presenting or discussing their views. Votes must be cast freely and in secret and must be counted honestly. Candidates who receive the numbers of votes needed to win must be installed for their proper terms of office until new elections are held. Within these guidelines, there is a great diversity of election systems. No two countries have identical arrangements in terms of voter qualifications and election procedures.

Requirements for Voting. While the world's major democracies have provided for universal adult suffrage, all have some minimum requirements that must be met in order to participate. For example, most democracies, including the United States, restrict the vote to citizens by birth or naturalization.

A Virginia voter is accompanied by her children as she casts her ballot in Virginia in 1996. (Reuters/Mike Theiler/Archive Photos)

Another restriction on suffrage is residency in the constituency or country for a specified period of time, which can vary from thirty days to a year. At one time these requirements were much greater. In the United States, the state of Mississippi had a two-year residency requirement. The Voting Rights Act of 1970 set a maximum residency requirement of thirty days for presidential elections. Two years later, the Supreme Court expanded the requirement for a reasonable residency requirement to all elections.

Voter Registration. Registration is another prerequisite for voter participation in many democracies. Before citizens are allowed to vote, their name must appear on an official list of eligible voters maintained by the government. In the United States, states began to require registration at the beginning of the twentieth century in order to prevent election fraud. Registration in the United States is the individual's responsibility. As a result, turnout in elections has declined since it was instituted. In contrast, most democracies place the responsibility of registration on government.

In most states, voters must be registered thirty days prior to an election. Several states, including Maine, Minnesota, and Wisconsin, allow voters to register at their polling place on election day. One state, North Dakota, does not require voters to register. These four states are generally among the states with the highest voter turnout in the United States.

In 1993 the U.S. Congress enacted a "Motor Voter" registration law that required states to permit individuals to register to vote when they apply for a driver's license, at certain state welfare offices, or by mail. The intent of the legislation was to increase participation by making registration easier.

Bibliography

Alvarez, R. Michael. *Information and Elections.* Ann Arbor: University of Michigan Press, 1997.

Christian, Spencer, and Tom Biracree. *Electing Our Government: Everything You Need to Know to Make Your Vote Really Count.* New York: St. Martin's Griffin, 1996.

Ginsberg, Benjamin, and Alan Stone, eds. *Do Elections Matter?* 3d ed. Armonk, N.Y.: M. E. Sharpe, 1996.

Menendez, Albert J. *The Perot Voters and the Future of American Politics.* Amherst, N.Y.: Prometheus Books, 1996.

Tolchin, Susan J. *The Angry American: How Voter Rage Is Changing the Nation.* Boulder, Colo.: Westview Press, 1996.

William V. Moore

Voting Rights

Voting is a fundamental right in a democracy; however, that right was only gradually extended to all American adults.

The right to vote is one of the most fundamental rights of American citizenship, and its widespread distribution is one of the essential features of American democracy. The expansion of voting rights has been an important theme in the evolution of American democracy, as has been the increasing role of the federal government in defining such rights.

Early Voting Rights. In colonial America,

Key Terms

ELECTORATE: members of a society who have the right to vote

ENFRANCHISE: to award the vote to a person or members of a group

FRANCHISE: the right to vote; also called suffrage

UNIVERSAL SUFFRAGE: situation in which all citizens have the right to vote

VOTING AGE: minimum age at which a citizen can vote in a public election

President Lyndon B. Johnson (right) holds the copy of the Voting Rights Act of 1965, which he has just signed, as he talks with House Speaker John McCormack (left); Vice President Hubert H. Humphrey, and Senator Everett Dirksen. (AP/Wide World Photos)

voting rights were limited to adult white males who could meet a property qualification. It was generally felt that ownership of property was necessary to prove a stake in society. During and after the American Revolution, property qualifications were reduced or replaced with a requirement that a voter be a taxpayer. Voting continued to be seen as a privilege rather than a basic right of citizenship.

The original U.S. CONSTITUTION said little about voting rights. The definition of who could vote was left to the states, with the con-

dition that the requirements for voting for members of the House of Representatives be the same as those for voting for members of the largest house of the state legislature. The franchise (right to vote) remained almost exclusively limited to white males.

Expansion of Voting Rights. By the 1830's there was a noticeable trend in the direction of manhood suffrage—that is, toward allowing adult white male citizens to vote whether they owned property or not. Though all women and most black men continued to be excluded from voting, manhood suffrage was an important step in establishing a connection between citizenship and voting rights.

The Civil War set the stage for a significant broadening of voting rights as well as for a growing federal role in their definition. During Reconstruction, Congress required that the former Confederate states allow adult male AFRICAN AMERICANS to vote. The Fourteenth Amendment (1868)—the second of the CIVIL WAR AMENDMENTS—reinforced this requirement by including a provision (never actually used) that allowed reduction of a state's representation in Congress if it denied the vote to its adult male citizens. The Fifteenth Amendment (1870) went further, saying that the right to vote could not be denied on the basis of race, color, or previous condition of servitude. Since blacks were already voting in the South under congressionally mandated changes in state constitutions, the most immediate effect of the Fifteenth Amendment was to enfranchise blacks in the North, where most states still limited suffrage to whites.

The Fifteenth Amendment illustrates the point that the right to vote and its actual use are two different things. By the 1890's southern states were finding ways to limit black voting without formally restricting the right to vote on a racial basis. Techniques such as unevenly applied literacy tests, poll taxes, and the all-white primary (sometimes backed up by the threat of violence) effectively reduced African American voting to insignificance.

During the same period, the WOMAN SUFFRAGE movement exerted increasing pressure in an effort to gain access to the ballot. Beginning with Wyoming in 1890, a number of states recognized the right of women to vote.

However, women could not vote on a nationwide basis until ratification of the Nineteenth Amendment in 1920.

The Civil Rights Movement. Reviving the Fifteenth Amendment and ending restrictions on black voting rights in the southern and border states became a major goal of the Civil Rights movement that developed after World War II. Early CIVIL RIGHTS ACTS made limited attempts to protect voting rights. In 1964 the Twenty-fourth Amendment banned the poll tax in federal elections. It was not, however, until the Selma-to-Montgomery civil rights

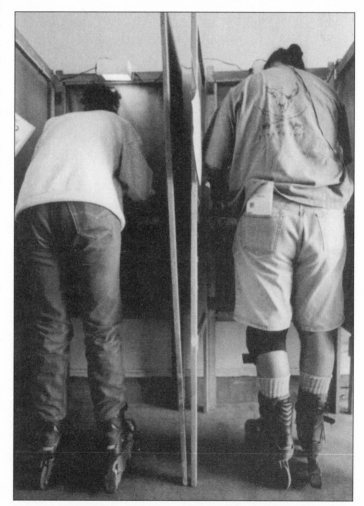

Young Californians wearing rollerblade skates while voting in the 1996 general election reflect the impact of the Twenty-sixth Amendment. (Reuters/Sam Mircovich/Archive Photos)

Major Expansions of Voting Rights

Date	Action	Significance or Intent
1870	Fifteenth Amendment	Guaranteed the vote to African Americans.
1920	Nineteenth Amendment	Guaranteed the vote to women.
1961	Twenty-third Amendment	Gave District of Columbia residents right to vote in presidential elections.
1964	Twenty-fourth Amendment	Prohibited use of poll taxes or other taxes to restrict voting rights.
1965	Voting Rights Act	Banned voting tests in the South and some other areas.
1970	Voting Rights Act	Suspended literacy tests for voting.
1971	Twenty-sixth Amendment	Extended vote to eighteen-year-olds.
1972	*Dunn v. Blumstein*	Supreme Court held that long residency requirements for voting were unconstitutional.
1975	Voting Rights Act	Required that voting information be bilingual in parts of twenty-four states.
1982	Voting Rights Act	Extended 1965 act for twenty-five years.

march dramatized the issue that Congress acted effectively. The result was the Voting Rights Act of 1965. The act provided for federal supervision of elections in southern counties where African Americans did not vote in numbers consistent with their presence in the population. Originally limited to five years, the act was subsequently renewed and extended to cover AMERICAN INDIANS and LATINOS.

The trend toward greater federal definition of voting rights continued in other ways. The Twenty-sixth Amendment (1971) enfranchised millions of new voters by lowering the voting age to eighteen. The federal courts also struck down many state laws limiting the vote to longtime residents. By the 1970's residency requirements of longer than thirty days were no longer permitted.

Bibliography

Peacock, Anthony A. *Affirmative Action and Representation: Shaw v. Reno and the Future of Voting Rights.* Durham, N.C.: Carolina Academic Press, 1997.

Rogers, Donald W., ed. *Voting and the Spirit of American Democracy.* Urbana: University of Illinois Press, 1992.

Rogers, Donald W., and Christine B. Scriabine. *Voting and the Spirit of American Democracy: Essays on the History of Voting and Voting Rights in America.* Urbana: University of Illinois Press, 1992.

Scher, Richard K., Jon L. Mills, and John J. Hotaling. *Voting Rights and Democracy: The Law and Politics of Districting.* Chicago: Nelson-Hall, 1997.

William C. Lowe

W

War Crimes

Although destruction and mass killing are integral parts of warfare, international law recognizes rules protecting noncombatants, wounded and disarmed soldiers, and prisoners of war, and the United States has played a major role in punishing combatants who violate those rules as war criminals.

The idea of war crimes, though rooted in a long tradition of efforts to ensure humane treatment for innocent parties, traces its modern development to the U.S. Civil War and subsequent efforts to codify (write down in a system of principles or rules) the laws and customs of war. Closely related to the evolution of war crimes is the development of the laws of war.

War Crimes and the Civil War. The Civil War saw the first effort to codify laws of war. It also saw one of the first war crimes trials, in which a southern army captain, Henri Wirz, was convicted of inhumane treatment of Union prisoners of war in Georgia's Andersonville prison. Wirz's trial was controversial, and many questioned whether he was not a scapegoat at a time when many other violators of the laws of war in both the North and South were not prosecuted. However, the terrible conditions at Andersonville stimulated considerable popular resentment, and this fact, combined with much testimony regarding barbarities committed personally by Wirz, led to his conviction and execution.

Codification of the Laws of War. A more important and influential development arising from the Civil War concerned the codification of the laws of war. In 1863 Francis Lieber, of Columbia University, at the request of President Abraham Lincoln, produced a manual which codified the existing principles and customs of land warfare. Lieber's *Instructions for the Government of the Armies of the United States in the Field* was adopted by the Union army in the same year.

By the beginning of the twentieth century, several other nations had modeled their national military manuals after the American code, even as momentum built to codify the international laws of war. This effort culminated in drafting of the 1907 Hague Convention Respecting the Laws and Customs of War on Land. Many of the rules codified in the 1907 convention had already been accepted by nations as binding customary laws. The convention merely clarified them and identified other areas of growing consensus.

War Crime Tribunals. The notion of trying war crimes by international tribunals (courts) did not emerge until after World War I. Until then, it was assumed that governments bore responsibility for compensating victims of war crimes committed by its armed forces and that war criminals would be dealt with by their own governments—or, if captured, by the injured belligerent government. After World War I, this began to change, as the Versailles Treaty called for the investigation and punishment of war crimes committed by the forces of the Axis powers (Germany, Austro-Hungarian Empire, and Turkey). Few were brought to trial, however, and those found guilty of various offenses received light sentences.

The traditional laws of war concerning punishment for war crimes rested on the notion that individuals are not direct subjects of international law. Trials for war crimes, then, took place under the jurisdiction of a country's military or civil jurisdiction. Soldiers ordered to commit war crimes could defend their actions by citing the *respondeat superior* principle, the defense of superior orders. In such cases the superior who gave the order was held responsible for the war crime. Soldiers who exceeded their orders could be held accountable when committing war crimes on their own authority. This traditional attitude changed rather dramatically in the wake of the Nuremberg trials after World War II.

Nuremberg Legacy. The wholesale violations of the laws of war that took place during World War II shocked the conscience of humanity. For the first time in history, the international community responded by bringing to justice several thousand persons who were found guilty of war crimes. The Nuremberg trials set a new precedent in regard to the *respondeat superior* question. No longer could soldiers simply follow illegal orders with impunity. To obey orders knowing that they called for commission of war crimes was to participate in the crime. In 1949 the International Committee for the Red Cross convinced governments that it was time to revise and update the laws of war as a result of their widespread violation during World War II.

Although the laws of war have been greatly augmented since World War II, acts of cruelty and barbarity, especially in the context of civil wars, are still quite prevalent. Individuals, for

Defendants at the Nuremberg trials included Adolf Hitler's Luftwaffe chief, Hermann Goering (seated next to guard holding baton), who committed suicide before he could be executed, and Hitler's deputy, Rudolf Hess (to Goering's right). (National Archives)

The My Lai Massacre

The war crime principles that emerged from World War II came into sharp focus in 1970-1971, when American army lieutenant William Calley was court-martialed and found guilty of the premeditated murder of twenty-two Vietnamese civilians at My Lai. The Vietnam War, like all guerrilla wars, blurred distinctions between armed combatants and civilians. This fact made observing laws of war difficult—a point to which Calley appealed in his defense. Nevertheless, the court-martial held that Calley had exceeded orders given to him by his superior officer. Enemy forces had evacuated My Lai, so it no longer held military significance. Even if one could say the massacre represented a reprisal, the laws of war specifically prohibit reprisals against innocent civilians. Under the Nuremberg principles, Calley was justifiably convicted. His life sentence was reduced on appeal, and he eventually became a federal parolee, illustrating that military and civil courts are reluctant to mete out harsh punishments even for those convicted of war crimes.

Bibliography

Anderson, David L., ed. *Facing My Lai: Moving Beyond the Massacre.* Lawrence: University Press of Kansas, 1998.

Clark, Ramsey. *The Fire This Time: U.S. War Crimes in the Gulf.* New York: Thunder's Mouth Press, 1994.

Dinstein, Yoram, and Mala Tabory. *War Crimes in International Law.* Boston: Martinus Nijhoff, 1996.

Goldstein, Joseph, Burke Marshall, and Jack Schwartz. *The My Lai Massacre and Its Cover-up: Beyond the Reach of Law?* New York: Free Press, 1976.

McCormack, Timothy L. H., and Gerry J. Simpson. *The Law of War Crimes: National and International Approaches.* Boston: Kluwer Law International, 1997.

Robert F. Gorman

Watergate

The political scandal known as "Watergate" created a major constitutional crisis when President Richard Nixon and his top aides obstructed justice while denying personal involvement in a criminal break-in at the Democratic Party campaign headquarters.

the first time in history, can be held directly accountable for violations of the laws of war and thus, in this sense, may be viewed as direct subjects of international law. If war crimes are to be deterred, however, governments must be willing, either collectively or through their national legal systems, to prosecute war crimes and punish the offenders. To this day, governments have been reluctant, for political reasons, to prosecute war crimes aggressively. Still, by aggressively training elements of their armed forces, providing instruction in the laws of war, and instilling principles of military justice and discipline, governments provide a foundation from which the brutalities and inhumanity of war, which is always an unfortunate and necessarily deadly exercise, can be mitigated.

Watergate cast a long shadow over the presidency and the government as a whole for many years. Both politicians and the public were suspicious of presidential power, and special prosecutors were appointed on a number of occasions to investigate possible wrongdoing. Among the activities investigated by special prosecutors were the Iran-Contra scandal that tainted the Reagan and Bush administrations and the Whitewater allegations against Bill Clinton and members of his administration.

Prelude to Watergate. In early 1972 PUBLIC OPINION POLLS indicated that President Richard Nixon would easily win reelection against the expected Democratic nominee, Senator George McGovern from South Dakota. Nevertheless, several members of the Committee to Reelect the President (CREEP) did not want to take chances. Hoping to learn the Democratic party's campaign strategy, they broke into the Party's national headquarters in Washington, D.C.'s Watergate Hotel. The operatives bungled the operation, however. A custodian who noticed a door ajar in the Democratic Party offices notified police, who arrested the would-be burglars.

Although three of those arrested in the break-in, E. Howard Hunt, James McCord, and G. Gordon Liddy, worked for CREEP, no one could prove at that time that anyone in the Nixon administration had been involved in planning the break-in or in paying money to the seven defendants to remain quiet. More than two years later it was proved that in June, 1972, Nixon himself had ordered the Central Intelligence Agency to interfere with the Federal Bureau of Investigation's probe of the break-in. Moreover, Nixon's main assistants, John Erlichman and Bob Haldeman, approved large secret payments to the seven defendants. Nixon hoped that the defendants would not reveal the participation of their superiors in the break-in. The cover-up was successful through the months leading up to the November, 1972, election, which Nixon won in a landslide.

Judge Sirica's Role. During their trial in January, 1973, the defendants falsely claimed they had acted alone. The cover-up began to unravel in March, however, when federal district court judge John Sirica sentenced the defendants (five of whom pleaded guilty and two of whom a jury found guilty). Suspecting that the defendants had lied during their trial, Sirica told them that if they cooperated with prosecutors and a recently formed U.S. Senate investigating committee, chaired by Senator Sam Ervin, Jr., they would not serve much time in jail. However, if they remained uncoopera-

tive, he would sentence them to forty-five years in federal prison.

One of the convicted felons, James McCord, wrote a letter to Sirica explaining that he and his partners had been paid to perjure themselves during the trial and that others had been involved in the cover-up. Nevertheless, President Nixon continued denying his personal involvement.

The Special Prosecutor and the Senate Hearings. On April 30, 1973, Nixon accepted the resignations of Erlichman, Haldeman, his personal counsel John Dean, and Attorney General Richard Kleindienst, all of whom had participated in the cover-up. He appointed a well-respected Republican, Elliot Richardson, as his new attorney general, authorizing him to appoint an independent special prosecutor. Nixon thought that he could somehow control Richardson and Archibald Cox, the new special prosecutor. However, Cox quickly made it clear that he would seek the truth, no matter where his search led him. Richardson strove to reestablish the integrity of the JUSTICE DEPARTMENT, which had been used for political purposes by Kleindienst and his predecessor, John Mitchell.

The Senate Investigating Committee. After Senator Ervin's committee began its televised hearings in May, 1973, it became clear that many morally questionable decisions had been made by influential people in the Nixon White House and that laws had probably been violated by many members of his administration. It still remained unclear, however, whether Nixon himself had been involved in the cover-up.

The White House Tapes. In July, 1973, a former White House assistant testified that from 1971 until at least March, 1973, all conversations in the president's Oval Office had been secretly recorded, and that these tapes had been kept by order of the president. Senators Ervin and Howard Baker and Special Prosecutor Cox immediately understood that these tapes could provide incontrovertible proof of the president's innocence or guilt. In response to subpoenas from the Senate Committee and Archibald Cox, President Nixon

poena in October. Unless the U.S. Supreme Court voted to overrule the decision of the appeals court, Nixon would have to turn over the relevant tapes or be held in contempt of

President Richard Nixon addressing the nation on Watergate on April 30, 1973—the day he accepted the resignations of his top assistants who participated in the Watergate cover-up. (AP/Wide World Photos)

invoked "executive privilege" and refused to turn over the relevant tapes.

After Nixon refused to comply with the subpoena, Cox asked Judge Sirica to enforce the subpoena. Sirica did so, and a federal appeals court upheld its validity of the sub-

court, which would most certainly cause his IMPEACHMENT by the House of Representatives and removal from office by the Senate.

In a desperate attempt to stop the special prosecutor, Nixon ordered Richardson to fire him and abolish the office in October. When

Shortly after Richard Nixon resigned the presidency to avoid impeachment, his successor, Gerald Ford, addressed the nation to announce he had pardoned Nixon for any or all crimes he may have committed during his administration. (Gerald R. Ford Library)

both Richardson and Assistant Attorney General William Ruckelshaus refused to fire Cox, Nixon fired them both. Robert Bork, then the U.S. solicitor general and third in command in the Department of Justice, complied with Nixon's wishes and fired Cox. Nixon's abuse of his presidential power came to be known as the "Saturday night massacre."

In November Nixon appointed yet another attorney general, Senator William Saxbe of Ohio. Leon Jaworski became the new special prosecutor. President Nixon's attempt to destroy the independence of the American JUDI-

CIAL SYSTEM had failed, and he was even forced to agree that he would not attempt to fire special prosecutor Jaworski without the approval of Republican and Democratic leaders from the House and the Senate.

Nixon's Resignation. Nixon's special counsel, James St. Clair, asked the U.S. SUPREME COURT to reverse the decision of a federal appeals court; however, in a unanimous decision written by Chief Justice Warren Burger the Court affirmed the decision of the lower court and ordered Nixon to turn over the subpoenaed tapes to the special prosecutor on July 24, 1974.

Nixon's guilt soon became obvious to almost everyone: In a conversation recorded on June 23, 1972, he had ordered the CIA to interfere with the FBI's investigation of the break-in. This action clearly constituted criminal obstruction of justice. On July 27, 1974, the House Judiciary Committee voted 27-11 to impeach Nixon. After Nixon learned that few Republicans would support him in either the House of Representatives or the Senate, he finally decided to resign in order to avoid the public humiliation of being impeached.

Vice President Gerald R. Ford was sworn in as president on August 9, 1974. A month later he granted Nixon a full pardon for all crimes which he had committed during his presidency. Many of Nixon's top assistants were later convicted of their crimes and sentenced to prison.

Bibliography

Emery, Fred. *Watergate: The Corruption of American Politics and the Fall of Richard Nixon.* New York: Times Books, 1994.

Ervin, Sam, Jr. *The Whole Truth: The Watergate Conspiracy.* New York: Random House, 1980.

Gormley, Ken. *Archibald Cox: Conscience of a Nation.* Reading, Mass.: Addison-Wesley, 1997.

Kutler, Stanley I., ed. *Abuse of Power: The New Nixon Tapes.* New York: Free Press, 1997.

_____. *Watergate: The Fall of Richard M. Nixon.* St. James, N.Y.: Brandywine Press, 1996.

Edmund J. Campion

Welfare

The United States, like most modern states, accepts that for the good of the whole community, government must plan and spend to provide whatever may be regarded as the basic conditions of social justice.

Governmental efforts to ensure social justice in the United States are best understood in the context of the politics of a complex federal system. This is a system involving fifty states, thousands of municipalities, and more than 100,000 other governmental units. Each has distinctive powers and important capacities to determine what revenues, if any, are redistributed to ensure measures of social justice. The views of the many communities that these governments represent are often disparate and subject to differing interpretations, a fact which has made the development of federally sponsored, nationwide programs of social justice uniquely difficult and highly politicized in the United States.

Nevertheless, long before the New Deal policies of President Franklin D. Roosevelt in the 1930's millions of Americans were beneficiaries of federal and state policies and expenditures directed toward the improvement of their social welfare.

Early American Experience. The American experience with extensions of social justice, beginning in the nineteenth century, was strikingly different from policies initiated in Great Britain and elsewhere. There were a number of reasons for this. Until the mid-1920's the United States remained predominantly an agricultural nation. Its trade union movements were small and weak; capitalists, corporations, and the business communities, including farmers, generally exercised dominant influences over government policymaking. Its civil service and bureaucracies were modest in size and in political influence; suspicions of governmental power traditionally were strong. Many Americans prided themselves on their individualism and their general capacity to care for themselves without government "interference." All these factors militated against national planning and the implementation of universalized social welfare programs.

Large, politically influential groups of Americans, nonetheless, received the benefits of social legislation enacted by federal and state governments during the nineteenth and early twentieth centuries—well prior to the New Deal. Since free or cheap land represented a capital subsidy, for example, millions of farmers (as well as speculators and other business interests, notably transcontinental railroads) profited from the distribution of the public domain—in other words, from federal land subsidies. Under such federal legislation as the Homestead Act (1862), more than 147 million acres were distributed free of charge between 1862 and 1904, and more than 610 million acres were sold cheaply—ostensibly to farmers. After the 1840's millions of American children likewise received free public educations—in the most comprehensive educational programs in the industrializing world—from state and local governments.

In addition, under the Arrears Pension Act (1879), the Dependent Pension Act (1890), and related federal legislation on behalf of Civil War veterans, their widows, and dependents, nearly a million pensioners by the mid-1890's received handsome service pensions (including land), as well as disability and old-age pensions. State governments invariably

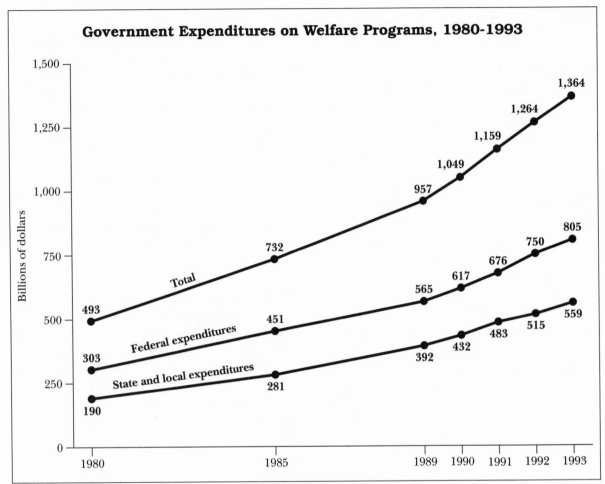

Government Expenditures on Welfare Programs, 1980-1993

Source: U.S. Bureau of the Census, *Statistical Abstract of the United States: 1997.* 117th ed. Washington, D.C.: U.S. Government Printing Office, 1997.

augmented these benefits. By the 1890's the federal government alone was spending 41 percent of its income on the relatively lavish veterans' benefits that were collected by more than one-third of northern men and by a substantial number of widowed women.

Middle- and working-class women's groups were primarily responsible in nearly every state for winning legislation limiting women's hours of labor and, in fifteen states by 1913, for winning minimum wage laws. In nearly every state women's groups secured pensions for widows with children and for aged women. U.S. Supreme Court decisions threw an additional protective mantle over some of this "ma-

ternalist protective labor legislation" years before male wage earners were covered by such laws. Thus, although the American political structure long ruled out universalized social welfare legislation, millions of its citizens benefited from federal and state aid designed to help them meet many basic needs.

The New Deal. The unprecedented social and economic disasters that attended the Great Depression during the decade after 1929 created the political pressures from which flowed the New Deal legislation of President Franklin D. Roosevelt. Between 1933 and 1938 New Deal policies, many experimental in character, took two major directions. Each necessitated unprecedented peacetime federal spending. The earliest programs were designed to alleviate the shocks of massive unemployment as well as to subsidize the rehabilitation of major banking and business failures and encourage job retention. To relieve unemployment, for example, federal agencies were established to create "public works" under the auspices of the Works Progress Administration, the Public Works Administration, the National Youth Administration, and the Civilian Conservation Corps.

Further legislation helped refinance homeowners' and farm mortgages, extended crop loans, set a floor under wages and a ceiling on hours for millions of workers, prevented mortgage foreclosures, initiated a national housing program for low-income families, instituted retirement pensions for railroad employees,

The modern American welfare system began during the 1930's, when the Social Security Act responded to the obvious needs of many older Americans for government assistance. (National Archives)

mandated minimum wages and maximum hours for employees working under government contracts, and paid adjusted pensions to World War I veterans. Intended as "relief" measures, little of this type of New Deal legislation contributed to a universalized effort to extend social welfare or social justice to all American citizens.

Social Security System. The enactment of one federal "entitlement" program, however, emerged as the nearest approximation to a genuinely national social welfare program: the Social Security Act of 1935, the centerpiece of New Deal welfare statism. Paid for by wage earners' contributions and by a payroll tax on their employers, the SOCIAL SECURITY SYSTEM assured wage earners retirement income based on their highest level of earnings, along with additional benefits for them and their dependents. Social Security established a framework for the United States' major programs of unemployment insurance, public assistance, and old-age retirement insurance at both federal and state levels.

Modest additions to social welfare legislation have included the G.I. Bill of 1944, which rewarded 13 million World War II veterans with educational benefits—a temporary measure—and the Medicare, Medicaid, and food stamp programs launched during the Great Society campaign of President Lyndon B. Johnson during the mid-1960's.

Reevaluations and Uncertainty. Beginning in the 1970's, as "big government" fell into popular—hence political—disfavor, and as

Typical welfare recipients are single mothers unable to earn the incomes necessary to keep up with the costs of raising children. (AP/Wide World Photos)

congressional struggles to achieve a balanced budget and cut the deficit curtailed spending, national social welfare entitlement programs, including Social Security, came under attack by the media, legislators, and Presidents Richard Nixon, Jimmy Carter, Ronald Reagan, and George Bush. Social Security, despite its inequities, appeared immune, largely because of its broad middle-class political base and support from well-organized interest groups such as the American Association of Retired Persons. However, those programs which popularly were stigmatized by the term "welfare"—implying government "handouts" for people who did not work—were more vulnerable.

Although facts were difficult to marshal and varied from state to state, there was widespread agreement among experts and legislators that "welfare" programs were not only inordinately expensive but also desperately in need of reform. Again without precise information, there were suspicions and estimations of widespread welfare fraud. Generally, such programs centered on aid to persons of low income, many of whom had been living for years in poverty and on public assistance, constituting what some sociologists called a "culture of poverty." Many were black, Hispanic, or immigrant residents of inner cities, poorly educated and often unemployable. Their vulnerability to the loss of public assistance was enhanced by their lack of political clout.

During the 1990's debate over the future of social welfare and entitlement programs intensified. While running for president in 1992, Bill Clinton vowed to push for a national health care program that would cover all Americans, some 25 million of whom still had neither public nor private health insurance. Public opinion polls indicated that a majority of Americans supported the idea. The plan his administration produced, however, was widely criticized and was defeated by a Congress that was trying to reduce the budget deficit. In the congressional elections of 1994, Republicans won a majority of the seats in both houses and began to examine all government social spending more critically than ever. Significant cuts to such long-standing programs as Medicare and Medicaid were heatedly debated, and even Social Security was subjected to reevaluation of such elements as its formula for computing cost-of-living increases. By the mid-1990's, while it appeared unlikely that such broad middle-class programs such as Social Security would be destroyed, it appeared equally unlikely that social welfare programs would soon be expanded.

Bibliography

Davies, Gareth. *From Opportunity to Entitlement: The Transformation and Decline of Great Society Liberalism.* Lawrence: University Press of Kansas, 1996.

Gensler, Howard. *The American Welfare System: Origins, Structure, and Effects.* Westport, Conn.: Praeger, 1996.

Hombs, Mary Ellen. *Welfare Reform: A Reference Handbook.* Santa Barbara, Calif.: ABC-Clio, 1996.

Jansson, Bruce S. *The Reluctant Welfare State: American Social Welfare Policies, Past, Present, and Future.* 3d ed. Pacific Grove, Calif.: Brooks/Cole, 1997.

Koon, Richard L. *Welfare Reform: Helping the Least Fortunate Become Less Dependent.* New York: Garland, 1997.

Noble, Charles. *Welfare as We Knew It: A Political History of the American Welfare State.* New York: Oxford University Press, 1997.

Clifton K. Yearley

Wills

Private legal documents directing who gets the property belonging to the estate of persons when they die, wills affect the redistribution of wealth in society and the extent to which the dead can influence the lives of their survivors.

Apart from certain tax questions, state laws govern wills, and the laws of the various states vary greatly. Some states have adopted some or all of the Uniform Probate Code (UPC), a statute designed as a model to both modernize and unify the law. Congress has established a federal tax law governing gifts, estates, and "generation-skipping transfers." One important distinction is between "probate" and "nonprobate" property. In general, probate property is property someone owns alone. Nonprobate property usually is shared. Joint bank accounts or stocks, life insurance, living trusts, and real property owned in joint tenancy all avoid the probate system. Avoiding probate, however, does not mean avoiding federal tax; they are two different systems.

Intestacy. Each state has an "intestate" statute that tells how to distribute probate property not covered by a will. The statute applies to people who never made wills, people whose wills are invalid, and people whose wills do not cover all their property. The details vary among states, but common patterns emerge. Principal problems include how much to presume about what distributions most people would prefer, and whether other public policies, such as fair treatment of surviving relatives, should override those presumed intentions.

Spouses and descendants have the first claims on estates. Many states share the estate between the surviving spouse and the descendants. Others give everything to surviving spouses and rely on the spouses to serve as conduits to the children. If a surviving spouse is not the parent of the children, as commonly happens in second-marriage situations, the children may get a larger intestate share. That approach protects the children against the possibility that they will get nothing at the stepparent's death. If no spouse or descendants exist, the property usually goes to various descendants of the deceased person's grandparents or to the next-closest surviving relative.

Wills. To change the result of an intestacy scheme, an individual makes a will, a formal document telling how to distribute property. A will may also name an executor to handle the estate or appoint a guardian for minors or incapacitated relatives. State laws vary on the elements involved in creating a valid will. In almost all situations, it must be in writing and signed by the person making it, but many states add other formal requirements.

One controversy is the extent to which the law should require a long list of formalities. Wills that fail on formal grounds may still reflect the maker's intention. To make will execution easier, some states have adopted the UPC's approach of shortening the list of formalities. Others allow wills executed in "substantial compliance" with the statute. A third approach is to recognize noncomplying wills if there is clear evidence that the testator intended the document to be a will.

Trusts. Trusts are flexible devices for holding property in a way to benefit families. One can create a trust by giving property to someone else (the trustee) with instructions to manage the property for the benefit of others. Testamentary trusts are created by will. Living trusts are created during the creator's lifetime, so the creators have the choice of giving the property to a trustee or naming themselves as trustees and thus keeping control of the property while they are still able. Trusts can provide solutions to a wide variety of planning problems: providing for college, supporting children with disabilities, caring for aging parents. Living trusts have become particularly popular as probate-evidence devices.

Bibliography

American Bar Association. *The American Bar Association Guide to Wills and Estates.* New York: Times Books, 1995.

Dukeminier, Jesse, and Stanley M. Johanson. *Wills, Trusts, and Estates.* 5th ed. Boston: Little, Brown, 1995.

Klueger, Robert F. *A Guide to Asset Protection: How to Keep What's Legally Yours.* New York: John Wiley & Sons, 1997.

Page, William H. *Page on the Law of Wills.* Rev. by Jeffrey A. Schoenblum. Cincinnati: Anderson, 1991.

Roger W. Andersen

Woman Suffrage

Winning the legal right to vote made American women the political equals of men, forever altering an old common-law prejudice that women were men's legal inferiors.

Ratification of the U.S. CONSTITUTION's Nineteenth Amendment in 1920 belatedly extended VOTING RIGHTS to American women in state and federal elections. As the ratification process began in 1918, women were completely without the vote in exactly half the states. However, only fifteen of these states—mostly in the West—extended full voting privileges to women. Twelve states permitted women to vote only in presidential elections, two others only in primaries.

Background. By 1920 agitation for granting woman suffrage (the right to vote) was more than a century old. True, the general estate of white females in the United States during the eighteenth and early nineteenth centuries was more fortunate than conditions most women endured elsewhere. Nevertheless, their denial of the vote for 120 years after the Constitution went into effect was perceived by a vocal minority of women and sympathetic men as a glaring anomaly in an ostensibly free and increasingly democratic society.

A few white women participated in voting during the colonial era, and some enjoyed voting rights, again locally, through the nineteenth century, but these were insignificant exceptions to the prevailing practices of a male-dominated society. Furthermore, general preclusion of woman suffrage contrasted sharply with extensions of male suffrage. Universal white manhood suffrage, for example, was a reality by the mid-1840's, a distinctively American achievement. Moreover, in 1870, as a part of post-Civil War Reconstruction, ratifi-

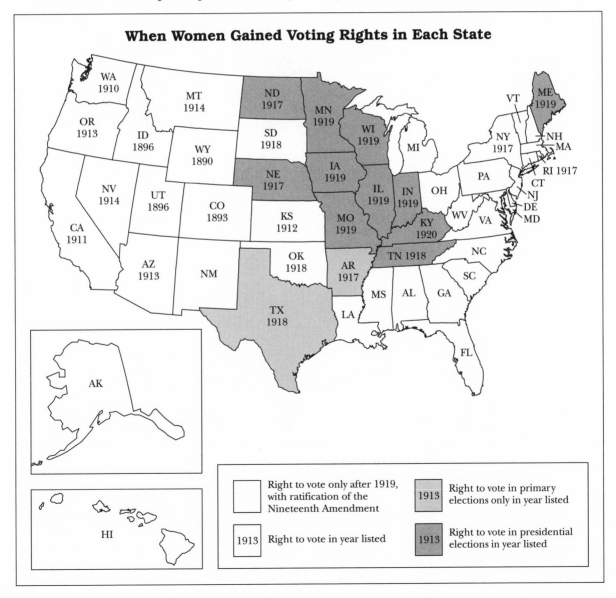

When Women Gained Voting Rights in Each State

cation of the Fifteenth Amendment prohibited denial of the vote because of race, color, or previous conditions of servitude, thus granting the franchise (the right to vote) to black males recently emancipated by the Thirteenth Amendment in 1865. Opinions held by a majority of eighteenth and nineteenth century women about the value of the franchise are unknown, but thousands of educated and articulate women certainly regarded denial of the vote as a glaring discontinuity in the overall advance of American democracy.

Early Pioneers. American women whose enthusiasm for equality remained latent at the end of the revolutionary era and the opening of the nineteenth century were receptive to the message of England's Mary Wollstonecraft. Her pathbreaking feminist writings enjoyed wide currency in North America. Wollstonecraft espoused women's full participation with men in a joint exercise of equal civil and political rights, along with women's liberation from their traditional status through access to education.

Women in the Abolitionist Movement. Among female reformers and their allies, woman suffrage had lower priority before the 1840's than legal reforms in married women's property rights and alterations in laws of divorce. Successes in these efforts opened wider vistas for them. In New York State, for example, victories in securing such changes encouraged a few women to participate in the utopian and reformist movements that flourished through the 1830's. In this context, women made impressive contributions to the abolitionist movement that worked to abolish SLAVERY.

The first Massachusetts woman to graduate from college, Lucy Stone was a leader in the early nineteenth century abolitionist movement and a pioneer in the women's rights movement. (Library of Congress)

Their eagerness to participate was signaled by the attendance of two American Quaker schoolteachers, Lucretia Mott and Elizabeth Cady Stanton, at the World Anti-Slavery Convention gathered in London in 1840. Though they were refused seats at the London convention, Mott and Stanton returned home with strengthened convictions. Within a few years, both women and male abolitionists were joined in American antislavery organizations by such reformers as Angelina and Sarah Grimké, Lucy Stone, Fanny Wright, and Abby Kelley Foster. Often a divisive element within abolitionist ranks and usually discriminated against, women nevertheless found abolitionism a training ground that equipped them to move on to suffrage and other feminist reforms.

Seneca Falls. A gathering of about three hundred women in the Wesleyan chapel at Seneca Falls, New York, in July, 1848, has been widely viewed as the beginning of the woman suffrage movement in the United States. Its leaders were Elizabeth Cady Stanton and Lucretia Mott. Modeling their own Declaration of Sentiments on the Declaration of Independence, the women at Seneca Falls proclaimed the equality of the sexes and proceeded to pass a dozen resolutions enumerating specific women's rights. Curiously, the only proposal not passed unanimously was the right to vote.

The extension of women's rights had been so long delayed that discussions of them caused divisions. In addition, many women were still committed overwhelmingly to domestic pursuits, and their energies were dispersed through other emancipating activities such as educational reform, temperance, and abolition. Nevertheless, the Seneca Falls declaration solicited wide public attention. Two years later Lucy Stone founded the Woman's Rights Convention in Worcester, Massachusetts. Containing both female and male reformers, that organization was dedicated primarily to woman suffrage. However, rancorous sectional controversies of the 1850's soon led to the Civil War and preempted public interest in all reforms except the antislavery movement.

Post-Civil War Campaigns. Suffragists had always believed that their close identification with the efforts of northern abolitionists to free the slaves would advance the suffrage cause and their own emancipation. Convinced by male antislavery leaders of the overwhelming importance of abolition, many suffragist leaders quietly took back seats during the turbulent 1850's until AFRICAN AMERICANS were freed and abolitionists could reciprocate by aiding women in their fight for the vote.

Suffragists were gratified by the Wyoming

Susan B. Anthony (standing) and her friend Julia Ward Howe, who used the fame she won as author of "The Battle Hymn of the Republic" to help advance the woman suffrage cause. (Library of Congress)

Territory's extension of the vote to women in 1869 but found themselves abandoned by postwar politicians and former abolitionists. The Reconstruction Act of 1867 enfranchised black men, not women, throughout the South. The Fourteenth Amendment imposed penalties for denying the black male vote. The Fifteenth Amendment, which proclaimed that the vote could not be denied because of race, color, or previous condition of servitude, notably lacked inclusion of the word "sex."

Suffragist Organizations. These Reconstruction battles changed the suffragists' misconception that they were automatically connected with former abolitionists, with black leaders, and with Republican politicians. Woman suffrage advocates split into two organizations, each established in 1869: Lucy Stone's American Woman Suffrage Association (AWSA) and Susan B. Anthony's and Elizabeth Stanton's National Woman Suffrage Association (NWSA). Thereafter, the two organizations concentrated upon securing constitutional amendments that would give the vote to women. Stone's AWSA sought amendments to state constitutions, while the NWSA fought for an amendment to the U.S. Constitution. After years of such tactical (and to some extent, personal) divisions, the two organizations combined as the National American Woman Suffrage Association (NAWSA) in 1890.

Between 1881 and 1922 Anthony and Stanton oversaw creation of a massive six-volume compilation of documents and essays entitled *The History of Woman Suffrage.* It became a mine of information—and inspiration—for future generations of feminists.

The tenacity, intrepidity, public protests, and spirited LOBBYING of these women won for them the vote in four Rocky Mountain states between 1869 and 1896, as well as in seventeen additional states between 1910 and 1918. In 1913 Lucy Burns and Alice Paul used the leverage of female voters in states with

woman suffrage and drew on the reform impetus of the Progressive era to form the National Woman's Party to press for an amendment to the federal Constitution. These efforts were boosted by the United States' entrance into World War I. The contributions women made to the war effort by taking over the industrial jobs of millions of men who went into military service were generally recognized. As a consequence, enough traditional attitudes were changed to secure passage of the Nineteenth Amendment in 1920.

Bibliography

Graham, Sara H. *Woman Suffrage and the New Democracy.* New Haven, Conn.: Yale University Press, 1996.

Marilley, Suzanne M. *Woman Suffrage and the Origins of Liberal Feminism in the United States, 1820-1920.* Cambridge, Mass.: Harvard University Press, 1996.

Monroe, Judy. *The Nineteenth Amendment: Women's Right to Vote.* Springfield, N.J.: Enslow, 1998.

Neuman, Nancy M., ed. *A Voice of Our Own: Leading American Women Celebrate the Right to Vote.* San Francisco, Calif.: Jossey-Bass, 1996.

Ryan, Barbara. *The Women's Movement: Reference and Resources.* New York: G. K. Hall, 1996.

Mary E. Virginia

Women in Politics

The fact that women constitute more than half of the population gives them a unique role in politics; however, as public officeholders, they are the most underrepresented social group in the United States.

In colonial America, political rights were granted largely on custom and usage, which implied that politics was for men only. This was rarely specified, however. Where specifications existed, they tended to be based on property,

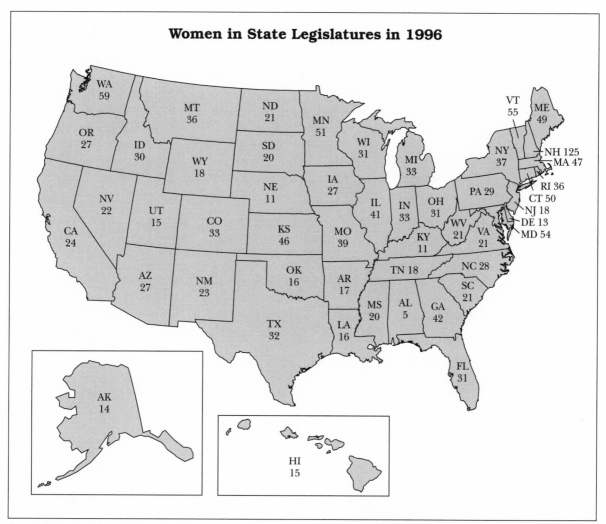

Women in State Legislatures in 1996

WA 59 · OR 27 · ID 30 · MT 36 · WY 18 · ND 21 · SD 20 · MN 51 · WI 31 · MI 33 · VT 55 · ME 49 · NY 37 · NH 125 · MA 47 · NV 22 · UT 15 · CO 33 · NE 11 · IA 27 · IL 41 · IN 33 · OH 31 · PA 29 · RI 36 · CT 50 · NJ 18 · DE 13 · MD 54 · CA 24 · AZ 27 · NM 23 · KS 46 · MO 39 · KY 11 · WV 21 · VA 21 · OK 16 · AR 17 · TN 18 · NC 28 · SC 21 · TX 32 · LA 16 · MS 20 · AL 5 · GA 42 · FL 31 · AK 14 · HI 15

Source: U.S. Bureau of the Census, *Statistical Abstract of the United States: 1997.* 117th ed. Washington, D.C.: U.S. Government Printing Office, 1997.

wealth, age, and religion, not gender. Land ownership was a particularly important qualification. Propertyholders generally were male, but conditions existed in which property could be held by women. Daughters and widows could inherit, divorced women could leave a marriage with their property, and women could even own property in their own names. Therefore, under certain circumstances, women were allowed to vote while some men were not. Few women, however, had the franchise (the right to vote) and fewer exercised it.

When the former colonies joined to form

the United States, each had its own written constitution, which specified the qualifications required for the franchise. Before the AMERICAN REVOLUTION, local governments were essentially private spheres. Local rights of political participation and the ability to hold elective office were lost when the national government began including local governments under the national system. This was accomplished by first specifying who had national or state political rights, and then limiting participation to those persons.

The American Revolution led to a general

One of two women senators representing California, Diane Feinstein and other female members of Congress gathered in early 1994 to speak out in favor of a ban on private possession of assault weapons. (AP/Wide World Photos)

loss of status for American women. Two reasons for this loss were the shift from custom, which allowed for conditions under which women could vote, to written constitutions, which did not; and the move from a property-based franchise toward universal manhood suffrage.

The process of restoring and expanding the female franchise was complex, because suffrage was controlled by individual states and because of the distinctive electoral bases of various local governmental units. Nevertheless, the movement toward women's suffrage (right to vote) began at the local level.

Political participation for women has been more readily available at the local level for two reasons. One concerns the functions and activities of local government, which include caring for the poor, education, sanitation, and the regulation of activities that affect the health and welfare of citizens. These fit within the scope of traditional roles and concerns of women. One reason advanced for female suffrage was women's concern for protecting and advancing the health and welfare of their families. A second reason was that local government was conducted close to home and required only part-time commitments. Women traditionally were tied to household and family obligations that permitted only a limited amount of free time and forced them to remain close to home. Women could participate in local government while still fulfilling their other roles.

Between 1807, when New Jersey withdrew woman suffrage, and 1838, when Kentucky granted it on a limited basis, no women voted legally anywhere in the United States. This was the longest period without WOMAN SUFFRAGE in American history. Nevertheless, even in states where women could not vote, many women were elected and appointed to local offices throughout U.S. history. In nonsuffragist states, women were elected to school-related positions in roughly the same numbers as in suffragist states.

The Nineteenth Amendment. On August 26, 1920, the Nineteenth Amendment became part of the U.S. Constitution, giving the right to vote to women. Suffragists had campaigned for the vote; they did not particularly want, nor did they seek in large numbers, to gain public office. Having the vote would facilitate two different strategies. First, women would have more influence over male politicians and would be able to LOBBY more effectively for

needed reforms. Second, women could use their votes through direct legislation, which allows citizens to petition to overrule legislation or initiate new legislation. As for holding public office, there was little difference after national suffrage from the situation beforehand. In 1929 there were 122 women serving in state legislatures; that number increased to only 140 by 1937.

The early leaders of the suffrage movement believed that with the vote, women would become the cutting edge of social change. They claimed that women would have a morally uplifting, life-enhancing, and liberalizing effect on the nation. They believed, too, that women could prevent wars. James D. Cox, the unsuccessful 1920 Democratic presidential candidate, greeted ratification of the Nineteenth Amendment by declaring that the civilization of the world was saved, because the mothers of the world would stay the hand of war. Although women tended to be more anti-

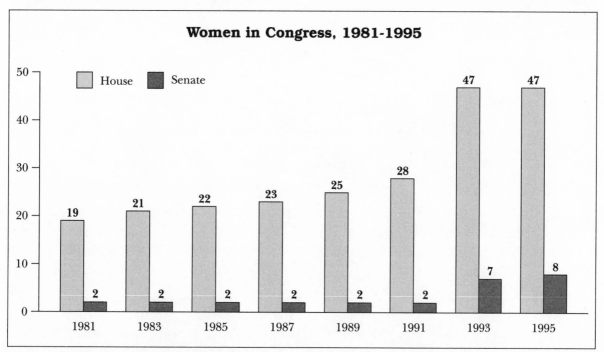

Source: U.S. Bureau of the Census, *Statistical Abstract of the United States: 1997.* 117th ed. Washington, D.C.: U.S. Government Printing Office, 1997.

Note: The Senate has a total of 100 members. Voting members of the House of Representatives total 435.

war than men, even with the right to vote they lacked the political power to prevent war.

This view echoed the message that suffragists had long been preaching. In the early days of the suffrage movement, many suffragists had focused on the sexual and social liberation of the individual woman as the key to equality. Suffrage was only one necessary reform in a long agenda that they hoped would revolutionize male-female relationships and society as a whole.

Women's "Roles." Suffrage leaders gradually began to emphasize women's roles as wife, mother, and homemaker. Women were the guardians of the family's spiritual values, while man's domain was the public world of com-

merce, work, and power. In arguing for the vote, suffragists asserted that women would bring their home-nurtured morality to the public sphere, and the reforms that they sought would preserve and protect the welfare and stability of the family. "Enlarged housekeeping" was the term temperance leader Frances Willard used to describe politics, and women were depicted in aprons wielding brooms, cleaning up public messes.

After gaining the vote, women's organizations lobbied for legislation affecting women and children. Their first victory was a controversial 1921 maternity and infancy bill that appropriated $1.25 million annually for educational instruction in the health care of moth-

First Lady Hillary Rodham Clinton's determination to play a much more direct role in government than previous presidents' wives made her one of the most admired and most detested women in America. (AP/Wide World Photos)

Members of various women's rights organizations gathered in July, 1995, to protest California governor Pete Wilson's stand on ending state affirmative action policies. (AP/Wide World Photos)

ers and infants. This was the forerunner of the late twentieth century Maternal and Child Health Block Grant, which serves nearly 12 million low-income women and children, and the Women, Infants, and Children (WIC) Program, which provides dietary supplements and health care to about 2.4 million needy pregnant women, nursing mothers, and children under five years of age.

Exercising the Franchise. In the mid-1920's many male politicians quit trying to win women's political favor. It had become clear that no female voting bloc existed, and women generally voted like their husbands, if they voted at all. Millions of women voted, but in far fewer numbers than men. Only about one-third of the eligible female electorate voted in 1920. Acquiring the habit of voting proved to be a slow process, particularly in what was still a hostile climate.

With the passage of the suffrage amendment, the energy seemed to drain out of the movement for women's political rights. Gaining the right to vote had been a single dramatic issue that unified and compelled women to action. Having won the vote, women could not find any comparable simple and universal issue around which to mobilize. Disillusionment set in when they found that winning the vote had not changed their lives significantly.

Some modern political scientists have concluded that the early suffragists were right: The real obstacle to equality was not the vote, but the division of lifestyles between men and women. It was not until women became self-supporting equal partners with men that women began to vote in large numbers. It was not the right to vote, but changes in the structure of society, that brought about changes in the political role of women.

The "Year of the Woman." The year 1992 was dubbed the "year of the woman" in American politics because female membership in the Senate and House of Representatives increased dramatically. The number of women in the House rose from twenty-eight to forty-seven and in the Senate from two to seven. It was also a year in which newly elected president Bill Clinton appointed women to 30 percent of the top jobs in his administration. Most women believed, however, that it would be at least another decade before any lasting political and electoral gains were made by women.

Redistricting and retirements had opened up many congressional seats that women captured. Twenty-two of the twenty-four newly elected women in the House won in open-seat races, as did four of the five new female senators. The 1993 races were more difficult for women than those of 1992. In 1992 women ran primarily for seats in Congress, but in 1993 women sought the offices of governor and mayor. Results indicate that fewer voters prefer women in executive offices than in legislative posts.

Voter Attitudes. Voters have been found to worry that women are not tough enough to be governors, yet feel uncomfortable when women come across as too tough. Women have to strive constantly for a comfortable middle ground of appearing strong enough to lead, but not so tough as to appear threatening. The issue agenda is also difficult for women. The economy and crime are two dominant political issues. Voters seem to have less confidence in women than men on both issues.

On the other hand, many voters view women as more in touch with their constituents and as caring more about people. They think women certainly know the price of a gallon of milk—an advantage in an environment where 86 percent of voters consider themselves middle class and three-fourths think that this class is having a difficult time. Overall, voters think women are more in touch, care more about the average person, are better listeners, and are better negotiators than men—all legislative traits. They also believe that women are not as good as men in handling crises, supervising big budgets and staffs, being tough, and managing—all executive traits.

Bibliography

Carroll, Susan J. *Women as Candidates in American Politics.* 2d ed. Bloomington: Indiana University Press, 1994.

Cox, Elizabeth. *Women in Modern American Politics: A Bibliography, 1900-1995.* Washington, D.C.: Congressional Quarterly, 1997.

Darcy, Robert, Susan Welch, and Janet Clark. *Women, Elections and Representation.* 2d ed. Lincoln: University of Nebraska Press, 1994.

Flammang, Janet A. *Women's Political Voice: How Women Are Transforming the Practice and Study of Politics.* Philadelphia: Temple University Press, 1997.

Gelb, Joyce, and Marian L. Palley. *Women and Public Policies: Reassessing Gender Politics.* Rev. ed. Charlottesville, Va.: University Press of Virginia, 1996.

Thomas, Sue, and Clyde Wilcox. *Women and Elective Office: Past, Present, and Future.* New York: Oxford University Press, 1998.

Allison L. Hayes

The Constitution of the United States of America

We the People of the United States, in Order to form a more perfect Union, establish Justice, insure domestic Tranquility, provide for the common defence, promote the general Welfare, and secure the Blessings of Liberty to ourselves and our Posterity, do ordain and establish this Constitution for the United States of America.

ARTICLE I.

SECTION 1. All legislative Powers herein granted shall be vested in a Congress of the United States, which shall consist of a Senate and House of Representatives.

SECTION 2. The House of Representatives shall be composed of Members chosen every second Year by the People of the several States, and the Electors in each State shall have the Qualifications requisite for Electors of the most numerous Branch of the State Legislature.

No Person shall be a Representative who shall not have attained to the Age of twenty five Years, and been seven Years a Citizen of the United States, and who shall not, when elected, be an Inhabitant of that State in which he shall be chosen.

Representatives and direct Taxes shall be apportioned among the several States which may be included within this Union, according to their respective Numbers, which shall be determined by adding to the whole Number of free Persons, including those bound to Service for a Term of Years, and excluding Indians not taxed, three fifths of all other Persons. The actual Enumeration shall be made within three Years after the first Meeting of the Congress of the United States, and within every subsequent Term of ten Years, in such Manner as they shall by Law direct. The number of Representatives shall not exceed one for every thirty Thousand, but each State shall have at Least one Representative; and until such enumeration shall be made, the State of New Hampshire shall be entitled to chuse three, Massachusetts eight, Rhode-Island and Providence Plantations one, Connecticut five, New-York six, New Jersey four, Pennsylvania eight, Delaware one, Maryland six, Virginia ten, North Carolina five, South Carolina five, and Georgia three.

When vacancies happen in the Representation from any State, the Executive Authority thereof shall issue Writs of Election to fill such Vacancies.

The House of Representatives shall chuse their Speaker and other Officers; and shall have the sole Power of Impeachment.

SECTION 3. The Senate of the United States shall be composed of two Senators from each State, chosen by the Legislature thereof, for six Years; and each Senator shall have one Vote.

Immediately after they shall be assembled in Consequence of the first Election, they shall be divided as equally as may be into three Classes. The Seats of the Senators of the first Class shall be vacated at the Expiration of the second Year, of the second Class at the Expiration of the fourth Year, and of the third Class at the Expiration of the sixth Year, so that one third may be chosen every second Year; and if Vacancies happen by Resignation, or otherwise, during the Recess of the Legislature of any State, the Executive thereof may make temporary Appointments until the next Meeting of the Legislature, which shall then fill such Vacancies.

No Person shall be a Senator who shall not have attained to the Age of thirty Years, and been nine Years a Citizen of the United States, and who shall not, when elected, be an Inhabitant of that State for which he shall be chosen.

The Vice President of the United States shall be President of the Senate, but shall have no Vote, unless they be equally divided.

The Senate shall chuse their other Officers, and also a President pro tempore, in the Absence of the Vice President, or when he shall exercise the Office of President of the United States.

The Senate shall have the sole Power to try all Impeachments. When sitting for that Purpose, they shall be on Oath or Affirmation. When the President of the United States is tried, the Chief Justice shall preside: And no Person shall be convicted without the Concurrence of two thirds of the Members present.

Judgment in Cases of Impeachment shall not extend further than to removal from Office, and disqualification to hold and enjoy any Office of honor, Trust or Profit under the United States: but the Party convicted shall nevertheless be liable and subject to Indictment, Trial, Judgment and Punishment, according to Law.

SECTION 4. The Times, Places and Manner of holding Elections for Senators and Representatives, shall be prescribed in each State by the Legislature thereof; but the Congress may at any time by Law make or alter such Regulations, except as to the Places of chusing Senators.

The Congress shall assemble at least once in every Year, and such Meeting shall be on the first Monday in December, unless they shall by Law appoint a different Day.

SECTION 5. Each House shall be the Judge of the Elections, Returns and Qualifications of its own Members, and a Majority of each shall constitute a Quorum to do Business; but a smaller Number may adjourn from day to day, and may be authorized to compel the Attendance of absent Members, in such Manner, and under such Penalties as each House may provide.

Each House may determine the Rules of its Proceedings, punish its Members for disorderly Behaviour, and, with the Concurrence of two thirds, expel a Member.

Each House shall keep a Journal of its Proceedings, and from time to time publish the same, excepting such Parts as may in their Judgment require Secrecy; and the Yeas and Nays of the Members of either House on any question shall, at the Desire of one fifth of those Present, be entered on the Journal.

Neither House, during the Session of Congress, shall, without the Consent of the other, adjourn for more than three days, nor to any other Place than that in which the two Houses shall be sitting.

SECTION 6. The Senators and Representatives shall receive a Compensation for their Services, to be ascertained by Law, and paid out of the Treasury of the United States. They shall in all Cases, except Treason, Felony and Breach of the Peace, be privileged from Arrest during their Attendance at the Session of their respective Houses, and in going to and returning from the same; and for any Speech or Debate in either House, they shall not be questioned in any other Place.

No Senator or Representative shall, during the Time for which he was elected, be appointed to any civil Office under the Authority of the United States, which shall have been created, or the Emoluments whereof shall have been encreased during such time; and no Person holding any Office under the United States, shall be a Member of either House during his Continuance in Office.

SECTION 7. All Bills for raising Revenue shall originate in the House of Representatives; but the Senate may propose or concur with Amendments as on other Bills.

Every Bill which shall have passed the House of Representatives and the Senate, shall, before it becomes a Law, be presented to the President of the United States; If he approve he shall sign it, but if not he shall return it, with his Objections to that House in which it shall have originated, who shall enter the Objections at large on their Journal, and proceed to reconsider it. If after such Reconsideration two thirds of that House shall agree to pass the Bill, it shall be sent, together with the Objections, to the other House, by which it shall likewise be reconsidered, and if approved by two thirds of that House, it shall become a Law. But in all such Cases the Votes of both Houses shall be determined by yeas and Nays, and the Names of the Persons voting for and against the Bill shall be entered on the Journal of each House respectively. If any Bill shall not be returned by the President within ten Days (Sundays excepted) after it shall have been presented to him, the Same shall be a Law, in like Manner as if he had signed it, unless the Congress by their Adjournment prevent its Return, in which Case it shall not be a Law.

Every Order, Resolution, or Vote to which the Concurrence of the Senate and House of Representatives may be necessary (except on a question of Adjournment) shall be presented to the President of the United States; and before the Same shall take Effect, shall be approved by him, or being disapproved by him, shall be repassed by two thirds of the Senate and House of Representatives, according to the Rules and Limitations prescribed in the Case of a Bill.

SECTION 8. The Congress shall have Power To lay and collect Taxes, Duties, Imposts and Excises, to pay the Debts and provide for the common Defence and general Welfare of the United States; but all Duties, Imposts and Excises shall be uniform throughout the United States;

To borrow Money on the credit of the United States;

To regulate Commerce with foreign Nations, and among the several States, and with the Indian Tribes;

To establish an uniform Rule of Naturalization, and uniform Laws on the subject of Bankruptcies throughout the United States;

To coin Money, regulate the Value thereof, and of foreign Coin, and fix the Standard of Weights and Measures;

To provide for the Punishment of counterfeiting the Securities and current Coin of the United States;

To establish Post Offices and post Roads;

To promote the Progress of Science and useful Arts, by securing for limited Times to Authors and Inventors the exclusive Right to their respective Writings and Discoveries;

To constitute Tribunals inferior to the supreme Court;

To define and punish Piracies and Felonies committed on the high Seas, and Offenses against the Law of Nations;

To declare War, grant Letters of Marque and Reprisal, and make Rules concerning Captures on Land and Water;

To raise and support Armies, but no Appropriation of Money to that Use shall be for a longer Term than two Years;

To provide and maintain a Navy;

To make Rules for the Government and Regulation of the land and naval Forces;

To provide for calling forth the Militia to execute the Laws of the Union, suppress Insurrections and repel Invasions;

To provide for organizing, arming, and disciplining, the Militia, and for governing such Part of them as may be employed in the Service of the United States, reserving to the States respectively, the Appointment of the Officers, and the Authority of training the Militia according to the discipline prescribed by Congress;

To exercise exclusive Legislation in all Cases whatsoever, over such District (not exceeding ten Miles square) as may, by Cession of particular States, and the Acceptance of Congress, become the Seat of the Government of the United States, and to exercise like Authority over all Places purchased by the Consent of the Legislature of the State in which the Same shall be, for the Erection of Forts, Magazines, Arsenals, dock-Yards and other needful Buildings;—And

To make all Laws which shall be necessary and proper for carrying into Execution the foregoing Powers, and all other Powers vested by this Constitution in the Government of the

United States, or in any Department or Officer thereof.

SECTION 9. The Migration or Importation of such Persons as any of the States now existing shall think proper to admit, shall not be prohibited by the Congress prior to the Year one thousand eight hundred and eight, but a Tax or duty may be imposed on such Importation, not exceeding ten dollars for each Person.

The Privilege of the Writ of Habeas Corpus shall not be suspended, unless when in Cases of Rebellion or Invasion the public Safety may require it.

No Bill of Attainder or ex post facto Law shall be passed.

No Capitation, or other direct, Tax shall be laid, unless in Proportion to the Census or Enumeration herein before directed to be taken.

No Tax or Duty shall be laid on Articles exported from any State.

No Preference shall be given by any Regulation of Commerce or Revenue to the Ports of one State over those of another: nor shall Vessels bound to, or from, one State, be obliged to enter, clear, or pay Duties in another.

No Money shall be drawn from the Treasury, but in Consequence of Appropriations made by Law; and a regular Statement and Account of the Receipts and Expenditures of all public Money shall be published from time to time.

No Title of Nobility shall be granted by the United States: And no Person holding any Office of Profit or Trust under them, shall, without the Consent of the Congress, accept of any present, Emolument, Office, or Title, of any kind whatever, from any King, Prince, or foreign State.

SECTION 10. No State shall enter into any Treaty, Alliance, or Confederation; grant Letters of Marque and Reprisal; coin Money; emit Bills of Credit; make any Thing but gold and silver Coin a Tender in Payment of Debts; pass any Bill of Attainder, ex post facto Law, or Law impairing the Obligation of Contracts, or grant any Title of Nobility.

No State shall, without the Consent of the Congress, lay any Imposts or Duties on Imports or Exports, except what may be absolutely necessary for executing it's inspection Laws: and the net Produce of all Duties and Imposts, laid by any State on Imports or Exports, shall be for the Use of the Treasury of the United States; and all such Laws shall be subject to the Revision and Control of the Congress.

No State shall, without the Consent of Congress, lay any Duty of Tonnage, keep Troops, or Ships of War in time of Peace, enter into any Agreement or Compact with another State, or with a foreign Power, or engage in War, unless actually invaded, or in such imminent Danger as will not admit of delay.

ARTICLE II.

SECTION 1. The executive Power shall be vested in a President of the United States of America. He shall hold his Office during the Term of four Years, and, together with the Vice President, chosen for the same Term, be elected, as follows

Each State shall appoint, in such Manner as the Legislature thereof may direct, a Number of Electors, equal to the whole Number of Senators and Representatives to which the State may be entitled in the Congress: but no Senator or Representative, or Person holding an Office of Trust or Profit under the United States, shall be appointed an Elector.

The Electors shall meet in their respective States, and vote by Ballot for two Persons, of whom one at least shall not be an Inhabitant of the same State with themselves. And they shall make a List of all the Persons voted for, and of the Number of Votes for each; which List they shall sign and certify, and transmit sealed to the Seat of the Government of the United States, directed to the President of the

Senate. The President of the Senate shall, in the Presence of the Senate and House of Representatives, open all the Certificates, and the Votes shall then be counted. The Person having the greatest Number of Votes shall be the President, if such Number be a Majority of the whole Number of Electors appointed; and if there be more than one who have such Majority, and have an equal Number of Votes, then the House of Representatives shall immediately chuse by Ballot one of them for President; and if no Person have a Majority, then from the five highest on the List the said House shall in like manner chuse the President. But in chusing the President, the Votes shall be taken by States, the Representation from each State having one Vote; A quorum for this Purpose shall consist of a Member or Members from two thirds of the States, and a Majority of all the States shall be necessary to a Choice. In every Case, after the Choice of the President, the Person having the greatest Number of Votes of the Electors shall be the Vice President. But if there should remain two or more who have equal Votes, the Senate shall chuse from them by Ballot the Vice President.

The Congress may determine the Time of chusing the Electors, and the Day on which they shall give their Votes; which Day shall be the same throughout the United States.

No Person except a natural born Citizen, or a Citizen of the United States, at the time of the Adoption of this Constitution, shall be eligible to the Office of the President; neither shall any person be eligible to that Office who shall not have attained to the Age of thirty five Years, and been fourteen Years a Resident within the United States.

In Case of the Removal of the President from Office, or of his Death, Resignation, or Inability to discharge the Powers and Duties of the said Office, the Same shall devolve on the Vice President, and the Congress may by Law provide for the Case of Removal, Death, Resignation or Inability, both of the President and Vice President, declaring what Officer shall then act as President, and such Officer shall act accordingly, until the Disability be removed, or a President shall be elected.

The President shall, at stated Times, receive for his Services, a Compensation, which shall neither be increased nor diminished during the Period for which he shall have been elected, and he shall not receive within that Period any other Emolument from the United States, or any of them.

Before he enter the Execution of his Office, he shall take the following Oath or Affirmation:—"I do solemnly swear (or affirm) that I will faithfully execute the Office of President of the United States, and will to the best of my Ability, preserve, protect and defend the Constitution of the United States."

SECTION 2. The President shall be Commander in Chief of the Army and Navy of the United States, and of the Militia of the several States, when called into the actual Service of the United States; he may require the Opinion, in writing, of the principal Officer in each of the executive Departments, upon any Subject relating to the Duties of their respective Offices, and he shall have Power to grant Reprieves and Pardons for Offenses against the United States, except in Cases of Impeachment.

He shall have Power, by and with the Advice and Consent of the Senate, to make Treaties, provided two thirds of the Senators present concur; and he shall nominate, and by and with the Advice and Consent of the Senate, shall appoint Ambassadors, other public Ministers and Consuls, Judges of the supreme Court, and all other Officers of the United States, whose Appointments are not herein otherwise provided for, and which shall be established by Law: but the Congress may by Law vest the Appointment of such inferior Officers, as they think proper, in the President alone, in the Courts of Law, or in the Heads of Departments.

The President shall have Power to fill up all Vacancies that may happen during the Recess of the Senate, by granting Commissions which shall expire at the End of their next Session.

SECTION 3. He shall from time to time give to the Congress Information of the State of the Union, and recommend to their Consideration such Measures as he shall judge necessary and expedient; he may, on extraordinary Occasions, convene both Houses, or either of them, and in Case of Disagreement between them, with Respect to the Time of Adjournment, he may adjourn them to such Time as he shall think proper; he shall receive Ambassadors and other public Ministers; he shall take Care that the Laws be faithfully executed, and shall Commission all the Officers of the United States.

SECTION 4. The President, Vice President and all civil Officers of the United States, shall be removed from Office on Impeachment for, and Conviction of, Treason, Bribery, or other high Crimes and Misdemeanors.

ARTICLE III.

SECTION 1. The judicial Power of the United States, shall be vested in one supreme Court, and in such inferior Courts as the Congress may from time to time ordain and establish. The Judges, both of the supreme and inferior Courts, shall hold their Offices during good Behaviour, and shall, at stated Times, receive for their Services, a Compensation, which shall not be diminished during their Continuance in Office.

SECTION 2. The judicial Power shall extend to all Cases, in Law and Equity, arising under this Constitution, the Laws of the United States, and Treaties made, or which shall be made, under their Authority;—to all Cases affecting Ambassadors, other public Ministers and Consuls;—to all Cases of admiralty and maritime Jurisdiction;—to Controversies to which the United States shall be a Party;—to Controversies between two or more States; be-

tween a State and Citizens of another State; between Citizens of different States,—between Citizens of the same State claiming Lands under Grants of different States, and between a State, or the Citizens thereof, and foreign States, Citizens or Subjects.

In all Cases affecting Ambassadors, other public Ministers and Consuls, and those in which a State shall be Party, the supreme Court shall have original Jurisdiction. In all the other Cases before mentioned, the supreme Court shall have appellate Jurisdiction, both as to Law and Fact, with such Exceptions, and under such Regulations as the Congress shall make.

The Trial of all Crimes, except in Cases of Impeachment, shall be by Jury; and such Trial shall be held in the State where the said Crimes shall have been committed; but when not committed within any State, the Trial shall be at such Place or Places as the Congress may by Law have directed.

SECTION 3. Treason against the United States, shall consist only in levying War against them, or in adhering to their Enemies, giving them Aid and Comfort. No Person shall be convicted of Treason unless on the Testimony of two Witnesses to the same overt Act, or on Confession in open Court.

The Congress shall have Power to declare the Punishment of Treason, but no Attainder of Treason shall work Corruption of Blood, or Forfeiture except during the Life of the Person attainted.

ARTICLE IV.

SECTION 1. Full Faith and Credit shall be given in each State to the public Acts, Records, and judicial Proceedings of every other State; And the Congress may by general Laws prescribe the Manner in which such Acts, Records and Proceedings shall be proved, and the Effect thereof.

SECTION 2. The Citizens of each State shall be entitled to all Privileges and Immunities of

Citizens in the several States.

A Person charged in any State with Treason, Felony, or other Crime, who shall flee from Justice, and be found in another State, shall on Demand of the executive Authority of the State from which he fled, be delivered up, to be removed to the State having Jurisdiction of the Crime.

No person held to Service or Labour in one State, under the Laws thereof, escaping into another, shall, in Consequence of any Law or Regulation therein, be discharged from such Service or Labour, but shall be delivered up on Claim of the Party to whom such Service or Labour may be due.

SECTION 3. New States may be admitted by the Congress into this Union; but no new State shall be formed or erected within the Jurisdiction of any other State; nor any State be formed by the Junction of two or more States, or Parts of States, without the Consent of the Legislatures of the States concerned as well as of the Congress.

The Congress shall have Power to dispose of and make all needful Rules and Regulations respecting the Territory or other Property belonging to the United States; and nothing in this Constitution shall be so construed as to Prejudice any Claims of the United States, or of any particular State.

SECTION 4. The United States shall guarantee to every State in this Union a Republican Form of Government, and shall protect each of them against Invasion; and on Application of the Legislature, or of the Executive (when the Legislature cannot be convened) against domestic Violence.

ARTICLE V.

The Congress, whenever two thirds of both Houses shall deem it necessary, shall propose Amendments to this Constitution, or, on the Application of the Legislatures of two thirds of the several States, shall call a Convention for proposing Amendments, which, in either Case, shall be valid to all Intents and Purposes, as Part of this Constitution, when ratified by the Legislatures of three fourths of the several States, or by Conventions in three fourths thereof, as the one or the other Mode of Ratification may be proposed by the Congress; Provided that no Amendment which may be made prior to the Year One thousand eight hundred and eight shall in any Manner affect the first and fourth Clauses in the Ninth Section of the first Article; and that no State, without its Consent, shall be deprived of it's equal Suffrage in the Senate.

ARTICLE VI.

All Debts contracted and Engagements entered into, before the Adoption of this Constitution, shall be as valid against the United States under this Constitution, as under the Confederation.

This Constitution, and the Laws of the United States which shall be made in Pursuance thereof; and all Treaties made, or which shall be made, under the Authority of the United States, shall be the supreme Law of the Land; and the Judges in every State shall be bound thereby, any Thing in the Constitution or Laws of any State to the Contrary notwithstanding.

The Senators and Representatives before mentioned, and the Members of the several State Legislatures, and all executive and judicial Officers, both of the United States and of the several States, shall be bound by Oath or Affirmation, to support this Constitution; but no religious Test shall ever be required as a Qualification to any Office or public Trust under the United States.

ARTICLE VII.

The Ratification of the Conventions of nine States, shall be sufficient for the Establishment of this Constitution between the States so ratifying the Same.

Done in Convention by the Unanimous

Consent of the States present the Seventeenth Day of September in the Year of our Lord one thousand seven hundred and Eighty seven and of the Independence of the United States of America the Twelfth. In Witness whereof We have hereunto subscribed our Names,

G°: Washington—Presid[t] and deputy from Virginia

New Hampshire { John Langdon
Nicholas Gilman

Massachusetts { Nathaniel Gorham
Rufus King

Connecticut { W[m] Sam[l] Johnson
Roger Sherman

New York { Alexander Hamilton

New Jersey { Wil: Livingston
David Brearley
W[m] Paterson
Jona: Dayton

Pennsylvania { B Franklin
Thomas Mifflin
Rob[t] Morris
Geo. Clymer
Tho[s]. FitzSimons
Jared Ingersoll
James Wilson
Gouv Morris

Delaware { Geo: Read
Gunning Bedord jun
John Dickinson
Richard Bassett
Jaco: Broom

Maryland { James McHenry
Dan of S[t] Tho[s]. Jenifer
Dan[l] Carroll

Virginia { John Blair—
James Madison Jr.

North Carolina { W[m]. Blount
Rich[d] Dobbs Spaight.
Hu Williamson

South Carolina { J. Rutledge
Charles Cotesworth Pinckney
Charles Pickney
Pierce Butler

Georgia { William Few
Abr Baldwin

Attest William Jackson Secretary

AMENDMENTS TO THE U.S. CONSTITUTION

AMENDMENT I.

Congress shall make no law respecting an establishment of religion, or prohibiting the free exercise thereof; or abridging the freedom of speech, or of the press, or the right of the people peaceably to assemble, and to petition the Government for a redress of grievances.

[ratified December, 1791]

AMENDMENT II.

A well regulated Militia, being necessary to the security of a free State, the right of the people to keep and bear Arms, shall not be infringed.

[ratified December, 1791]

AMENDMENT III.

No Soldier shall, in time of peace be quartered in any house, without the consent of the Owner, nor in time of war, but in a manner to be prescribed by law.

[ratified December, 1791]

AMENDMENT IV.

The right of the people to be secure in their persons, houses, papers, and effects, against unreasonable searches and seizures, shall not be violated, and no Warrants shall issue, but upon probable cause, supported by Oath or affirmation, and particularly describing the place to be searched, and the persons or things to be seized.

[ratified December, 1791]

AMENDMENT V.

No person shall be held to answer for a capital, or otherwise infamous crime, unless on a presentment or indictment of a Grand Jury, except in cases arising in the land or naval forces, or in the Militia, when in actual service in time of War or public danger; nor shall any person be subject for the same offence to be twice put in jeopardy of life or limb, nor shall be compelled in any criminal case to be a witness against himself, nor be deprived of life, liberty, or property, without due process of law; nor shall private property be taken for public use without just compensation.

[ratified December, 1791]

AMENDMENT VI.

In all criminal prosecutions, the accused shall enjoy the right to a speedy and public trial, by an impartial jury of the State and district wherein the crime shall have been committed; which district shall have been previously ascertained by law, and to be informed of the nature and cause of the accusation; to be confronted with the witnesses against him; to have compulsory process for obtaining witnesses in his favor, and to have the assistance of counsel for his defence.

[ratified December, 1791]

AMENDMENT VII.

In Suits at common law, where the value in controversy shall exceed twenty dollars, the right of trial by jury shall be preserved, and no fact tried by a jury shall be otherwise reexamined in any Court of the United States, than according to the rules of the common law.

[ratified December, 1791]

AMENDMENT VIII.

Excessive bail shall not be required, nor excessive fines imposed, nor cruel and unusual punishments inflicted.

[ratified December, 1791]

AMENDMENT IX.

The enumeration in the Constitution, of certain rights, shall not be construed to deny or disparage others retained by the people.

[ratified December, 1791]

AMENDMENT X.

The powers not delegated to the United States by the Constitution, nor prohibited by it to the States, are reserved to the States respectively, or to the people.

[ratified December, 1791]

AMENDMENT XI.

The Judicial power of the United States shall not be construed to extend to any suit in law or equity, commenced or prosecuted against one of the United States by Citizens of another State, or by Citizens or Subjects of any Foreign State.

[ratified February, 1795]

AMENDMENT XII.

The Electors shall meet in their respective states, and vote by ballot for President and Vice President, one of whom, at least, shall not be an inhabitant of the same state with themselves; they shall name in their ballots the person voted for as President, and in distinct ballots the person voted for as Vice-President, and they shall make distinct lists of all persons voted for as President, and of all persons voted for as Vice-President, and of the number of votes for each, which lists they shall sign and certify, and transmit sealed to the seat of the government of the United States, directed to the President of the Senate;—The President of the Senate shall, in the presence of the Senate and House of Representatives, open all the certificates and the votes shall then be counted;—The person having the greatest number of votes for President, shall be the President, if such number be a majority of the whole number of Electors appointed; and if no person have such majority, then from the persons having the highest numbers not exceeding three on the list of those voted for as President, the House of Representatives shall choose immediately, by ballot, the President. But in choosing the President, the votes shall be taken by states, the representation from each state having one vote; a quorum for this purpose shall consist of a member or members from two-thirds of the states, and a majority of all the states shall be necessary to a choice. And if the House of Representatives shall not choose a President whenever the right of choice shall devolve upon them, before the fourth day of March next following, then the Vice-President shall act as President, as in the case of the death or other constitutional disability of the President.—The person having the greatest number of votes as Vice-President, shall be the Vice-President, if such number be a majority of the whole number of Electors appointed, and if no person have a majority, then from the two highest numbers on the list, the Senate shall choose the Vice-President; a quorum for the purpose shall consist of two-thirds of the whole number of Senators, and a majority of the whole number shall be necessary to a choice. But no person constitutionally ineligible to the office of President shall be eligible to that of Vice-President of the United States.

[ratified June, 1804]

AMENDMENT XIII.

SECTION 1. Neither slavery nor involuntary servitude, except as a punishment for crime whereof the party shall have been duly convicted, shall exist within the United States, or any place subject to their jurisdiction.

SECTION 2. Congress shall have power to enforce this article by appropriate legislation.

[ratified December, 1865]

AMENDMENT XIV.

SECTION 1. All persons born or naturalized in the United States and subject to the jurisdiction thereof, are citizens of the United States and of the State wherein they reside. No State shall make or enforce any law which shall abridge the privileges or immunities of citizens of the United States; nor shall any State deprive any person of life, liberty, or property, without due process of law; nor deny to any person within its jurisdiction the equal protection of the laws.

SECTION 2. Representatives shall be apportioned among the several States according to their respective numbers, counting the whole number of persons in each State, excluding Indians not taxed. But when the right to vote at any election for the choice of electors for President and Vice President of the United States, Representatives in Congress, the Executive and Judicial officers of a State, or the members of the Legislature thereof, is denied to any of the male inhabitants of such State, being twenty-one years of age, and citizens of the United States, or in any way abridged, except for participation in rebellion, or other crime, the basis of representation therein shall be reduced in the proportion which the number of such male citizens shall bear to the whole number of male citizens twenty-one years of age in such State.

SECTION 3. No person shall be a Senator or Representative in Congress, or elector of President and Vice President, or hold any office, civil or military, under the United States, or under any State, who, having previously taken an oath, as a member of Congress, or as an officer of the United States, or as a member of any State legislature, or as an executive or judicial officer of any State, to support the Constitution of the United States, shall have engaged in insurrection or rebellion against the same, or given aid or comfort to the enemies thereof. But Congress may by a vote of two-thirds of each House, remove such disability.

SECTION 4. The validity of the public debt of the United States, authorized by law, including debts incurred for payment of pensions and bounties for services in suppressing insurrection or rebellion, shall not be questioned. But neither the United States nor any State shall assume or pay any debt or obligation incurred in aid of insurrection or rebellion

against the United States, or any claim for the loss or emancipation of any slave; but all such debts, obligations and claims shall be held illegal and void.

SECTION 5. The Congress shall have power to enforce, by appropriate legislation, the provisions of this article.

[ratified July, 1868]

AMENDMENT XV.

SECTION 1. The right of citizens of the United States to vote shall not be denied or abridged by the United States or by any State on account of race, color, or previous condition of servitude.

SECTION 2. The Congress shall have power to enforce this article by appropriate legislation.

[ratified February, 1870]

AMENDMENT XVI.

The Congress shall have power to lay and collect taxes on incomes, from whatever source derived, without apportionment among the several States, and without regard to any census or enumeration.

[ratified February, 1913]

AMENDMENT XVII.

The Senate of the United States shall be composed of two Senators from each State, elected by the people thereof, for six years; and each Senator shall have one vote. The electors in each State shall have the qualifications requisite for electors of the most numerous branch of the State legislatures.

When vacancies happen in the representation of any State in the Senate, the executive authority of such State shall issue writs of election to fill such vacancies: *Provided*, That the legislature of any State may empower the executive thereof to make temporary appointments until the people fill the vacancies by election as the legislature may direct.

This amendment shall not be so construed

as to affect the election or term of any Senator chosen before it becomes valid as part of the Constitution.

[ratified April, 1913]

AMENDMENT XVIII.

SECTION 1. After one year from the ratification of this article the manufacture, sale, or transportation of intoxicating liquors within, the importation thereof into, or the exportation thereof from the United States and all territory subject to the jurisdiction thereof for beverage purposes is hereby prohibited.

SECTION 2. The Congress and the several States shall have concurrent power to enforce this article by appropriate legislation.

SECTION 3. This article shall be inoperative unless it shall have been ratified as an amendment to the Constitution by the legislatures of the several States, as provided in the Constitution, within seven years from the date of the submission hereof to the States by the Congress.

[ratified January, 1919, repealed December, 1933]

AMENDMENT XIX.

The right of citizens of the United States to vote shall not be denied or abridged by the United States or by any State on account of sex.

Congress shall have power to enforce this article by appropriate legislation.

[ratified August, 1920]

AMENDMENT XX.

SECTION 1. The terms of the President and Vice President shall end at noon on the 20th day of January, and the terms of Senators and Representatives at noon on the 3d day of January, of the years in which such terms would have ended if this article had not been ratified; and the terms of their successors shall then begin.

SECTION 2. The Congress shall assemble at least once in every year, and such meeting shall begin at noon on the 3d day of January, unless they shall by law appoint a different day.

SECTION 3. If, at the time fixed for the beginning of the term of the President, the President elect shall have died, the Vice President elect shall become President. If a President shall not have been chosen before the time fixed for the beginning of his term, or if the President elect shall have failed to qualify, then the Vice President elect shall act as President until a President shall have qualified; and the Congress may by law provide for the case wherein neither a President elect nor a Vice President elect shall have qualified, declaring who shall then act as President, or the manner in which one who is to act shall be selected, and such person shall act accordingly until a President or Vice President shall have qualified.

SECTION 4. The Congress may by law provide for the case of the death of any of the persons from whom the House of Representatives may choose a President whenever the right of choice shall have devolved upon them, and for the case of the death of any of the persons from whom the Senate may choose a Vice President whenever the right of choice shall have devolved upon them.

SECTION 5. Sections 1 and 2 shall take effect on the 15th day of October following the ratification of this article.

SECTION 6. This article shall be inoperative unless it shall have been ratified as an amendment to the Constitution by the legislatures of three-fourths of the several States within seven years from the date of its submission.

[ratified January, 1933]

AMENDMENT XXI.

SECTION 1. The eighteenth article of amendment to the Constitution of the United States is hereby repealed.

SECTION 2. The transportation or importation into any State, Territory, or possession of the United States for delivery or use therein of intoxicating liquors, in violation of the laws thereof, is hereby prohibited.

SECTION 3. This article shall be inoperative unless it shall have been ratified as an amendment to the Constitution by conventions in the several States, as provided in the Constitution, within seven years from the date of the submission hereof to the States by the Congress.

[ratified December, 1933]

AMENDMENT XXII.

SECTION 1. No person shall be elected to the office of the President more than twice, and no person who has held the office of President, or acted as President, for more than two years of a term to which some other person was elected President shall be elected to the office of the President more than once. But this Article shall not apply to any person holding the office of President when this Article was proposed by the Congress, and shall not prevent any person who may be holding the office of President, or acting as President, during the term within which this Article becomes operative from holding the office of President or acting as President during the remainder of such term.

SECTION 2. This article shall be inoperative unless it shall have been ratified as an amendment to the Constitution by the legislatures of three-fourths of the several States within seven years from the date of its submission to the States by the Congress.

[ratified February, 1951]

AMENDMENT XXIII.

SECTION 1. The District constituting the seat of Government of the United States shall appoint in such manner as the Congress may direct:

A number of electors of President and Vice President equal to the whole number of Senators and Representatives in Congress to which the District would be entitled if it were a State, but in no event more than the least populous State; they shall be in addition to those appointed by the States, but they shall be considered, for the purposes of the election of President and Vice President, to be electors appointed by a State; and they shall meet in the District and perform such duties as provided by the twelfth article of amendment.

SECTION 2. The Congress shall have power to enforce this article by appropriate legislation.

[ratified March, 1961]

AMENDMENT XXIV.

SECTION 1. The right of citizens of the United States to vote in any primary or other election for President or Vice President, for electors for President or Vice President, or for Senator or Representative in Congress, shall not be denied or abridged by the United States or any State by reason of failure to pay any poll tax or other tax.

SECTION 2. The Congress shall have power to enforce this article by appropriate legislation.

[ratified January, 1964]

AMENDMENT XXV.

SECTION 1. In case of the removal of the President from office or of his death or resignation, the Vice President shall become President.

SECTION 2. Whenever there is a vacancy in the office of the Vice President, the President shall nominate a Vice President who shall take office upon confirmation by a majority vote of both Houses of Congress.

SECTION 3. Whenever the President transmits to the President pro tempore of the Senate and the Speaker of the House of Representatives his written declaration that he is unable to discharge the powers and duties of his office, and until he transmits to them a written declaration to the contrary, such powers and duties shall be discharged by the Vice President as Acting President.

SECTION 4. Whenever the Vice President and a majority of either the principal officers of the executive departments or of such other body as Congress may by law provide, transmit to the President pro tempore of the Senate and the Speaker of the House of Representatives their written declaration that the President is unable to discharge the powers and duties of his office, the Vice President shall immediately assume the powers and duties of the office as Acting President.

Thereafter, when the President transmits to the President pro tempore of the Senate and the Speaker of the House of Representatives his written declaration that no inability exists, he shall resume the powers and duties of his office unless the Vice President and a majority of either the principal officers of the executive department or of such other body as Congress may by law provide, transmit within four days to the President pro tempore of the Senate and the Speaker of the House of Representatives their written declaration that the President is unable to discharge the powers and duties of his office. Thereupon Congress shall decide the issue, assembling within forty-eight hours for that purpose if not in session. If the Congress, within twenty-one days after receipt of the latter written declaration, or, if Congress is not in session, within twenty-one days after Congress is required to assemble, determines by two-thirds vote of both Houses that the President is unable to discharge the powers and duties of his office, the Vice President shall continue to discharge the same as Acting President; otherwise, the President shall resume the powers and duties of his office.

[ratified February, 1967]

AMENDMENT XXVI.

SECTION 1. The right of citizens of the United States, who are eighteen years of age or older, to vote shall not be denied or abridged by the United States or by any State on account of age.

SECTION 2. The Congress shall have power to enforce this article by appropriate legislation.

[ratified July, 1971]

AMENDMENT XXVII.

No law, varying the compensation for the services of the Senators and Representatives, shall take effect, until an election of Representatives shall have intervened.

[ratified May 7, 1992]

Glossary

Small-caps (including some headwords) indicate the subjects of core essays in the encyclopedia.

Abortion: Medical procedure that terminates human pregnancy, usually before a fetus is viable.

Accountability: Requirement that public officials be answerable for their actions through elections, impeachment, or other mechanisms to enforce the public will.

Activist politics: Conventional and unconventional ways in which members of the public participate in political systems.

Adjudication: Application of existing laws or rules to special situations through case-by-case decision making.

Administration: Managing the tasks of government with economy and efficiency.

Administrative law: Area of law dealing with the powers and ADMINISTRATIVE PROCEDURES of government agencies.

AFFIRMATIVE ACTION: Government policies promoting and requiring preferential treatment of minorities to redress the effects of past discrimination or to promote diversity in workplaces, schools, and other sectors.

Agricultural management: Government intervention in farming for the purpose of helping to make farming more prosperous, while protecting national interests.

Alien: Immigrant resident who is not a citizen or national of the United States.

Alliance: Agreement among states in which each participant pledges to assist the others in security matters.

Ally: State that coordinates its defense policies with those of one or more other states, frequently on the basis of formal treaties.

AMBASSADOR: Highest-ranking diplomatic representative appointed by one country to represent it in one or more other countries.

American Revolution: Period during the 1770's and 1780's when Great Britain's North American colonies fought for independence and created the United States of America.

Anarchism: View that all forms of government are oppressive and intolerable to free and rational people.

Anarchy: Absence of rule, lawlessness; associated in classical thought with direct democracy.

ANTITRUST LAW: Body of federal law dealing with the unreasonable restraint of trade in commercial activity.

Appeal: Application to a higher court to review a lower court decision in a case.

Appellate court: Court of review to determine the validity of the rulings of lower courts.

Appropriation: Spending or obligation of public funds for authorized purposes.

Arbitration: Method of resolving disagreements between two parties in which a third party makes a decision after hearing both sides of the dispute.

Armed forces: Personnel trained and outfitted by government to conduct armed conflict.

Arms control: Attempts to reduce the risk of war—especially nuclear war—by regulating arms competition among nations and by reducing incentives for war.

Arms race: Rivalry among countries to outdo one another in the level or quality of their weapons systems.

Arraignment: The hearing at which a criminal defendant is formally charged with a crime.

Arrest: The process of detaining an alleged criminal, pursuant to an arrest warrant or because police officers have probable cause to believe that a crime has been committed.

Articles of Confederation: Agreement ratified by the thirteen original U.S. states in 1781, forming a government in which the states retained important powers while the national government received only limited power; replaced by the U.S. CONSTITUTION in 1789.

Assault: At common law, the placing of another person in fear of imminent peril. States define assault statutorily and generally divide it into subcategories based on type and severity of assault.

At-large election: Election in which all voters from all districts select candidates from a common list to fill the seats of a representative body such as a city council. At-large representatives represent entire electorates, rather than residents of individual districts.

ATTORNEY GENERAL OF THE UNITED STATES: Cabinet-level officer heading the federal JUSTICE DEPARTMENT; a politically appointed officer responsible for impartial enforcement of federal law.

Authoritarianism: Nondemocratic government by arbitrary authority that ignores fundamental rights of individuals and rules through force rather than consent.

Authority: Legitimate rule of a government over its citizens.

Autonomy: Self-rule of a nation or of a community or group within a state.

Balance of power: Condition in which the military and economic strength of competing countries or alliances is approximately equal.

Ballot: Piece of paper on which the names of candidates or proposals appear for voter selection.

Bankruptcy: The process by which a debtor's debts are discharged (known as a Chapter 7 bankruptcy) or reorganized (known as a Chapter 11 bankruptcy). Federal bankruptcy law is designed to give the debtor a "fresh start" while providing fairness among classes of creditors in access to the debtor's assets.

Bargaining: Actions and negotiations in which two or more parties seek to resolve conflicts while pursuing their interests.

Battery: At common law, an unlawful beating or other wrongful touching of another person inflicted without his or her consent. States define battery statutorily and subdivide it into various categories, such as sexual battery.

Bicameralism: Having two houses or chambers, particularly in a legislative body, such as the U.S. CONGRESS, which consist of the House of Representatives and the Senate.

BILL OF RIGHTS: First ten amendments to the U.S. CONSTITUTION, listing basic CIVIL LIBERTIES that the federal government cannot abridge; these include FREEDOM OF SPEECH and religion, protection against arbitrary searches and seizures, and certain rights guaranteed to citizens accused of crimes.

BIRTH CONTROL: Employment of methods or devices to prevent pregnancy.

Block grant: Grant of funds usually from a higher level of government to a lower level that specifies a range of activities for which monies may be used, with recipients allowed broad discretion to spend within these limits.

Bond: Certificate of indebtedness, tendered by a unit of government (the borrower) to a lender, that provides written recognition of the legal obligation to repay the loan plus interest.

Budget: Document that describes a government's plans for spending and specifies taxation and deficit policies for a single fiscal period.

Budget deficit: Amount by which expenditures exceed receipts within a fiscal year, an amount the government must borrow.

Bureaucracy: Administrative organization usually staffed by career employees and characterized by a division of labor, specialization of tasks, hierarchical chain of command, standard operation procedure, and formal record keeping.

Burglary: At common law, breaking and entering the house of another with intent to commit a felony while inside.

BUSINESS: Commercial and industrial enterprises in the private (nongovernment) sector.

BUSING: Government policy of shifting children among schools to achieve racial and ethnic balance in order to overcome effects of de facto SEGREGATION.

Bylaw: Local ordinance passed by town meeting and having the force of law.

Cabinet: Heads of the major government departments, who advise the head of the government, such as the president.

Campaign: Activities—such as speeches, television advertising, and rallies—engaged in by a candidate seeking public office, or by others active on the candidate's behalf during POLITICAL CAMPAIGNING.

CAPITAL PUNISHMENT: Execution of persons convicted of capital crimes, such as murder or TREASON.

CAPITALISM: Economic system allowing private ownership of property and open competition between businesses in a free market.

Caucus: Meeting of key political party leaders, usually to decide party policy or select a candidate; also, meeting of registered party members to select representatives who will attend conventions at which delegates will select the party's presidential candidate.

CENSORSHIP: Suppression of the publication or dissemination of any form of expression regarded as objectionable.

Certiorari **(writ of):** The appellate proceeding for the U.S. SUPREME COURT to review a decision of one of the appellate COURTS of the U.S. system.

CHECKS AND BALANCES: Principle that the judicial, legislative, and executive branches of government have the power to limit and counteract one another's decisions.

Chief executive: Top officer in the executive branch of a government, such as a state governor or president of the United States.

Citizen: Member of a state or nation by birth or naturalization.

CITIZEN MOVEMENT: Organized effort by people with common goals and values who engage in collective political action to change, or to resist change in, some aspect of society.

CITIZENSHIP: Membership in a political state—a status that gives persons in representative democracies both rights and responsibilities as active participants within the civil community.

City manager: Appointed officer who carries out the executive duties of a municipality in a council-manager form of government.

Civic education: Education of the members of a nation in the rights and responsibilities of citizenship.

CIVIL DISOBEDIENCE: Refusal to obey a law that one considers morally unjust or unconstitutional.

CIVIL LAW: Division of law, sometimes called "private law," applying to the rights governing conduct between individuals who use courts for redress.

CIVIL LIBERTIES: Freedoms or rights guaranteed to all individuals by law, custom, or judicial interpretation.

CIVIL PROCEDURE: The set of rules governing the process of pretrial, trial, and post-trial litigation in civil cases. Federal rules of civil procedure govern litigation in federal courts, and each state has its own set of rules for state proceedings.

CIVIL RIGHTS: Explicit acts of government, either constitutionally derived or promulgated as statutory law, that protect citizens from unfair, arbitrary, and discriminatory treatment at the hands of government or other citizens.

CIVIL RIGHTS MOVEMENT: Predominantly black-led movement of the 1950's and 1960's based in churches and legal-action groups that worked to extend full social and political rights to all Americans.

CIVIL SERVICE: Body of individuals chosen by merit and protected from improper political interference who administer a government's programs.

Civil War, U.S.: War fought between the northern and southern states between 1861 and 1865, primarily over the issue of whether the southern states could secede from the Union.

CIVIL WAR AMENDMENTS: The Thirteenth, Fourteenth, and Fifteenth Amendments to the U.S. CONSTITUTION, adopted between the end of the Civil War in 1865 and 1870, primarily in order to protect the rights of AFRICAN AMERICANS.

Class: Group sharing a common economic or social status.

Class conflict: Marxist notion that society tends to polarize into two dominant conflicting groups, impoverished workers and wealthy capitalists.

Closed primary: Election in which only citizens who registered as party members before the election are permitted to vote.

Cloture: Procedure used to close off debate so that a legislature can move to a vote on a bill.

Coalition: Temporary alliance or association of groups to advance a common cause.

Cold War: Period of conflict and competition between the United States and the Soviet Union, and their allies, which lasted more than four decades after World War II.

Collective bargaining: Negotiations between employees, through their labor unions, and their employers regarding wages and working conditions.

Collective security: System in which nations agree to defend one another against attack; an attack against one is considered an attack against all.

Colonialism: System whereby a country exploits economic and political control over a foreign country for self-serving reasons.

Commander in chief: Ultimate governor of a military entity, usually a highly placed civilian executive officer.

COMMERCE REGULATION: Government intervention in the marketplace to protect consumers against fraud and monopoly, to protect sellers against unfair competition, and to raise revenue for itself.

COMMON LAW: The body of case law which, as an evolving whole, sets forth the governing law. Common law has been supplanted by statutory law in many instances, but it continues to be of importance in American law in a number of areas, such as tort law. The American common-law tradition is descended from English common law.

Communism: In theory, a classless society managed by the dictatorship of the working class, and with most property owned by the state. In practice, communist governments, such as that of the former Soviet Union, have tended to be authoritarian.

CONGRESS: Lawmaking branch of the U.S. government, consisting of the House of Representatives and the Senate.

CONSCIENTIOUS OBJECTION: Refusal to serve in the military on grounds of religious beliefs or conscience.

Consensus: Unanimous agreement among members of a group. Consensus agreements are typically reached through series of compromises.

Consent of the governed: Agreement of those being governed to a form of government or political system.

CONSERVATISM: Political belief that stresses individual freedom, the free market, and minimum state intervention in social and economic life (also called classical liberalism). Modern conservatives also emphasize political and cultural traditions as well as personal virtue and character formation.

Constituency: Citizens whom a political leader formally represents.

Constitution: Basic or fundamental law of a politically organized body, such as a nation, it defines the structure and powers of government; it may include limitations on governmental powers, such as descriptions of individuals' civil rights and liberties. Individual states have constitutions, and the U.S. CONSTITUTION is considered the most fundamental law of the nation as a whole.

Constitutional democracy: Form of democratic government in which the majority is limited by rights assured to all, such as freedom of speech and religion.

CONSTITUTIONAL LAW: Area of jurisprudence in which laws, governmental actions, and judicial decisions are examined to determine whether they violate constitutional principles that are intended to limit governmental abuses.

Constitutionalism: Belief in limited government guaranteed through a written or understood contract.

Consulate: Extension of an embassy serving to protect its citizens abroad and to perform administrative tasks.

CONSUMERISM: Public activism to protect the interests of consumers against dishonest and unfair practices of manufacturers and retailers.

Contract: Binding mutual promises between parties to take specified actions. In order for there to be a valid contract, there must be a promise and "consideration" (something given in exchange for that promise). FREEDOM OF CONTRACT is considered an essential component of a DEMOCRACY.

Corporation: Legal "person" created and recognized under state law that is owned by its shareholders; it carries on business in perpetuity. The shareholders of a corporation are not liable for the debts incurred by the entity unless they specifically undertake a guarantee of those debts.

County: Large territorial division of local government. COUNTY GOVERNMENTS are considered extensions of the state.

COURTS, FEDERAL: As the major components of the judicial branch of the United States government, federal courts operate independently of state judicial systems and are responsible for hearing cases and administering justice respecting federal law; they are organized in three levels that include district courts, courts of appeals, and the Supreme Court.

COURTS, STATE AND LOCAL: Judicial branch of state governments; as the systems that try most civil and criminal cases in the United States, they apply state laws and local ordinances in individual cases and issue decisions that control the acts of local authorities, state officials, and all the citizens within their jurisdictions.

CRIME: Any behavior that violates the LAW, thereby making offenders subject to PUNISHMENT.

CRIMINAL JUSTICE SYSTEM: The total complex of local, state, and federal laws, policing forces, prosecuting offices, court systems, and correctional programs.

Criminal procedure: The set of rules governing the process of pretrial, trial, and appeal of litigation in criminal cases.

CRUEL AND UNUSUAL PUNISHMENT: PUNISHMENT that is considered, by the standards of the time, to be more painful or tormenting than is appropriate for the offense committed.

DECLARATION OF INDEPENDENCE: Document signed by American patriots and sent to the British crown in 1776 on which the independence of the United States is founded.

Defendant: The responding party in a civil matter, or the person charged with the crime in a criminal matter.

Demagogue: Political figure who achieves personal power by appealing to the baser instincts of the masses through a rhetoric of ethnic or racial hatred or class envy.

Democracy: Government of, for, and by the people of a political unit, usually through elected representatives.

DEMOCRATIC PARTY: The oldest major political party in the United States; traditionally identified with the lower and middle classes and racial minorities. It has pursued a liberal agenda on issues of racial, social, and criminal justice.

Deposition: The process for obtaining testimony from a witness in a civil trial prior to trial, in which the witness is placed under oath, a record is kept, and opposing counsel poses a series of questions to the party and receives his or her answers. The rules of evidence are relaxed in depositions.

Deregulation: Removal or restricting governmental regulation usually of economic or business activity.

Deterrence: Strategy that seeks to prevent an adversary from attacking by threatening to retaliate with equal or greater force.

Dillon's Rule: Legal notion that because American local governments are "creatures of the state," they may exercise only such powers as are granted to them by their state constitutions or state legislatures.

Diplomacy: Communication between states through formal channels according to established rules.

Direct action: Boycotts, marches, and demonstrations undertaken to help force political or legal change.

Direct democracy: Political power exercised directly by the people, rather than exercised for them by elected representatives.

Disarmament: Policies designed to reduce existing armaments.

DISASTER RELIEF: Governmental response efforts at the local, state, and federal levels to disaster and emergency situations.

Discrimination: The treatment of members of one class or group of persons differently from another, based on some characteristic such as race, gender, or national origin.

DISTRICT ATTORNEY: Government official responsible for instituting criminal proceedings on behalf of a local jurisdiction, such as a COUNTY GOVERNMENT.

Double jeopardy: At common law and in U.S. constitutional law, the prohibition against trying a defendant twice for the same crime. The prohibition prevents an unsuccessful prosecutor from subjecting the defendant to successive retrials by marginally changing the charging crime.

Dual federalism: Form of federal government in which each of the different levels of government is rigidly restricted to the powers explicitly assigned to it.

DUE PROCESS OF LAW: Principle articulated in the Fifth and Fourteenth amendments of the U.S. Constitution declaring that government cannot deprive citizens of "life, liberty, and property" without following carefully applied legal procedures.

EDUCATION MANAGEMENT: Government participation in the funding, organization, and curricula of public schools.

Egalitarianism: Social system practicing, or philosophy advocating, complete equality among all members of a society.

ELECTION: Process through which citizens select government leaders and rule on issues that may be put before them.

ELECTORAL COLLEGE: Body of electors chosen by the voters of each U.S. state to select the president and vice president.

Electorate: Set of persons who are qualified to vote in an election.

Elitism: Belief that a small class of superior persons should have the power to rule or dominate the rest of an entire society.

Embargo: Order by a government prohibiting the sale of goods to another country.

Embassy: Permanent mission established by a national government in a foreign country to represent the government's interests in that country.

Departure from one's home country in order to establish residence elsewhere.

Eminent domain: Government's power to take private land for public purposes, usually with the owners receiving monetary compensation.

Empowerment: Movement encouraging average citizens to take responsibility for and control of actions that occur in the public's name; often applied to specific groups, such as women or the disabled.

ENTITLEMENTS: Governmental benefits to which citizens are entitled because they meet certain criteria specified by law, such as low income or advanced age.

ENVIRONMENTAL PROTECTION: Government laws and programs designed to preserve the environment against uncontrolled development and exploitation.

Equal protection of the laws: Principle embodied in the Fourteenth Amendment to the U.S. Constitution that citizens are to be treated equally by government with regard to laws and their application.

EQUAL RIGHTS AMENDMENT: Amendment guaranteeing equal rights to all regardless of sex that failed to win ratification during the early 1980's.

Equality of opportunity: Equal chances for all citizens to better their lot in life.

Equality under law: Principle that all citizens are equal before the law.

ESPIONAGE: Use of spies to obtain information or steal secrets about the activities of a foreign government.

Ethics: Principles identifying good and bad behavior and promoting moral duties and obligations.

Ethnicity: Racial, national, or cultural characteristics that set a group apart from other groups.

Euthanasia: Also known as "mercy killing," the ending of another person's life at that person's request or to end painful suffering when there is no hope of remission.

Evidence: The body of information presented at a trial to the "fact finder" (the judge or jury) upon which the fact finder makes the determinations required.

Exclusionary rule: Concept established by the U.S. Supreme Court that prevents evidence obtained in violation of a citizen's civil liberties from being introduced in a court of law.

Executive agreement: In the United States, an international agreement made by the president without the consent of the Senate.

Executive branch: In the United States, the president and the major departments of the government such as state, defense, treasury, and justice.

Executive order: Rule or regulation issued by the president usually to other administrative officials.

Executive privilege: Implicit authority for the executive to withhold information from the legislative or judicial branches.

Expert witness: Person who, because of his or her specialized area of knowledge, is capable of examining evidence and providing an explanation of that evidence and its meaning to the trier of fact (the judge or jury).

Faction: In James Madison's famous formulation, "a number of citizens, whether amounting to a majority or minority of the whole, who are united and actuated by some common impulse of passion, or of interest, adverse to the rights of other citizens, or to the permanent and aggregate interests of the community."

Fairness doctrine: Long-standing requirement in U.S. telecommunications law, no longer enforced, that requires that radio and television stations cover issues of public concern in a manner reflecting divergent relevant viewpoints.

FEDERAL MANDATE: Federal directive to state governments regarding implementation of laws, regulations, or policies in accordance with guidelines established by the federal government.

Federal Reserve: Central bank of the United States, created in 1913 to act as the lender (to banks) of last resort and as the nation's monetary authority.

FEDERALISM: System of government in which a central government and local or subunit governments have separate bases of authority and distinct powers as defined by written constitutions.

Federalists: Americans who supported adoption of the new U.S. Constitution between 1787 and 1789, and who favored a strong central government.

Felony: More serious crime than a misdemeanor, punishable by imprisonment in a state penitentiary or by death. Rape, burglary, robbery, murder, and some types of assault are felonies.

FEMINISM: Advocacy of the rights of women and their social, political, and economic equality with men.

FILIBUSTER: Form of legislative obstruction by which a parliamentary minority attempts through continuous talking to defeat or alter a measure favored by the majority.

Fiscal policy: Tax, spending, and debt policies of the government, intended to improve the performance of the economy with respect to employment, inflation, and economic growth.

Fiscal year: Twelve-month period covered by a single budget; the fiscal year of the U.S. government runs from October 1 to September 30.

Food stamps: Credit slips provided to lower-income families to help finance basic food needs.

FOREIGN POLICY: Plans and actions that a government undertakes to achieve its goals in the international environment.

Formula grant: Categorical grant distributed automatically according to a preestablished eligibility formula.

Founders: Statespersons, politicians, and community leaders who helped to found the United States in the late eighteenth century; not to be confused with Framers.

Fourteenth Amendment: Amendment to the U.S. Constitution that requires states to provide all persons within their jurisdiction "due process" and "equal protection" under law.

Framers: Participants in the conventions that framed the U.S. Constitution and Bill of Rights in the late eighteenth century; not to be confused with Founders.

Franchise: The right to vote in public elections. In the United States all adult citizens not disqualified by certain conditions (such as conviction of felonies) have the franchise.

Fraud: Intentional misrepresentation designed to induce another person to take some detrimental action, such as pay money or purchase an item.

Free speech: Right protected by the First Amendment to the U.S. Constitution, guaranteeing the right to speak out politically.

Free trade: Trade in which goods and services can be exchanged without tariff or nontariff barriers.

Freedom: In government and politics the right of individual citizens to decide how to live their lives, including the acquisition of property and involvement in political activities, subject to the necessities of social order and the protection of the rights of others.

FREEDOM OF ASSEMBLY AND ASSOCIATION: CIVIL LIBERTIES protected by the First Amendment to the U.S. Constitution that give citizens the right freely to gather and associate with anyone they choose.

FREEDOM OF SPEECH AND PRESS: CIVIL LIBERTIES protected by the First Amendment to the U.S. Constitution that give people the right to express themselves freely, both in speech and in print, without fear of government restriction on the content of what they say.

Full employment: Situation in which everyone willing and able to work is able to find a job.

G.I. Bill of Rights: Federal legislation enacted in 1944 to ease the transition back into civilian life for servicemen returning home from World War II.

GATT: *See* **General Agreement on Tariffs and Trade**.

Gay: Person with a homosexual orientation who is attracted to members of the same sex. As a noun "gay" is usually applied to male homosexuals, but as an adjective is also applied to lesbians.

General Agreement on Tariffs and Trade (GATT): 1947 agreement among twenty-three nations (including the United States) that reduced tariffs and other trade barriers in order to facilitate global economic growth and development. Now involves more than one hundred nations.

General election: Regular election to choose the holder or holders of an office or offices; contrasts with a primary election, in which political parties choose the candidates who will represent them in a general election.

General revenue sharing: Grants provided by the federal government to state and local governments with few federal limitations.

GOP: Acronym for "Grand Old Party," the popular nickname for the Republican Party.

Government: All the people or institutions that administer or control the affairs of a territorial unit, such as a nation.

GRAND JURY: Group of persons who hear evidence presented by the prosecution to determine whether there is sufficient likelihood that a crime has been committed to charge a defendant with a crime.

GRANT-IN-AID: Financial assistance paid by one level of government to another for particular purposes articulated in legislation or administrative regulation.

GRASSROOTS POLITICS: Political activity initiated at the lowest level of political systems.

Great Society: series of domestic social programs originated by the Lyndon B. Johnson administration.

Gross domestic product (GDP): Market value of the final goods and services produced within a nation in one year.

Gun control: Regulations or limits on the ownership, manufacture, use, and sale of firearms.

Habeas corpus: Writ ordering a person holding or detaining another person to produce the latter and to submit himself or herself to the judgment of the court as to the propriety of detention. It is used in criminal proceedings on behalf of detained defendants and, though less often, in child custody matters.

Home rule: Freedom of local governments to run their own affairs with little or no state interference.

House of Representatives: One branch of the U.S. Congress, comprising 435 voting members serving two-year terms who are apportioned among the states according to their populations.

Human rights: Held inherently by each human being, identified as individual civil and political rights, group economic and social rights, and people's collective rights.

Ideology: Consistent philosophy or system of beliefs that guides the actions of those who adopt it.

IMMIGRATION: Act of entering a region or country of which one is not a native for the purpose of establishing permanent residence.

IMPEACHMENT: Legal process by which a legislative body, such as Congress, accuses, tries, and removes government officials (such as the president, vice president, federal judges, or federal officials) who are judged to be corrupt.

Imperialism: Extension of a state's power through conquest and colonialism, with the goal of creating or extending an empire.

Implementation: Process of putting into effect the laws of legislatures and the directives of chief executives.

Impoundment: Choice by a chief executive not to spend certain money that the legislature has appropriated.

Incorporation doctrine: Process by which the Supreme Court has used the Fourteenth Amendment to make the provisions of the BILL OF RIGHTS apply to the states; also called absorption.

Incumbent: The current holder of an elected office.

Indictment: The grand jury's written charge that a person named in an indictment has done some illegal and punishable act.

Individualism: Concept that each person's interests should take precedence over interests of the state or group, and that people should be free to pursue economic initiative and a personal philosophy.

Industrial policy: Government policies aimed at improving the performance of industry.

Information superhighway: Electronic interconnection of thousands of computers and information sources, making vast databases available to non-computer experts.

Infrastructure: Installations or facilities such as paved roads, sewers, piped water systems, and electricity supplies that provide the foundation for economic development.

INITIATIVES: Process by which citizens enact their own laws or constitutional amendments by placing them on the ballot to be approved or rejected by popular vote.

Injunction: Court order instructing a person to refrain from taking some action.

INTEREST GROUP: Organized group that seeks to influence public policy.

INTERGOVERNMENTAL RELATIONS: Interrelationships among the federal, state, and local governments.

INTERNATIONAL LAW: Rules and principles of law that regulate the interrelationships of nations and their conduct toward one another.

International organization: Institution created by two or more nations to pursue common objectives.

Internet: Worldwide network of local computer networks, allowing all users to share information resources and to communicate directly with one another.

Interposition: Intervention of one government or agency into the actions of another, as when a state interposes itself between the federal government and its own citizens.

IRON TRIANGLE: Close relationship which is formed among business, regulators, and legislators.

Jim Crow law: Law mandating or supporting the physical SEGREGATION of African Americans from other Americans; they were particularly characteristic of southern states.

Judgment: Final ruling on the issues in a case, supported by findings of fact and conclusions of law.

Judicial branch: Federal judiciary, headed by the Supreme Court, and including courts of appeals, district courts, and a few specialized courts.

JUDICIAL REVIEW: Power of courts to decide whether a statute or executive act is in accordance with the Constitution.

Judicial system: The complete system of federal and state courts.

Jurisdiction: The set of controversies over which a court may lawfully render judgment. Proper jurisdiction is a prerequisite to a valid judgment. The petitioner to a court must plead valid jurisdiction, and the parties cannot waive defects in jurisdiction.

JURISPRUDENCE: Science of law that deals with ascertaining the principles on which legal rules should be based.

JURY: The persons (usually six or twelve in number) charged by the court with the task of fact finding in a trial, including the determination of guilt in a criminal trial.

Justice: The administration of rewards and punishments according to rules and principles that society considers fair and equitable, justice encompasses criminal law and the criminal justice system, civil law and civil courts, and social justice.

Laissez-faire: Doctrine that government should intervene as little as possible in the political or economic affairs of its citizens.

Law: Body of rules based on statutes, judicial decisions, and custom that are enacted by government and backed by sanctions.

LAW ENFORCEMENT: The carrying out of statutes by professionals hired for that purpose, particularly refers to enforcement of the criminal law.

Law enforcement agencies: National, state, and local entities engaged in crime prevention, law enforcement, and apprehension of criminals.

Leadership: Ability of political officeholders to have their positions accepted and adopted as the proper course of action by a group or society.

LEFT, THE: Individuals and political groups seeking progressive political and social change, emphasizing equality over freedom.

Legislative branch of government: Elected or appointed deliberative body with authority to enact, amend, and repeal laws, such as Congress.

Legislative oversight: Monitoring by legislative bodies of the rules and regulations formulated by administrative agencies.

Legislative veto: Power of legislatures to negate or invalidate decisions by members of the executive branch of government without employing the constitutionally required process of lawmaking.

Legitimacy: Widely shared acceptance by a society that those who govern do so with lawful authority; the feeling that the political process deserves public respect.

Lesbian: Female homosexual.

LIBERALISM: Political doctrine or movement that affirms and seeks social progress and the promotion of the social and political liberties of the individual.

Lien: Claim or liability against a person's property to secure payment of a debt. In order to be enforceable, a lien must meet certain requirements, generally relating to its filing of record, and multiple liens generally follow the "first in time, first in right" rule.

Limited government: Government whose structure prevents official acts that violate the rights of individuals or minorities.

Line-item veto: Power of an official to veto individual sections or lines of a bill.

Literacy test: Requirement that prospective voters be able to read and write in order to register to vote.

Litigation: The contesting of legal disputes in the courts through lawsuits.

LOBBYING: Attempting to influence government policy, particularly in legislatures, by applying public pressure or employing professional lobbyists.

McCARTHYISM: Political style characterized by public hysteria over communism during the early 1950's.

Machine politics: Nonideological form of politics dominated by a small elite, usually corrupt, based on the exchange of material benefits for political support.

Majority leader: Floor leader of the U.S. Senate, elected by the members of the majority party in the Senate, who has little real power and leads through negotiations with fellow senators.

Majority party: Political party holding a majority of the seats within the legislature.

Mandatory arrest laws: State laws requiring the arrest of alleged criminals when the police find that certain conditions exist. Such laws are enacted in response to a perception that police are improperly exercising their discretion not to arrest, such as in domestic violence situations.

Mandatory sentencing laws: Laws requiring specific sentences for particular crimes. Mandatory sentences generally depend on the type of crime, its context, and characteristics of the defendant such as the number of previous crimes committed.

Manslaughter: At common law, the unlawful killing of a human being without malice, as in a violent quarrel or in the heat of passion.

Market economy: Economic system characterized by private ownership of resources, a limited government role, and competitive markets for goods and services.

Martial law: Temporary form of government operated by the armed forces when civilian authorities cannot function.

Marxism: Doctrine derived from Karl Marx, holding that class struggle is the heart of the historical process and that ownership of the means of production and distribution determines the nature of the social order; collective ownership will follow a class revolution.

Mass media: Organs of mass communication, including newspapers and magazines, radio, and television.

Mayor: Chief executive, normally elected, of a municipality.

Media: Agencies of mass communications, such as newspapers, radio, television, and films.

Mediation: Process of alternative dispute resolution in which a neutral third party assists the disputants in reaching a settlement of their case.

Medicaid: U.S. government program that provides health insurance to the poor; administered and partially paid by the states.

Medicare: U.S. government program that provides health insurance to persons sixty-five years of age and older and to others entitled to Social Security benefits.

Melting pot: Common metaphor for assimilation, involving the idea that different ethnic groups melt and blend together to form a uniform American culture.

Merit system: Selection and advancement in public employment based on competitive examinations and ability, knowledge, and skills.

Military conscription: Government power to require citizens to serve in armed forces; also known as the "draft."

Militia: In early U.S. history, the entire population of adult males who were physically fit and politically eligible for military service.

Miranda rights: The requirement of U.S. constitutional law that, upon arrest, a person be informed of his or her rights in custody: generally, the rights to contact a lawyer and not to speak to the police (and a notice that any communications to the police can be used in court). Named from the 1966 Supreme Court case *Miranda v. Arizona.*

Misdemeanor: Crime of a less serious nature than a felony, generally punishable by a fine or imprisonment in a county jail.

Mobilization: Act of bringing individuals together for the purpose of collective political action; usually accomplished through emotional rhetoric and appeals for unity.

Monopoly: Any economic entity that controls the entire supply of a good or service, thereby destroying free market exchange.

Monroe Doctrine: U.S. policy of opposing European intervention in the Western Hemisphere, articulated by President James Monroe.

Morality: Quality of correct conduct.

Multiculturalism: Movement that promotes the merits of embracing cultural, racial, or ethnic diversity, especially in politics and education.

Multinational corporation: Business with operations in more than one country.

Murder: At common law, the killing of a human being with malice aforethought.

NAFTA: *See* **North American Free Trade Agreement.**

National debt: Amount that a national government has borrowed, and not yet repaid, to cover past deficits.

National Guard: Military organizations affiliated with the U.S. Army and Air Force that serve at the call of both state and national governments.

National health insurance: Any health insurance program that a national government organizes in order to guarantee coverage to all citizens for health services.

National liberation movement: Rebellions, often armed, of national or minority groups against colonial governments or native governments under foreign control.

NATIONAL SECURITY: Safety of a government and its society from threats by foreign nations.

Nationalism: Devotion to one's nation and an ideology stressing the unity of a people based on their cultural, linguistic, historical, religious, or ethnic similarity; major movement of the nineteenth century.

Nativism: Cultural and political discrimination against newly arrived immigrants in favor of the interests of citizens who have been in the country for several generations.

NATO. *See* **North Atlantic Treaty Organization.**

NATURAL LAW: System of ethics and political philosophy that sees right and wrong as universal and sees human law as based on morality.

Natural rights: Rights belonging to all human beings, received from nature, rather than a human institution.

Naturalization: Legal process by which a person can acquire a new nationality or citizenship.

New Deal: Domestic programs of President Franklin D. Roosevelt, designed to combat the effects of the Great Depression.

New Left: Term used to define the radical youth movement of the 1960's emphasizing economic equality and participatory democracy.

NEW RIGHT: Advocates of freedom in economic matters and a social order with strong emphasis on traditional moral values.

NONPARTISAN: Free from party affiliation, association, or designation.

Nonpartisan primary: Election in which candidates are not permitted to list their party affiliation on the ballot.

Nonproliferation: Preventing the transfer of nuclear weapons or technology to countries that do not have nuclear weapons.

Nonviolent direct action: Method of protest in which the protagonist initiates conflict nonviolently by doing or refusing to do certain things.

North American Free Trade Agreement (NAFTA): 1993 agreement that provides for Mexico, the United States, and Canada to reduce tariffs and other barriers to trade.

North Atlantic Treaty Organization (NATO): Mutual defense alliance among North American and Western European nations.

One-party rule: System in which a single political party runs the government and often suppresses competing parties.

Open primary: Form of direct primary in which any qualified voter may participate, regardless of party affiliation.

Order: Directive by a court to a person, usually a party to a dispute, governing future conduct.

Original intent: In constitutional interpretation, the emphasis on what the authors of the U.S. Constitution meant, their original intent, when deciding contemporary constitutional controversies.

Pacifism: Refusal to settle disputes with violence, usually based on moral or religious grounds; often used interchangeably with passive resistance and nonviolent resistance.

Partisan politics: Behavior of politicians in support of the principles or interests of their own political party.

Party: *See* **Political party.**

Party whip: Member of a legislative party who is responsible for party discipline in voting.

Patriotism: Political virtue that encourages strong devotion and readiness to make sacrifices for the welfare of one's homeland and fellow citizens.

Patronage: Jobs and other material rewards which are provided in exchange for political support.

Petitioning: Process by which a requisite number of signatures is obtained to initiate a ballot proposition.

Plea: Criminal defendant's answer to being charged with a crime: guilty, not guilty, or *Nolo contendere* (no contest).

Plea bargain: Agreement between a prosecutor and criminal defendant that settles the defendant's case before it goes to trial.

Plural society: Society composing distinct racial, linguistic, and religious groups.

Pluralism: The view that democracy and fairness are preserved when a political organization comprises multiple and distinct groups and interests; also condition of society in which diverse cultural, ethnic, racial, religious, and minority groups, and a diversity of private interests, are tolerated.

Plurality: When a candidate or proposition receives more votes than the alternative, but not a majority of the votes cast.

Police: Principal LAW ENFORCEMENT agencies in cities and towns.

Police power: Right of government to regulate the public health, safety, and welfare.

POLITICAL ACTION COMMITTEE (PAC): Legally constituted committee that can raise and donate money to candidates' political campaigns, subject to the restrictions of federal law.

Political boss: Local or state leader of the party machinery who delivers votes on election day in return for favors.

Political correctness: Loosely defined term for the notion that speech should respect civility and the dignity of members of recognized minorities by not using any words that might be perceived as offensive.

Political machine: Powerful political organization that operates through a local political party and dominates the politics of a city or state.

Political party: Association of people who hold similar views and come together to establish their priorities by gaining control of the machinery of government.

POLITICAL PARTY CONVENTION: Gathering of delegates representing members of a political party, who adopt a party platform and nominate candidates for office.

Political philosophy: Inquiry into the fundamental concepts concerning political life, such as the nature of the state, justice, law, liberty, authority, community, citizenship, and political obligation.

Political platforms: Statements of principles and programs that parties pledge to support during POLITICAL CAMPAIGNS.

Political science: Academic discipline akin to economics, psychology, and sociology that studies government institutions, political processes, and political behavior.

Political system: Institutions a society uses to run the government.

Politics: Institutions and processes by which laws are enacted, decisions are made, and people are governed.

Poll tax: Payment required as a condition for voting; formerly used in some parts of the United States.

Pollution: Waste put into the environment above the level that the environment can absorb or recycle.

Populism, populist: Political ideology that emphasizes the clash between the common peoples and the ruling elites and that promotes greater democracy as well as social and economic equality.

Positivism: Doctrine that holds that human knowledge is based on what is known through actual practice, sense perceptions, and reliance on scientific methods, not on moral values or ideals.

Power: The ability to get what one wants from someone else, by force or by getting someone to think in accordance with one's interests; also, the ability of a state to pursue its strategic interests based on factors such as the size of its armed forces, or its industrial capacity.

PRESIDENCY: Head of the executive branch of government in the United States.

Presidential system: Government in which the executive powers of administering laws are distinct from the legislative powers of making laws, and are carried out by different officials.

PRIMARY ELECTION: Election during which the members of a political party cast their ballots for the candidates they wish to represent the party in the general election.

Privacy: The right of individuals to be free from unwarranted publicity or uninvited intrusions into their personal affairs.

Privatization: Assumption of public functions and services by private business enterprise.

Probation: Judicial act permitting convicted criminals to remain free in society under conditions set by officers appointed by the court.

"Pro-choice" movements: Umbrella term for organized groups whose aim is to preserve and broaden women's right to choose to obtain an abortion.

Progressive movement: Reform movement started in the late nineteenth century in the United States in reaction to the growth of business power in politics and the marketplace; emphasized civil service reform, greater popular control over elections and lawmaking, and regulating industrial activity.

Progressive tax: Tax in which people with higher incomes pay a larger proportion of income or wealth as tax.

Propaganda: Information or education systematically provided by governments, often false or misleading, designed to enhance patriotism and foster support for government policies.

Property rights: Rights relating to the ownership and control of real property.

Prosecutor: The representative of the state in a criminal matter whose responsibilities include appearing before the grand jury to seek indictments, determining what charges to bring against a defendant, and representing the state at trial.

Protectionism: Policy of raising tariff and nontariff barriers on products coming from other countries in order to shield domestic industries from competition.

Protest movements: Organized expressions of dissent from governmental actions or policy.

Public administration: Processes and organizations that carry out the laws and policies of government; also a field of academic study and an area of professional training.

Public defender: Attorney paid by government to provide legal representation to criminal defendants who cannot afford their own lawyers.

Public good: Good that is provided to everyone at once, and from which no one can be excluded, such as national security or clean air.

Public interest: Shared or common interests of members of a political society, as opposed to private, or individual, interests.

Public opinion polling: Surveys of sample members of population groups to determine how the groups as a whole view certain political issues.

Public policy: Laws and actions taken by authorized governing bodies.

Public prosecutor: Public official responsible for overseeing prosecution of criminal cases.

Public utilities: Providers of basic public services, such as electricity, natural gas, telephone, water, and sewer services.

Quorum: Minimum number of members of a legislature who must be present for the valid transaction of business; often a majority of members, but may be lower.

Racism: Belief that one's own racial group is superior to other groups.

Radicalism: In the context of social and political philosophy and practice, behavior or theory that attempts to go to the root of a problem through intellectual analysis or practical policy; also sometimes refers to the degree of departure from previous or familiar practice.

Radicals: Group that seeks great changes in society.

Rape: At common law, the unlawful carnal knowledge of a woman against her will. "Statutory rape" is sexual conduct with a woman under a certain age.

Rationalism: Belief that there are logical principles at work in the universe that are discernible by human reason.

Real property: Fixed, or immovable, property, such as land, as opposed to personal property, such as clothes, furniture, and vehicles.

Recall election: Election in which the public decides whether to retain or dismiss an elected official prior to the expiration of the official's term.

Redistributive policies: Policies that take money from one group to allocate to another group.

Referendum: Procedure by which a proposal passed by a legislative body is presented to the voters for approval.

Reform: Fundamental change in the government, constitution, socioeconomic order, or basic values of society that does not involve the violent overthrow of the existing government; also, change within a political system that is consistent with established political rules.

Regime: Type or form of government.

Regressive tax: Tax that places a proportionately larger tax burden on people of lower income or wealth.

Regulation: Rule or procedure made by a governmental agency, usually affecting business activity, and having the force of law.

Regulatory agencies: Government agencies that set and enforce standards of behavior for other governmental units, businesses, and citizens.

Relativism: Theory that conceptions of moral values and truth are not absolute, but are relative to the institutions, people, and groups holding such values.

Representation: Standing in for individuals and groups to promote and protect their interests.

Representative democracy: System of governance in which the citizens elect representatives to an assembly or legislative body that is charged with the task of making laws.

Republic: State in which the supreme power belongs to the citizens and is exercised by representatives chosen by them.

Republican Party: Major political party with a tradition of limited government action in human and social service programs, a conservative approach to civil rights, and a close alliance with big business.

Reserved powers: Powers that are held to be exclusive within a specified level of government.

Restraining order: The order by a court to the respondent to refrain from doing a particular action.

Revolution: Overthrow of an established government, usually in a brief time and often by violence.

Revolutionary government: Regime that claims authority as deriving from its successes in overthrowing an illegitimate regime, and its ongoing efforts to remove counterrevolutionary forces.

Right, the: Individuals and political groups that tend to favor order and stability over change, emphasizing freedom over equality.

RIGHT TO BEAR ARMS: Legal right to possess lethal weapons, including firearms.

Right to die: Right of individuals to choose suicide or euthanasia as alternatives to natural deaths.

"Right to life" movement: Umbrella term for organized groups who advocate restricting or eliminating the right to abortion in order to protect fetal life.

Right-to-work laws: Laws making it illegal to require a job applicant or employee to be a member of a union in order to obtain or keep a job.

Rights: Those things to which individuals, groups, or nations have a just claim, as an individual's right to life, liberty, and the pursuit of happiness as expressed in the Declaration of Independence.

Rights of the accused: Based on the idea that citizens are innocent of crimes until they are convicted, these rights guarantee due process procedures and other protections for those accused of crimes.

Robbery: At common law, the forceful taking of another person's property in his or her presence and against his or her will. States often define robbery statutorily, altering the common-law definition.

Rule making: An agency's working interpretation of a law and issuance of binding directives to affected parties.

Rule of law: The general principle that society should be governed by laws, not persons; the laws should be prospective, predictable, as clear as possible, formally written, and enacted through orderly procedures.

School board: Elected or appointed group of citizens who administer school districts.

School prayer: Religious prayers that occur within public schools.

Search and seizure: Right of government LAW ENFORCEMENT agents to search for, and seize, evidence needed in criminal investigations.

Secession: Voluntary separation of a region or a people from a larger polity.

SEGREGATION: Physical separation of people according to such characteristics as race, religion, gender, or social class membership. In the United States, most often associated with discrimination against AFRICAN AMERICANS. De jure segregation is segregation by law, whereas de facto segregation is that sanctioned by social custom or accidental circumstances.

Self-determination: Right of a people to achieve sovereignty and independence.

Senate: One branch of the U.S. Congress, comprising two members from each state of the union who serve six-year terms.

Seneca Falls Convention: Meeting held in Seneca Falls, New York, in 1848, that marked the beginning of the women's rights movement in the United States.

Separate but equal: Doctrine used by the courts to justify publicly enforcing segregation of the white and black races in southern states in the U.S. in the late nineteenth and early twentieth centuries. If separate facilities were equal, the courts maintained, they did not violate the "equal protection" clause requirement of the Fourteenth Amendment.

SEPARATION OF POWERS: System in which legislative and judicial powers are placed in different institutions and are exercised by different people.

Settlement: The process by which a dispute is resolved by the parties themselves, without the need for trial, usually through negotiation or mediation. Ninety-five percent of all civil matters are settled prior to trial.

Sheriff: Chief LAW ENFORCEMENT official in a COUNTY GOVERNMENT.

Single-member district: System in which a candidate is elected to office by the voters of that district; commonly found in the United States.

SLAVERY: Forced labor of people who are considered property, not free.

SOCIAL SECURITY SYSTEM: Basic national American social insurance program, Old-Age, Survivors, and Disability Insurance (OASDI), as well as health insurance (Medicare). OASDI is the largest income maintenance program in the country, covering nine out of every ten labor force participants.

Socialization: Process by which the opinions and behavior of individuals are formed to be consistent with those of a large group.

Sovereignty: Principle that an entity (usually a national government) wields supreme authority over its designated territory.

Spoils system: Granting of government jobs to political supporters by elected officials; the opposite of the merit system.

Stare decisis: Judicial principle requiring courts to follow the precedents of earlier court decisions on the same legal issues.

State: In its broadest sense, any sovereign unit of government, such as an independent nation. Within the U.S. system of federal government, the fifty states are the largest units of government below the national government.

State police: Statewide police forces with jurisdiction over motor vehicle traffic laws.

States' rights: Doctrine holding that individual states retain certain rights, liberties, and authority that the federal government cannot take from them.

Statesmanship: In the traditional or classical understanding, the high art of political leadership by which certain gifted individuals who possess superior political knowledge and skills promote a nation's comprehensive interests and the common good of its citizens.

Statute of limitations: The period of time during which an action may be brought for a particular dispute.

Strategic Arms Limitation Talks (SALT): Negotiations held between the United States and the Soviet Union between 1969 and 1985, attempting to limit strategic weapons.

Subpoena: The document (and process) used to require a witness to appear and give testimony.

Suffrage movement: Historical struggle to win for women the right to vote.

Suffragette: Derisive term for activist female supporters of woman suffrage applied to suffragists by their opponents.

Sunset law: Requirement that a specified government program periodically demonstrate its effectiveness or be dissolved.

Sunshine law: Requirement that elected officials engaged in official government business do so in public meetings to facilitate public and media oversight.

Superpowers: States whose power exceeds that of other powers in the military, economic, and political spheres, and who therefore exercise enormous influence throughout the world; during the Cold War, the superpowers were the United States and the Soviet Union.

Supply-side economics: Economic theory behind the view that less government and lower marginal tax rates will provide greater opportunities and incentives, thus promoting economic growth.

Supremacy clause: Article 6 of the U.S. Constitution, which states that federal law will prevail in cases of conflict with state law.

SUPREME COURT, U.S.: The highest U.S. federal court, composed of nine members nominated by the president and confirmed by the Senate.

TARIFFS: Tax on the value of a commodity being imported into a country.

TAXATION: Compulsory mechanism used by government to acquire money from people by force of law.

Term limits: Formal or informal restrictions on how long elected officials may stay in office.

TERRORISM: Unlawful use of force or violence against persons or property to intimidate or coerce a government or its people in furtherance of the terrorist's political or social objectives.

Testimony: Oral evidence presented at trial regarding the issues in the case.

Third party: Minor political party that tries to challenge the major parties in a two-party system.

Tort: Civil wrong done by one party against another, excluding breaches of contract. Tort law concerns wrongful acts that are actionable in civil courts for which damages can be recovered.

TOWN MEETING: The practice in which all citizens of a town meet, discuss issues, and decide on a course of action.

Treason: Betrayal of one's nation through activities jeopardizing its interests or security; traditionally regarded as the highest crime known to society.

Treaty: Formal agreement among sovereign states on some matter of mutual interest such as trade and defense.

Trial: The process of judicial examination of a criminal or civil dispute in which the parties or their counsel bring the facts and law before the court for final determination.

Trust: An arrangement whereby legal title to property is held by one person (the trustee) for the benefit of another (the beneficiary).

TWO-PARTY SYSTEM: System in which only two parties have a realistic chance of winning control of the government.

Unicameral legislature: Lawmaking body composed of one chamber of elected representatives.

United Nations: Formal association of nations created in 1945 to succeed the League of Nations as an international peacekeeping body.

Universal Declaration of Human Rights: Seminal human rights charter passed by the United Nations on December 10, 1948, annually celebrated as Human Rights Days.

Universal suffrage: Situation pertaining in a political community that gives all adult citizens the right to vote.

Verdict: The formal decision by a jury as to the matters submitted to it in a case.

VETERANS: Former members of branches of the ARMED FORCES who meet minimal length-of-service requirements.

VETO POWER: Power of an official to prevent authoritative actions by a lawmaking or policymaking body, such as the power of the U.S. president to veto congressional enactments subject to an override by two-thirds of each branch.

VIGILANTISM: Unofficial and illegal pursuit of justice, usually by organized groups.

Voir dire: The process of choosing jurors, in which judges and counsel for each party ask questions of potential jurors to determine their suitability for the case.

War Crimes: Violation of internationally accepted rules of conduct toward civilians and prisoners during times of war.

Warrant: An order issued by a court to a law enforcement officer requiring him or her to perform a particular act, such as an arrest warrant requiring the arrest of a particular person.

WATERGATE: Political scandal of the early 1970's that led to President Richard Nixon's resignation after his complicity in an attempt to cover up a burglary became publicly known.

WELFARE STATE: Form of government in which the state takes on the responsibility of protecting and promoting the basic well-being of its members through legislation that guarantees support for individuals and families.

Whistle-blower: Person who brings public attention to instances of corruption and maladministration in government or business.

WILL: Legal instrument directing how the estate of a deceased person is to be distributed.

Witness: Person whose first-hand knowledge is relevant to the issues in a trial.

Woman suffrage: Right of women to vote.

Zero-sum: Situation in which negative and positive changes balance out, as when the introduction of a new form of pollution into the environment is offset by an equivalent pollution reduction elsewhere.

Bibliography

Compiled by Kevin Bochynski

General Sources 795
Armed Forces 797
Civil Liberties 797
Civil Rights 798
Congress 799
The Constitution 800
Criminal Justice 801
Economic Issues 802
Family, Health, and Gender Issues 803
Government Agencies 803
The Judiciary 804

The Legal System 805
Legislation and Government
   Regulation 805
The Media 806
Political Campaigns and Elections 807
Political Parties and Interest Groups . . . 809
The Presidency 810
Racial and Ethnic Groups 811
State and Local Government 812
The Supreme Court 813
Women 814

General Sources

Anglim, Christopher. *Labor, Employment, and the Law: A Dictionary.* Santa Barbara, Calif.: ABC-Clio, 1997.

Baca, Polly. *Consumer's Resource Handbook 1994.* Washington, D.C.: U.S. Office of Consumer Affairs; Pueblo, Colo., 1994.

Bailey, William G. *The Encyclopedia of Police Science.* 2d ed. New York: Garland, 1995.

Barone, Michael, and Grant Ujifusa. *The Almanac of American Politics.* Washington, D.C.: National Journal, yearly.

Barthelmas, Della G. *The Signers of the Declaration of Independence: A Biographical and Genealogical Reference.* Jefferson, N.C.: McFarland, 1997.

Brobeck, Stephen, Robert N. Mayer, and Robert O. Herrmann. *Encyclopedia of the Consumer Movement.* Santa Barbara, Calif.: ABC-Clio, 1997.

Chabran, Richard, and Raphael Chabran, eds. *The Latino Encyclopedia.* 6 vols. New York: Marshall Cavendish, 1996.

Champagne, Duane, ed. *The Native North American Almanac: A Reference Work on Native North Americans in the United States and Canada.* Detroit: Gale Research, 1994.

Critchlow, Donald T., ed. *The Politics of Abortion and Birth Control in Historical Perspective.* University Park: Pennsylvania State University Press, 1996.

Filler, Louis. *Dictionary of American Conservatism.* New York: Philosophical Library, 1987.

Fishkin, James S. *The Voice of the People: Public Opinion and Democracy.* New Haven, Conn.: Yale University Press, 1995.

Fleming, Thomas J. *Liberty! The American Revolution.* New York: Viking Press, 1997.

Fliegelman, Jay. *Declaring Independence: Jefferson, Natural Language, and the Culture of Performance.* Stanford, Calif.: Stanford University Press, 1993.

Foerstel, Herbert N. *Banned in the U.S.A.: A Reference Guide to Book Censorship in Schools and Public Libraries.* Westport, Conn.: Greenwood Press, 1994.

_____. *Free Expression and Censorship in America: An Encyclopedia.* Westport, Conn.: Greenwood Press, 1997.

Hamilton, Alexander, John Jay, and James Madison. *The Federalist Papers,* edited by Clinton Rossiter. New York: New American Library, 1961.

Hawkesworth, Mary, and Maurice Kogan, eds. *Encyclopedia of Government and Politics.* 2 vols. New York: Routledge, 1992.

Hoxie, Frederick E. *Encyclopedia of North American Indians.* Boston: Houghton Mifflin, 1996.

Johansen, Bruce E., and Donald A. Grinde. *The Encyclopedia of Native American Biography: Six Hundred Life Stories of Important People from Powhatan to Wilma Mankiller.* New York: Henry Holt, 1997.

Katz, Bernard S., and C. Daniel Vencill. *Biographical Dictionary of the United States Secretaries of the Treasury, 1789-1995.* Westport, Conn.: Greenwood Press, 1996.

Kausler, Donald H. *The Graying of America: An Encyclopedia of Aging, Health, Mind, and Behavior.* Urbana: University of Illinois Press, 1996.

Kittrie, Nicholas N., and Eldon D. Wedlock. *The Tree of Liberty: A Documentary History of Rebellion and Political Crime in America.* Rev. ed. Baltimore: Johns Hopkins University Press, 1998.

Klein, Barry T. *Reference Encyclopedia of the American Indian.* 8th ed. Nyack, N.Y.: Todd, 1998.

Kohn, George C. *Encyclopedia of American Scandal.* New York: Facts on File, 1989.

Leahy, James E. *The First Amendment, 1791-1991: Two Hundred Years of Freedom.* Jefferson, N.C.: McFarland, 1991.

McShane, Marilyn D., and Frank P. Williams, III, eds. *Encyclopedia of American Prisons.* New York: Garland, 1996.

Maier, Pauline. *American Scripture: Making the Declaration of Independence.* New York: Alfred A. Knopf: Distributed by Random House, Inc., 1997.

Maranto, Robert., and David Schultz. *A Short History of the United States Civil Service.* Lanham, Md.: University Press of America, 1991.

Markowitz, Harvey, ed. *Ready Reference: American Indians.* 3 vols. Pasadena, Calif.: Salem Press, 1995.

Miller, Randall M., and John D. Smith, eds. *Dictionary of Afro-American Slavery.* Westport, Conn.: Praeger, 1997.

Nolan, Cathal J. *Notable U.S. Ambassadors Since 1775: A Biographical Dictionary.* Westport, Conn.: Greenwood Press, 1997.

Notess, Greg R. *Government Information on the Internet.* Lanham, Md.: Bernan Press, 1997.

Powers, Roger S., William B. Vogele, Christopher Kruegler, and Ronald M. McCarthy, eds. *Protest, Power, and Change: An Encyclopedia of Nonviolent Action from ACT-UP to Women's Suffrage.* New York: Garland, 1997.

Safire, William. *Safire's Political Dictionary.* 3d ed. New York: Random House, 1993.

Seo, Danny. *Generation React: Activism for Beginners.* New York: Ballantine Books, 1997.

Stillman, Richard J. *The American Bureaucracy: The Core of Modern Government.* 2d ed. Chicago: Nelson-Hall, 1996.

Sullivan, Thomas F. P., ed. *Official Telecommunications Dictionary: Legal and Regulatory Definitions.* Rockville, Md.: Government Institutes, 1997.

Tomajczyk, Stephen F. *Dictionary of the Modern United States Military: Over 15,000 Weapons, Agencies, Acronyms, Slang, Installations, Medical Terms, and Other Lexical Units of Warfare.* Jefferson, N.C.: McFarland, 1996.

Trigger, Bruce G., et al., eds. *The Cambridge History of the Native Peoples of the Americas.* 3 vols. Cambridge, Eng.: Cambridge University Press, 1996.

Wagman, Robert J., and Angela E. Lauria. *The World Almanac of U.S. Politics.* Mahwah, N.J.: World Almanac Books, 1997.

West Publishing Company. *West's Encyclopedia of American Law.* Saint Paul, Minn.: Author, 1998.

Wetterau, Bruce. *Congressional Quarterly's Desk Reference on the Federal Budget.* Washington, D.C.: Author, 1998.

Williams, Vergil L. *Dictionary of American Penology.* Rev. ed. Westport, Conn.: Greenwood Press, 1996.

Zwirn, Jerrold, ed. *Accessing U.S. Government Information: Subject Guide to Jurisdiction of the Executive and Legislative Branches.* Rev. ed. Westport, Conn.: Greenwood Press, 1996.

Armed Forces

Aukofer, Frank. *America's Team—The Odd Couple: A Report on the Relationship Between the Media and the Military.* Nashville, Tenn.: The Freedom Forum First Amendment Center, 1995.

Aycock, William B., and Seymour W. Wurfel. *Military Law Under the Uniform Code of Military Justice.* Westport, Conn.: Greenwood Press, 1972.

Cooper, Jerry M. *The Rise of the National Guard: The Evolution of the American Militia, 1865-1920.* Lincoln: University of Nebraska Press, 1997.

Duncan, Stephen M. *Citizen Warriors: America's National Guard and Reserve Forces and the Politics of National Security.* Novato, Calif.: Presidio Press, 1997.

Fotion, Nicholas, and Gerard Elfstrom. *Military Ethics: Guidelines for Peace and War.* London: Routledge & Kegan Paul, 1986.

Gross, Charles J. *The Air National Guard and the Persian Gulf Crisis: From Shield to Storm.* Washington, D.C.: NGB Historical Services Division, 1995.

Karsten, Peter. *The Military in America.* New York: Free Press, 1986.

Kaufmann, J. E. *The Sleeping Giant: American Armed Forces Between the Wars.* Westport, Conn.: Praeger, 1996.

Morris, James M. *America's Armed Forces: A History.* 2d ed. Upper Saddle River, N.J.: Prentice Hall, 1996.

Sarkesian, Sam C., and Robert E. Connor. *America's Armed Forces: A Handbook of Current and Future Capabilities.* Westport, Conn.: Greenwood Press, 1996.

Schlueter, David A. *Military Criminal Justice: Practice and Procedure.* 4th ed. Charlottesville, Va.: Michie, 1996.

Shanor, Charles A., and Lynn L. Hogue. *Military Law in a Nutshell.* 2d ed. St. Paul, Minn.: West, 1996.

Shepard's/McGraw-Hill. *Shepard's Military Justice Citations.* 2d ed. Colorado Springs, Colo.: Author, 1994.

Stacewicz, Richard. *Winter Soldiers: An Oral History of the Vietnam Veterans Against the War.* New York: Twayne, 1997.

Tomajczyk, Stephen F. *Dictionary of the Modern United States Military: Over 15,000 Weapons, Agencies, Acronyms, Slang, Installations, Medical Terms, and Other Lexical Units of Warfare.* Jefferson, N.C.: McFarland, 1996.

Weigley, Russell. *History of the United States Army.* Bloomington: Indiana University Press, 1984.

Civil Liberties

Alderman, Ellen, and Caroline Kennedy. *The Right to Privacy.* New York: Alfred A. Knopf, 1995.

Barker, Lucius J., and Twiley W. Barker, Jr. *Civil Liberties and the Constitution.* 7th ed. Englewood Cliffs, N.J.: Prentice-Hall, 1994.

Berger, Raoul. *The Fourteenth Amendment and the Bill of Rights.* Oklahoma City: University of Oklahoma Press, 1989.

Bodenhamer, David. *Fair Trial: Rights of the Accused in American History.* New York: Oxford University Press, 1992.

Bracken, Harry M. *Freedom of Speech: Words Are Not Deeds.* Westport, Conn.: Praeger, 1994.

Cohen, William, and David J. Danelski. *Constitutional Law: Civil Liberty and Individual Rights.* 3d ed. Westbury, N.Y.: Foundation Press, 1994.

Cortner, Richard. *The Supreme Court and the Second Bill of Rights: The Fourteenth Amendment and the Nationalization of Civil Liberties.* Madison: University of Wisconsin Press, 1981.

Dickinson, Philip D. *Employee Privacy Rights and Wrongs.* Nashville, Tenn.: M. Lee Smith, 1996.

Ely, James W. *The Guardian of Every Other Right: A Constitutional History of Property Rights.* 2d ed. New York: Oxford University Press, 1998.

_____. *Property Rights in American History: From the Colonial Era to the Present.* New York: Garland, 1997.

Foerstel, Herbert N. *Free Expression and Censorship in America: An Encyclopedia.* Westport, Conn.: Greenwood Press, 1997.

Frankel, Marvin E. *Faith and Freedom: Religious Liberty in America.* New York: Hill & Wang, 1994.

Garvey, John H., and Frederick F. Schauer. *The First Amendment: A Reader.* 2d ed. St. Paul, Minn.: West, 1996.

Halbrook, Stephen P. *A Right to Bear Arms: State and Federal Bills of Rights and Constitutional Guarantees.* New York: Greenwood Press, 1989.

Ingelhart, Louis E. *Press and Speech Freedoms in America, 1619-1995: A Chronology.* Westport, Conn.: Greenwood Press, 1997.

Kirk, Russell, and Mitchell S. Muncy. *Rights and Duties: Reflections on Our Conservative Constitution.* Dallas, Tex.: Spence, 1997.

Levy, Leonard. *Freedom of the Press from Zenger to Jefferson: Early American Libertarian Theories.* Indianapolis, Ind.: Bobbs-Merrill, 1966.

Lynn, Barry W., Marc D. Stern, and Oliver S. Thomas. *The Right to Religious Liberty: The Basic ACLU Guide to Religious Rights.* 2d ed. Carbondale: Southern Illinois University Press, 1995.

Malcolm, Joyce L. *To Keep and Bear Arms: The Origins of an Anglo-American Right.* Cambridge, Mass.: Harvard University Press, 1994.

Mendelson, Wallace. *The American Constitution and Civil Liberties.* Homewood, Ill.: Dorsey Press, 1981

Reynolds, Moira D. *Women Advocates of Reproductive Rights: Eleven Who Led the Struggle in the United States and Great Britain.* Jefferson, N.C.: McFarland, 1994.

Scher, Richard K., Jon L. Mills, and John J. Hotaling. *Voting Rights and Democracy: The Law and Politics of Districting.* Chicago: Nelson-Hall, 1997.

Smith, F. LaGard. *ACLU—The Devil's Advocate: The Seduction of Civil Liberties in America.* Colorado Springs, Colo.: Marcon, 1996.

Smith, Steven D. *Foreordained Failure: The Quest for a Constitutional Principle of Religious Freedom.* New York: Oxford University Press, 1995.

Yates, Michael. *Power on the Job: The Legal Rights of Working People.* Boston: South End Press, 1994.

Civil Rights

Abraham, Henry J., and Barbara A. Perry. *Freedom and the Court: Civil Rights and Liberties in the United States.* 7th ed. New York: Oxford University Press, 1998.

Ashmore, Harry S. *Civil Rights and Wrongs: A Memoir of Race and Politics, 1944-1996.* Rev. ed. Columbia: University of South Carolina Press, 1997.

Blumberg, Rhoda L. *Civil Rights: The 1960's Freedom Struggle.* Boston: Twayne, 1991.

Bradley, David, and Shelley Fisher Fishkin, eds. *The Encyclopedia of Civil Rights in America.* New York: M. E. Sharpe, 1997.

Branch, Taylor. *Parting the Waters: America in the King Years, 1954-63.* New York: Simon & Schuster, 1988.

_____. *Pillar of Fire: America in the King Years, 1963-65.* New York: Simon & Schuster, 1998.

Bullock, Charles S., III, and Charles M. Lamb. *Implementation of Civil Rights Policy.* Monterey, Calif.: Brooks-Cole, 1984.

Cashman, Sean D. *African-Americans and the Quest for Civil Rights, 1900-1990.* New York: New York University Press, 1991.

Davis, Townsend. *Weary Feet, Rested Souls: A Guided History of the Civil Rights Movement.* New York: W. W. Norton, 1998.

Dent, Thomas C. *Southern Journey: A Return to the Civil Rights Movement.* New York: Willam Morrow, 1997.

Gates, Henry Louis, ed. *Speaking of Race, Speaking of Sex: Hate Speech, Civil Rights, and Civil Liberties.* New York: New York University Press, 1994.

Graham, Hugh D., ed. *Civil Rights in the United States.* University Park: Pennsylvania State University Press, 1994.

Kasher, Steven. *The Civil Rights Movement: A Photographic History, 1954-68.* New York: Abbeville Press, 1996.

Lawson, Steven F. *Running for Freedom: Civil Rights and Black Politics in America Since 1941.* 2d ed. New York: McGraw-Hill, 1997.

Levine, Michael L. *African Americans and Civil Rights: From 1619 to the Present.* Phoenix, Ariz.: Oryx Press, 1996.

Lewis, David L., and Charles W. Eagles. *The Civil Rights Movement in America: Essays.* Jackson: University Press of Mississippi, 1986.

Loevy, Robert D. *The Civil Rights Act of 1964: The Passage of the Law That Ended Racial Segregation.* Albany: State University of New York Press, 1997.

Luker, Ralph. *Historical Dictionary of the Civil Rights Movement.* Lanham, Md.: Scarecrow Press, 1997.

Murray, Paul T. *The Civil Rights Movement: References and Resources.* New York: G. K. Hall, 1993.

Olson, James S., and Mark Baxter, eds. *Encyclopedia of American Indian Civil Rights.* Westport, Conn.: Greenwood Press, 1997.

Powledge, Fred. *Free at Last? The Civil Rights Movement and the People Who Made It.* Boston: Little, Brown, 1991.

Rasmussen, R. Kent. *Farewell to Jim Crow: The Rise and Fall of Segregation in America.* New York: Facts on File, 1997.

Rediger, Pat. *Great African Americans in Civil Rights.* New York: Crabtree, 1996.

Riches, William T. M. *The Civil Rights Movement: Struggle and Resistance.* New York: St. Martin's Press, 1997.

Rosales, Francisco A. *Chicano! The History of the Mexican American Civil Rights Movement.* Houston, Tex.: Arte Publico Press, 1996.

Salmond, John A. *"My Mind Set on Freedom": A History of the Civil Rights Movement, 1954-1968.* Chicago: Ivan R. Dee, 1997.

Thomas, Brook. *Plessy v. Ferguson: A Brief History with Documents.* Boston: Bedford Books, 1997.

Weisbrot, Robert. *Freedom Bound: A History of America's Civil Rights Movement.* New York: Plume, 1991.

Wexler, Sanford. *The Civil Rights Movement: An Eyewitness History.* New York: Facts on File, 1993.

Williams, Juan. *Eyes on the Prize: America's Civil Rights Years, 1954-1965.* New York: Penguin, 1988.

Young, Andrew. *An Easy Burden: The Civil Rights Movement and the Transformation of America.* New York: HarperCollins, 1996.

Congress

Bacon, Donald C., Roger H. Davidson, and Morton Keller. *The Encyclopedia of the United States Congress.* New York: Simon & Schuster, 1995.

Baker, Ross K. *House and Senate.* New York: W. W. Norton, 1989.

Binder, Sarah A., and Steven S. Smith. *Politics or Principle? Filibustering in the United States Senate.* Washington, D.C.: Brookings Institution, 1997.

Congressional Quarterly, Inc. *Congress A to Z: A Ready Reference Encyclopedia.* 2d ed. Washington, D.C.: Author, 1993.

DeKieffer, Donald E. *The Citizen's Guide to Lobbying Congress.* Chicago: Chicago Review Press, 1997.

Greenberg, Ellen. *The House and Senate Explained: The People's Guide to Congress.* New York: W. W. Norton, 1996.

Hernon, Joseph M. *Profiles in Character: Hubris and Heroism in the U.S. Senate, 1789-1990.* Armonk, N.Y.: M. E. Sharpe, 1997.

Kessler, Ronald. *Inside Congress: The Shocking Scandals, Corruption, and Abuse of Power Behind the Scenes on Capitol Hill.* New York: Pocket Books, 1997.

Kravitz, Walter. *Congressional Quarterly's American Congressional Dictionary.* 2d ed. Washington, D.C.: Congressional Quarterly, 1997.

Peters, Ronald M. *The American Speakership: The Office in Historical Perspective.* 2d ed. Baltimore: Johns Hopkins University Press, 1997.

Schroedel, Jean R. *Congress, the President, and Policymaking: A Historical Analysis.* Armonk, N.Y.: M. E. Sharpe, 1994.

Sinclair, Barbara. *The Transformation of the U.S. Senate.* Baltimore: Johns Hopkins University Press, 1989.

Stern, Philip M. *The Best Congress Money Can Buy.* New York: Pantheon, 1988.

Thompson, Dennis F. *Ethics in Congress: From Individual to Institutional Corruption.* Washington, D.C.: Brookings Institution, 1995.

United States. Congress. Joint Committee on Printing. *The Capitol: A Pictorial History of the Capitol and of the Congress.* 9th ed. Washington, D.C.: U.S. Government Printing Office, 1988.

Will, George F. *Restoration: Congress, Term Limits, and the Recovery of Deliberative Democracy.* New York: Free Press, 1992.

Wolpe, Bruce C., and Bertram J. Levine. *Lobbying Congress: How the System Works.* 2d ed. Washington, D.C.: Congressional Quarterly, 1996.

The Constitution

Anastaplo, George. *The Constitution of 1787: A Commentary.* Baltimore: Johns Hopkins University Press, 1989.

Baker, Thomas E. *"The Most Wonderful Work": Our Constitution Interpreted.* St. Paul, Minn.: West, 1996.

Bizzoco, Dennis, ed. *The Exhaustive Concordance to the United States Constitution.* Chattanooga, Tenn.: Firm Foundation Press, 1994.

Burger, Warren E. *It Is so Ordered: A Constitution Unfolds.* New York: William Morrow, 1995.

Dworkin, R. M. *Freedom's Law: The Moral Reading of the American Constitution.* Cambridge, Mass.: Harvard University Press, 1996.

Farber, Daniel A., and Suzanna Sherry. *A History of the American Constitution.* St. Paul, Minn.: West, 1990.

Friendly, Fred, and Martha Elliot. *The Constitution: That Delicate Balance.* New York: Random House, 1984.

Galloway, Russell, and Rose E. Bird. *A Student's Guide to Basic Constitutional Analysis.* New York: Matthew Bender/Irwin, 1996.

Kammen, Michael, ed. *The Origins of the American Constitution: A Documentary History.* New York: Penguin Books, 1986.

Kluge, Dave. *The People's Guide to the United States Constitution.* New York: Carol, 1994.

Kramnick, Isaac, and Laurence R. Moore. *The Godless Constitution: The Case Against Religious Correctness.* New York: Norton, 1996.

Kyvig, David E. *Explicit and Authentic Acts: Amending the U.S. Constitution, 1776-1995.* Lawrence: University Press of Kansas, 1996.

Lamm, Barbara. *The American Constitution in Context.* Commack, N.Y.: Nova Science Publishers, 1996.

Levy, Leonard W., et al., eds. *Encyclopedia of the American Constitution.* 4 vols. New York: Macmillan, 1986.

Mitchell, Ralph. *CQ's Guide to the U.S. Constitution.* 2d ed. Washington, D.C.: Congressional Quarterly, 1994.

Padover, Saul K., and Jacob W. Landynski. *The Living U.S. Constitution: Historical Background, Landmark Supreme Court Decisions—With Introductions, Indexed Guide, Pen Portraits of the Signers.* 3d rev. ed. by Jacob W. Landynski. New York: Meridian, 1995.

Peltason, J. W. *Corwin and Peltason's Understanding the Constitution.* 13th ed. San Diego, Calif.: Harcourt Brace, 1994.

Rakove, Jack N. *Original Meanings: Politics and Ideas in the Making of the Constitution.* New York: Alfred A. Knopf, 1996.

Stevens, Richard G. *The American Constitution and Its Provenance.* Lanham, Md.: Rowman & Littlefield, 1997.

Vile, John R. *A Companion to the United States Constitution and Its Amendments.* 2d ed. Westport, Conn.: Praeger, 1997.

Wolfe, Christopher. *How to Read the Constitution: Originalism, Constitutional Interpretation, and Judicial Power.* Lanham, Md.: Rowman & Littlefield, 1996.

Criminal Justice

Abadinsky, Howard. *Crime and Justice: An Introduction.* Chicago: Nelson-Hall, 1987.

_____. *Law and Justice.* Chicago: Nelson-Hall, 1988.

Anderson, David C. *Crime and the Politics of Hysteria: How the Willie Horton Story Changed American Justice.* New York: Times Books, 1995.

Bedau, Hugo A. *The Death Penalty in America: Current Controversies.* New York: Oxford University Press, 1997.

Bidinotto, Robert J. *Criminal Justice? The Legal System Versus Individual Responsibility.* 2d ed. Irvington-on-Hudson, N.Y.: Foundation for Economic Education, 1996.

Bureau of Justice Statistics. *Criminal Victimization in the United States.* Washington, D.C.: U.S. Government Printing Office, annual.

Champion, Dean J. *Criminal Justice in the United States.* Columbus, Ohio: Merrill, 1990.

_____. *Felony Probation: Problems and Prospects.* Westport, Conn.: Praeger, 1988.

_____. *Probation and Parole in the United States.* Columbus, Ohio: Merrill, 1990.

Cole, George F. *The American System of Criminal Justice.* 7th ed. Belmont, Calif.: Wadsworth, 1995.

Cornelius, William J. *Swift and Sure: Bringing Certainty and Finality to Criminal Punishment.* Irvington-on-Hudson, N.Y.: Bridge Street Books, Inc., 1997.

Currie, Elliott. *Crime and Punishment in America.* New York: Henry Holt, 1998.

Durham, Jennifer L. *Crime in America: A Reference Handbook.* Santa Barbara, Calif.: ABC-Clio, 1996.

Federal Bureau of Investigation. *Crime in the United States: Uniform Crime Reports.* Washington, D.C.: U.S. Government Printing Office, annual.

Free, Marvin D. *African Americans and the Criminal Justice System.* New York: Garland, 1996.

Friedman, Lawrence M. *Crime and Punishment in American History.* New York: Basic Books, 1993.

Kender, Suzanne E., ed. *Crime in America.* New York: H. W. Wilson, 1996.

Keve, Paul W. *Crime Control and Justice in America: Searching for Facts and Answers.* Chicago: American Library Association, 1995.

Katz, Burton S. *Justice Overruled: Unmasking the Criminal Justice System.* New York: Warner Books, 1997.

Megivern, James J. *The Death Penalty: A Historical and Theological Survey.* New York: Paulist Press, 1997.

Randa, Laura E. *Society's Final Solution: A History and Discussion of the Death Penalty.* Lanham, Md.: University Press of America, 1997.

Roberson, Cliff, and Max Futrell. *An Introduction to Criminal Justice Research.* Springfield, Ill.: Charles C Thomas, 1988.

Samaha, Joel. *Criminal Justice.* 3d ed. St. Paul, Minn.: West, 1994.

Schmalleger, Frank, and Gordon M. Armstrong. *Crime and the Justice Systems in America: An Encyclopedia.* Westport, Conn.: Greenwood Press, 1997.

Smith, Christopher E. *The Rehnquist Court and Criminal Punishment.* New York: Garland, 1997.

Van den Haag, Ernest. *Punishing Criminals: Concerning a Very Old and Painful Question.* Lanham, Md.: University Press of America, 1991.

Vila, Bryan, and Cynthia Morris. *Capital Punishment in the United States: A Documentary History.* Westport, Conn.: Greenwood Press, 1997.

Walker, Samuel. *Popular Justice: A History of American Criminal Justice.* 2d ed. New York: Oxford University Press, 1998.

Whitebread, Charles, and Christopher Slobogin. *Criminal Procedure: An Analysis of Cases and Concepts.* 3d ed. Westbury, N.Y.: Foundation Press, 1993.

Williams, Vergil L. *Dictionary of American Penology.* Westport, Conn.: Greenwood Press, 1996.

Economic Issues

Brown, Karen B., and Mary L. Fellows. *Taxing America.* New York: New York University Press, 1996.

Brownlee, W. Elliot. *Federal Taxation in America: A Short History.* Washington, D.C.: Woodrow Wilson Center Press, 1996.

Carter, Marshall N., and William G. Shipman. *Promises to Keep: Saving Social Security's Dream.* Washington, D.C.: Regnery, 1996.

Cogan, John F., Timothy J. Muris, and Allen Schick. *The Budget Puzzle: Understanding Federal Spending.* Stanford, Calif.: Stanford University Press, 1994.

Collender, Stanley E. *The Guide to the Federal Budget.* 10th ed. Washington, D.C.: Urban Institute Press, 1991.

D'Arista, Jane W. *The Evolution of U.S. Finance.* Armonk, N.Y.: M. E. Sharpe, 1994.

Evans, Gary R. *Red Ink: The Budget, Deficit, and Debt of the U.S. Government.* San Diego, Calif.: Academic Press, 1997.

Friedman, Milton. *Capitalism and Freedom.* Chicago: University of Chicago Press, 1965.

Gordon, John S. *Hamilton's Blessing: The Extraordinary Life and Times of Our National Debt.* New York: Walker, 1997.

Hodge, Scott A., ed. *Balancing America's Budget: Ending the Era of Big Government.* Washington, D.C.: Heritage Foundation, 1997.

Kaufman, George G. *The U.S. Financial System: Money, Markets, and Institutions.* 6th ed. Englewood Cliffs, N.J.: Prentice Hall, 1995.

Kingson, Eric R., and James H. Schulz, eds. *Social Security in the 21st Century.* New York: Oxford University Press, 1997.

Krohn, Lauren. *Consumer Protection and the Law: A Dictionary.* Santa Barbara, Calif.: ABC-Clio, 1995.

Mack, Charles S. *Business, Politics, and the Practice of Government Relations.* Westport, Conn.: Quorum, 1997.

McQuaid, Kim. *Uneasy Partners: Big Business in American Politics, 1945-1990.* Baltimore: Johns Hopkins University Press, 1994.

Maltese, G. I., ed. *The U.S. Federal Budget Process: An Overview and Glossary of Terms.* Commack, N.Y.: Nova Science Publishers, 1995.

Morgan, Iwan W. *Deficit Government: Taxing and Spending in Modern America.* Chicago: Ivan R. Dee, 1995.

Rosenberg, Jerry M. *Encyclopedia of the North American Free Trade Agreement, the New American Community, and Latin-American Trade.* Westport, Conn.: Greenwood Press, 1995.

Rubin, Irene S. *The Politics of Public Budgeting: Getting and Spending, Borrowing, and Balancing.* Chatham, N.J.: Chatham House, 1990.

Samuelson, Robert J. *The Good Life and Its Discontents: The American Dream in the Age of Entitlement, 1945-1995.* New York: Times Books, 1995.

Sandak, Cass R. *The National Debt.* New York: Twenty-First Century Books, 1996.

Schick, Allen. *The Federal Budget: Politics, Policy, Process.* Washington, D.C.: Brookings Institution, 1995.

Thurow, Lester C. *The Future of Capitalism: How Today's Economic Forces Shape Tomorrow's World.* New York: Penguin Books, 1996.

Wildavsky, Aaron B., and Naomi Caiden. *The New Politics of the Budgetary Process.* 3d ed. New York: Longman, 1997.

Family, Health, and Gender Issues

Abalos, David T. *The Latino Family and the Politics of Transformation.* Westport, Conn.: Praeger, 1993.

Aulino, Charles M. *The Family Trust: A Financial Consultant's Guide to Trust Funds and Estate Planning.* 2d ed. Chicago: CCH Inc., 1995.

Blasius, Mark, and Shane Phelan, eds. *We Are Everywhere: A Historical Sourcebook in Gay and Lesbian Politics.* New York: Routledge, 1997.

Clinton, Hillary Rodham. *It Takes a Village: And Other Lessons Children Teach Us.* New York: Simon & Schuster, 1996.

Critchlow, Donald T., ed. *The Politics of Abortion and Birth Control in Historical Perspective.* University Park: Pennsylvania State University Press, 1996.

Crockett, Paul H. *HIV Law: A Survival Guide to the Legal System for People Living with HIV.* New York: Three Rivers Press, 1997.

Dychtwald, Ken, and Joe Flower. *Age Wave: The Challenges and Opportunities of an Aging America.* New York: Bantam Books, 1990.

Fox, Richard L. *Gender Dynamics in Congressional Elections.* Thousand Oaks, Calif.: Sage Publications, 1997.

Garrow, David J. *Liberty and Sexuality: The Right to Privacy and the Making of Roe v. Wade.* New York: Macmillan, 1994.

Gelb, Joyce, and Marian L. Palley. *Women and Public Policies: Reassessing Gender Politics.* Rev. ed. Charlottesville, Va: University Press of Virginia, 1996.

Gordon, Linda. *Woman's Body, Woman's Right: A Social History of Birth Control in America.* New York: Penguin Books, 1977.

Humm, S. Randall, et al., eds. *Child, Parent, and State: Law and Policy Reader.* Philadelphia: Temple University Press, 1994.

Kausler, Donald H. *The Graying of America: An Encyclopedia of Aging, Health, Mind, and Behavior.* Urbana: University of Illinois Press, 1996.

Klueger, Robert F. *A Guide to Asset Protection: How to Keep What's Legally Yours.* New York: John Wiley & Sons, 1997.

Krause, Harry D. *Family Law.* St. Paul, Minn.: West, 1988.

Lesbian and Gay Community Services Center. *The Gay Almanac.* New York: Berkley Books, 1996.

Meyer, Cheryl L. *The Wandering Uterus: Politics and the Reproductive Rights of Women.* New York: New York University Press, 1997.

Quayle, Dan, and Diane Medved. *The American Family: Discovering the Values That Make Us Strong.* New York: HarperCollins, 1996.

Reynolds, Moira D. *Women Advocates of Reproductive Rights: Eleven Who Led the Struggle in the United States and Great Britain.* Jefferson, N.C.: McFarland, 1994.

Riddle, John M. *Eve's Herbs: A History of Contraception and Abortion in the West.* Cambridge, Mass.: Harvard University Press, 1997.

Tone, Andrea. *Controlling Reproduction: An American History.* Wilmington, Del.: SR Books, 1997.

Urofsky, Melvin I., and Philip E. Urofsky, eds. *The Right to Die: A Two-Volume Anthology of Scholarly Articles.* New York: Garland, 1996.

Government Agencies

Bardach, Eugene, and Robert A. Kagan. *Going by the Book: The Problem of Regulatory Unreasonableness.* Philadelphia: Temple University Press, 1982.

Batten, Donna, ed. *Encyclopedia of Governmental Advisory Organizations.* Detroit: Gale, 1997.

Burkholz, Herbert. *The FDA Follies.* New York: Basic Books, 1994.

Congressional Quarterly. *Who's Who in Federal Regulation*. Washington, D.C.: Author, 1995.

Cooke, David C. *Your Treasury Department*. New York: W. W. Norton, 1964.

Daugherty, Duane A. *The New OSHA: Blueprints for Effective Training and Written Programs*. New York: American Management Association, 1996.

Davis, Shelley L. *Unbridled Power: Inside the Secret Culture of the IRS*. New York: HarperBusiness, 1997.

Higgs, Robert. *Hazardous to Our Health? FDA Regulation of Health Care Products*. Oakland, Calif.: Independent Institute, 1995.

Hoogenboom, Ari, and Olive Hoogenboom. *A History of the ICC: From Panacea to Palliative*. New York: W. W. Norton, 1976.

Huston, Luther A. *The Department of Justice*. New York: Praeger, 1967.

Jeffreys, Diarmuid. *The Bureau: Inside the Modern FBI*. Boston: Houghton Mifflin, 1995.

John, Richard R. *Spreading the News: The American Postal System from Franklin to Morse*. Cambridge, Mass.: Harvard University Press, 1995.

Kerwin, Cornelius M. *Rulemaking: How Government Agencies Write Law and Make Policy*. Washington, D.C.: Congressional Quarterly Press, 1994.

King, James J., ed. *The Environmental Dictionary: and Regulatory Cross Reference*. 3d ed. New York: John Wiley & Sons, 1995.

Light, Paul C. *Monitoring Government: Inspectors General and the Search for Accountability*. Washington, D.C.: Brookings Institution, Governance Institute, 1993.

Luebke, Thomas E., ed. *Department of the Treasury*. U.S. Government Printing Office, 1986.

Mackay, Robert J., James C. Miller, and Bruce Yandle, eds. *Public Choice and Regulation: A View from Inside the Federal Trade Commission*. Stanford, Calif.: Hoover Institution Press, 1987.

O'Toole, G. J. A. *Honorable Treachery: A History of U.S. Intelligence, Espionage, and Covert Action from the American Revolution to the CIA*. New York: Atlantic Monthly Press, 1991.

Patrick, William. *The Food and Drug Administration*. New York: Chelsea House, 1988.

Ranelagh, John. *The Agency: The Rise and Decline of the CIA*. New York: Simon & Schuster/Touchstone, 1987.

Riebling, Mark. *Wedge: The Secret War Between the FBI and CIA*. New York: Alfred A. Knopf, 1994.

Stefoff, Rebecca. *The Drug Enforcement Administration*. New York: Chelsea House, 1989.

Theoharis, Athan G. *The FBI: An Annotated Bibliography and Research Guide*. New York: Garland, 1994.

Trask, Roger R. *Defender of the Public Interest: The General Accounting Office, 1921-1966*. Washington, D.C.: U.S. Government Printing Office, 1996.

Ungar, Sanford J. *FBI*. Boston: Atlantic Monthly Press, 1976.

Vincoli, Jeffrey W. *Making Sense of OSHA Compliance*. Rockville, Md.: Government Institutes, 1997.

Watson, Patrick. *The FBI's Changing Missions in the 1990s*. Washington, D.C: Consortium for the Study of Intelligence, 1993.

Willmann, John B. *The Department of Housing and Urban Development*. New York: Praeger, 1967.

Wilson, James Q. *Bureaucracy: What Government Agencies Do and Why They Do It*. New York: Basic Books, 1989.

The Judiciary

Abraham, Henry J. *The Judicial Process*. 6th ed. New York: Oxford University Press, 1993.

Abramson, Jeffrey. *We, the Jury: Justice and the Democratic Ideal*. New York: Basic Books, 1994.

Bator, Paul M., and Daniel J. Meltzer, eds. *Hart and Wechsler's The Federal Courts and the Fed-*

eral System. 3d ed. Westbury, N.Y.: Foundation Press, 1988.

Berger, Raoul. *Government by Judiciary: The Transformation of the Fourteenth Amendment.* Cambridge, Mass.: Harvard University Press, 1977.

Blank, Blanche D. *The Not So Grand Jury: The Story of the Federal Grand Jury System.* Lanham, Md.: University Press of America, 1993.

Brenner, Susan W., and Gregory G. Lockhart. *Federal Grand Jury Practice.* St. Paul, Minn.: West, 1996.

Carp, Robert A., and Ronald Stidham. *The Federal Courts.* 2d ed. Washington, D.C.: Congressional Quarterly Press, 1991.

Clement, Mary. *The Juvenile Justice System: Law and Process.* Boston: Butterworth-Heinemann, 1997.

Fino, Susan P. *The Role of State Supreme Courts in the New Judicial Federalism.* New York: Greenwood, 1987.

Glick, Henry R. *State Court Systems.* Englewood Cliffs, N.J.: Prentice-Hall, 1973.

Lesser, Maximus A., and William S. Hein. *The Historical Development of the Jury System.* Buffalo, N.Y.: W. S. Hein, 1992.

Marcus, Maeva. *Origins of the Federal Judiciary: Essays on the Judiciary Act of 1789.* New York: Oxford University Press, 1992.

Meador, Daniel J. *American Courts.* St. Paul, Minn.: West, 1991.

Posner, Richard A. *The Federal Courts: Crisis and Reform.* Cambridge, Mass.: Harvard University Press, 1985.

Surrency, Erwin C. *History of the Federal Courts.* New York: Oceana, 1987.

Wheeler, Russell R., and Cynthia E. Harrison. *Creating the Federal Judicial System.* 2d ed. Washington, D.C.: Federal Judicial Center, 1994.

Williams, Mary E., ed. *The Jury System.* San Diego, Calif.: Greenhaven Press, 1997.

Wright, Charles A. *The Law of Federal Courts.* 5th ed. St. Paul, Minn.: West, 1994.

The Legal System

Barron, Jerome A., and C. Thomas Dienes. *Constitutional Law in a Nutshell.* 3d ed. St. Paul, Minn.: West, 1995.

Braveman, Daan, William C. Banks, and Rodney A. Smolla. *Constitutional Law: Structure and Rights in Our Federal System.* 3d ed. New York: Matthew Bender, 1996.

Calvi, James V., and Susan E. Coleman. *American Law and Legal Systems.* 3d ed. Upper Saddle River, N.J.: Prentice Hall, 1997.

Cantor, Norman F. *Imagining the Law: Common Law and the Foundations of the American Legal System.* New York: HarperCollins, 1997.

Cappalli, Richard B. *The American Common Law Method.* Irvington, N.Y.: Transnational, 1997.

Chemerinsky, Erwin. *Constitutional Law: Principles and Policies.* New York: Aspen Law & Business, 1997.

Coleman, Jules L., and Anthony J. Sebok, eds. *Constitutional Law and Its Interpretation.* New York: Garland, 1994.

Farnsworth, E. Allan. *An Introduction to the Legal System of the United States.* 3d ed. Dobbs Ferry, N.Y.: Oceana, 1996.

Fine, Toni M. *American Legal Systems: A Resource and Reference Guide.* Cincinnati, Ohio: Anderson, 1997.

Fisher, Louis. *American Constitutional Law.* 2d ed. New York: McGraw-Hill, 1995.

Grasso, Kenneth L., and Cecilia Rodriguez Castillo, eds. *Liberty Under Law: American Constitutionalism, Yesterday, Today, and Tomorrow.* Lanham, Md.: University Press of America, 1997.

Matthews, Elizabeth W. *The Law Library Reference Shelf: Annotated Subject Guide.* 3d ed. Buffalo, N.Y.: W. S. Hein, 1996.

Legislation and Government Regulation

Anderson, Ronald A. *Cyclopedia of Insurance Law.* 2d ed. Rochester, N.Y.: Lawyers Cooperative, 1984.

Apple, James G. *A Primer on the Civil-Law System.* Washington, D.C.: Federal Judicial Center, 1995.

Batten, Donna, ed. *Encyclopedia of Governmental Advisory Organizations.* Detroit: Gale, 1997.

Congressional Quarterly. *Who's Who in Federal Regulation.* Washington, D.C.: Author, 1995.

Cooper, Richard M., ed. *Food and Drug Law.* Washington, D.C.: Food and Drug Law Institute, 1991.

Dobbyn, John F. *Insurance Law in a Nutshell.* 3d ed. St. Paul, Minn.: West, 1996.

Fast, Julius, and Timothy Fast. *The Legal Atlas of the United States.* New York: Facts on File, 1997.

Feldacker, Bruce. *Labor Guide to Labor Law.* 3d ed. Englewood Cliffs, N.J.: Prentice-Hall, 1990.

Gardner, Martin R. *Understanding Juvenile Law.* New York: Matthew Bender, 1997.

Goldman, Alvin L. *Labor and Employment Law in the United States.* Boston: Kluwer Law International, 1996.

Gould, William B. *A Primer on American Labor Law.* 3d ed. Cambridge, Mass.: MIT Press, 1993.

Higgs, Robert. *Hazardous to Our Health? FDA Regulation of Health Care Products.* Oakland, Calif.: Independent Institute, 1995.

Jerry, Robert H. *Understanding Insurance Law.* 2d ed. New York: Matthew Bender, 1996.

Kennedy, Charles H. *An Introduction to U.S. Telecommunications Law.* Boston: Artech House, 1994.

Kozolchyk, Boris, Gary T. Doyle, and Martin G. Olea Amaya. *Transportation Law and Practice in North America.* Tucson, Ariz.: National Law Center for Inter-American Free Trade, 1996.

Lowenstein, Daniel H. *Election Law: Cases and Materials.* Durham, N.C.: Carolina Academic Press, 1995.

McCarthy, Martha M., Nelda H. Cambron-McCabe, and Stephen B. Thomas. *Public School Law: Teachers' and Students' Rights.* 4th ed. Boston: Allyn & Bacon, 1998.

Mackay, Robert J., James C. Miller, and Bruce Yandle, eds. *Public Choice and Regulation: A View from Inside the Federal Trade Commission.* Stanford, Calif.: Hoover Institution Press, 1987.

Mackenthun, Kenneth M., and Jacob I. Bregman. *Environmental Regulations Handbook.* Boca Raton, Fla.: Lewis, 1992.

Rosenberg, Jerry M. *Encyclopedia of the North American Free Trade Agreement, the New American Community, and Latin-American Trade.* Westport, Conn.: Greenwood Press, 1995.

Shenefield, John H. *The Antitrust Laws: A Primer.* 2d ed. Washington, D.C.: AEI Press, 1996.

The Media

Abramson, Jeffrey. *Postmortem—The O.J. Simpson Case: Justice Confronts Race, Domestic Violence, Lawyers, Money, and the Media.* New York: Basic Books, 1996.

Abramson, Jeffrey B., F. Christopher Arterton, and Gary R. Orren. *The Electronic Commonwealth: The Impact of New Media Technologies on Democratic Politics.* New York: Basic Books, 1988.

Aukofer, Frank. *America's Team—The Odd Couple: A Report on the Relationship Between the Media and the Military.* Nashville, Tenn.: The Freedom Forum First Amendment Center, 1995.

Bennett, W. Lance, and David L. Paletz, eds. *Taken by Storm: The Media, Public Opinion, and U.S. Foreign Policy in the Gulf War.* Chicago: University of Chicago Press, 1994.

Braden, Maria. *Women Politicians and the Media.* Lexington: University Press of Kentucky, 1996.

Cook, Timothy E. *Governing with the News: The News Media as a Political Institution.* Chicago: The University of Chicago Press, 1998.

_____. *Making Laws and Making News: Media Strategies in the U.S. House of Representatives.*

Washington, D.C.: Brookings Institution, 1989.

Croteau, David, and William Hoynes. *By Invitation Only: How the Media Limit Political Debate.* Monroe, Maine: Common Courage, 1994.

Davis, Richard. *The Press and American Politics: The New Mediator.* 2d ed. Upper Saddle River, N.J.: Prentice Hall, 1996.

Diamond, Edwin, and Robert A. Silverman. *White House to Your House: Media and Politics in Virtual America.* Cambridge, Mass.: MIT Press, 1995.

Dye, Thomas, Harmon Zeigler, and S. Robert Lichter. *American Politics in the Media Age.* 4th ed. Monterey, Calif.: Brooks/Cole, 1992.

Entman, Robert M. *Democracy Without Citizens: Media and the Decay of American Politics.* New York: Oxford University Press, 1989.

Fiske, John. *Media Matters: Everyday Culture and Political Change.* Rev. ed. Minneapolis: University of Minnesota Press, 1996.

Freedom Forum Media Studies Center. *The Presidency in the New Media Age.* New York: Author, 1994.

Graber, Doris A. *Mass Media and American Politics.* 5th ed. Washington, D.C.: Congressional Quarterly Press, 1997.

Just, Marion R. *Crosstalk: Citizens, Candidates, and the Media in a Presidential Campaign.* Chicago: The University of Chicago Press, 1996.

Kerbel, Matthew R. *Remote and Controlled: Media Politics in a Cynical Age.* Boulder, Colo.: Westview Press, 1995.

Kurtz, Howard. *Spin Cycle: Inside the Clinton Propaganda Machine.* New York: Free Press, 1998.

Lavrakas, Paul J., Michael W. Traugott, and Peter V. Miller., eds. *Presidential Polls and the News Media.* Boulder, Colo.: Westview Press, 1995.

Mann, Thomas E., and Gary R. Orren, eds. *Media Polls in American Politics.* Washington, D.C.: Brookings Institution, 1992.

Mazzocco, Dennis. *Networks of Power: Corporate TV's Threat to Democracy.* Boston: South End Press, 1994.

Page, Benjamin I. *Who Deliberates? Mass Media in Modern Democracy.* Chicago: University of Chicago Press, 1996.

Sproule, J. Michael. *Propaganda and Democracy: The American Experience of Media and Mass Persuasion.* New York: Cambridge University Press, 1997.

Trend, David. *Cultural Democracy: Politics, Media, New Technology.* Albany: State University of New York Press, 1997.

Voters, and Reporters in America. Thousand Oaks, Calif.: Sage Publications, 1997.

Wittenberg, Ernest, and Elisabeth Wittenberg. *How to Win in Washington: Very Practical Advice About Lobbying, the Grassroots, and the Media.* 2d ed. Cambridge, Mass.: B. Blackwell, 1994.

Political Campaigns and Elections

Abramson, Paul R., John H. Aldrich, and David W. Rohde. *Change and Continuity in the 1988 Elections.* Rev. ed. Washington, D.C.: Congressional Quarterly Press, 1991.

Alexander, Herbert E. *Financing Politics: Money, Elections, and Political Reform.* 4th ed. Washington, D.C.: Congressional Quarterly Press, 1992.

Archer, Jules. *Winners and Losers: How Elections Work in America.* San Diego, Calif.: Harcourt Brace Jovanovich, 1984.

Asher, Herbert B. *Presidential Elections and American Politics.* 5th ed. Pacific Grove, Calif.: Brooks/Cole, 1992.

Bennett, W. Lance. *The Governing Crisis: Media, Money, and Marketing in American Elections.* New York: St. Martin's Press, 1992.

Best, Judith. *The Choice of the People? Debating the Electoral College.* Lanham, Md.: Rowman & Littlefield, 1996.

Boller, Paul F. *Presidential Campaigns.* Rev. ed. New York: Oxford University Press, 1996.

Brady, David W., John F. Cogan, and Douglas Rivers. *The 1996 House Elections: Reaffirming the Conservative Trend.* Stanford, Calif.: Hoover Institution on War, Revolution, and Peace, 1997.

Butler, David, Howard R. Penniman, and Austin Ranney, eds. *Democracy at the Polls: A Comparative Study of Competitive National Elections.* Washington, D.C.: American Enterprise Institute for Public Policy Research, 1981.

Campbell, James E. *The Presidential Pulse of Congressional Elections.* 2d ed. Lexington: University Press of Kentucky, 1997.

Congressional Quarterly's Guide to U.S. Elections. 3d ed. Washington, D.C.: Congressional Quarterly Press, 1993.

Corrado, Anthony, ed. *Campaign Finance Reform: A Sourcebook.* Washington, D.C.: Brookings Institution, 1997.

Dubin, Michael J. *United States Congressional Elections, 1788-1994: The Official Results of the Elections of the 1st Through 104th Congresses.* Jefferson, N.C.: McFarland, 1996.

Fenno, Richard F. *Senators on the Campaign Trail: The Politics of Representation.* Norman: University of Oklahoma Press, 1996.

Hardaway, Robert M. *The Electoral College and the Constitution: The Case for Preserving Federalism.* Westport, Conn.: Praeger, 1994.

Havel, James T. *U.S. Presidential Candidates and the Elections: A Biographical and Historical Guide.* New York: Macmillan, 1996.

Holbrook, Thomas M. *Do Campaigns Matter?* Thousand Oaks: Sage Publications, 1996.

Kamber, Victor. *Poison Politics: Are Negative Campaigns Destroying Democracy?* New York: Insight Books, 1997.

Kimberling, William C. *The Electoral College.* Washington, D.C.: National Clearinghouse on Election Administration, Federal Election Commission, 1992.

Kubiak, Greg D. *The Gilded Dome: The U.S. Senate and Campaign Finance Reform.* Norman: University of Oklahoma Press, 1994.

Kuroda, Tadahisa. *The Origins of the Twelfth Amendment: The Electoral College in the Early Republic, 1787-1804.* Westport, Conn.: Greenwood Press, 1994.

Longley, Lawrence D., and Neal R. Peirce. *The Electoral College Primer.* New Haven, Conn.: Yale University Press, 1996.

McCubbins, Mathew D., ed. *Under the Watchful Eye: Managing Presidential Campaigns in the Television Era.* San Diego, Calif.: Congressional Quarterly Press, 1992.

McGillivray, Alice V., and Richard M. Scammon. *America at the Polls: A Handbook of American Presidential Election Statistics.* Washington, D.C.: Congressional Quarterly, 1994.

McWilliams, Wilson C. *The Politics of Disappointment: American Elections, 1976-94.* Chatham, N.J.: Chatham House, 1995.

Maisel, Sandy L. *Parties and Elections in America: The Electoral Process.* 2d ed. New York: McGraw Hill, 1993.

Miller, Arthur H., and Bruce E. Gronbeck, eds. *Presidential Campaigns and American Self Images.* Boulder, Colo.: Westview Press, 1994.

Nelson, Michael, ed. *The Elections of 1992.* Washington, D.C.: Congressional Quarterly Press, 1993.

Palmer, Niall A. *The New Hampshire Primary and the American Electoral Process.* Westport, Conn.: Praeger, 1997.

Pika, Joseph A., and Richard A. Watson. *The Presidential Contest: With a Guide to the 1996 Presidential Race.* 5th ed. Washington, D.C.: Congressional Quarterly Press, 1995.

Popkin, Samuel L. *The Reasoning Voter: Communication and Persuasion in Presidential Campaigns.* Chicago: University of Chicago Press, 1991.

Regens, James L., and Ronald K. Gaddie. *The Economic Realities of Political Reform: Elections and the U.S. Senate.* New York: Cambridge University Press, 1995.

Roseboom, Eugene, and Alfred E. Eckes, Jr. *A History of Presidential Elections, from George*

Washington to Jimmy Carter. 4th ed. New York: Macmillan, 1979.

Sabato, Larry, ed. *Toward the Millennium: The Elections of 1996.* Boston: Allyn & Bacon, 1997.

Salmore, Stephen A., and Barbara G. Salmore. *Candidates, Parties, and Campaigns: Electoral Politics in America.* 2d rev. ed. Washington, D.C.: Congressional Quarterly Press, 1989.

Scher, Richard K. *The Modern Political Campaign: Mudslinging, Bombast, and the Vitality of American Politics.* Armonk, N.Y.: M. E. Sharpe, 1997.

Selnow, Gary W. *High-tech Campaigns: Computer Technology in Political Communication.* Westport, Conn.: Praeger, 1994.

Shields-West, Eileen. *The World Almanac of Presidential Campaigns.* New York: World Almanac, 1992.

Sorauf, Frank J. *Inside Campaign Finance.* New Haven, Conn.: Yale University Press, 1992.

_____. *Money in American Elections.* Glenview, Ill.: Scott, Foresman, Little, Brown College Division, 1988.

Thurber, James A., and Candice J. Nelson. *Campaigns and Elections American Style.* Boulder, Colo.: Westview Press, 1995.

Traugott, Michael W., and Paul J. Lavrakas. *The Voter's Guide to Election Polls.* Chatham, N.J.: Chatham House, 1996.

Wattenberg, Martin P. *The Rise of Candidate-Centered Politics: Presidential Elections of the 1980s.* Cambridge, Mass.: Harvard University Press, 1991.

Wayne, Stephen J. *The Road to the White House, 1992: The Politics of Presidential Elections.* 3d ed. New York: St. Martin's Press, 1992.

West, Darrell M. *Air Wars: Television Advertising in Election Campaigns, 1952-1996.* 2d ed. Washington, D.C.: Congressional Quarterly, 1997.

Woodward, Bob. *The Choice: How Clinton Won.* New York: Simon & Schuster, 1997.

Wright, Russell O. *Presidential Elections in the United States: A Statistical History, 1860-1992.* Jefferson, N.C.: McFarland, 1995.

Political Parties and Interest Groups

Batchelor, John C. *Ain't You Glad You Joined the Republicans? A Short History of the GOP.* New York: Henry Holt, 1996.

Baumgartner, Frank R., and Beth L. Leech. *Basic Interests: The Importance of Groups in Politics and in Political Science.* Princeton, N.J.: Princeton University Press, 1998.

Berry, Jeffrey M. *The Interest Group Society.* 3d ed. New York: Longman, 1997.

Browne, William P. *Groups, Interests, and U.S. Public Policy.* Washington, D.C.: Georgetown University Press, 1998.

Bykerk, Loree G., and Ardith Maney. *U.S. Consumer Interest Groups: Institutional Profiles.* Westport, Conn.: Greenwood, 1995.

Campbell, James E. *Cheap Seats: The Democratic Party's Advantage in U.S. House Elections.* Columbus: Ohio State University Press, 1996.

Congressional Quarterly. *National Party Conventions, 1831-1996.* Washington, D.C.: Author, 1997.

Gais, Thomas. *Improper Influence: Campaign Finance Law, Political Interest Groups, and the Problem of Equality.* Ann Arbor: University of Michigan Press, 1996.

Herrnson, Paul S., Ronald G. Shaiko, and Clyde Wilcox, eds. *The Interest Group Connection: Electioneering, Lobbying, and Policymaking in Washington.* Chatham, N.J.: Chatham House, 1998.

Hrebenar, Ronald J. *Interest Group Politics in America.* 3d ed. Armonk, N.Y.: M. E. Sharpe, 1997.

Killian, Linda. *The Freshmen: What Happened to the Republican Revolution?* Boulder, Colo.: Westview Press, 1998.

Kurian, George T. *The Encyclopedia of the Democratic Party.* Armonk, N.Y.: M. E. Sharpe, 1997.

————. *The Encyclopedia of the Republican Party.* Armonk, N.Y.: M. E. Sharpe, 1997.

Maney, Ardith, and Loree G. Bykerk. *Consumer Politics: Protecting Public Interests on Capitol Hill.* Westport, Conn.: Greenwood Press, 1994.

Mayer, George H. *The Republican Party, 1854-1966.* 2d ed. New York: Oxford University Press, 1967.

Radosh, Ronald. *Divided They Fell: The Demise of the Democratic Party, 1964-1996.* New York: Free Press, 1996.

Reynolds, David. *Democracy Unbound: Progressive Challenges to the Two Party System.* Boston: South End Press, 1997.

Rosenstone, Steven J., Roy L. Behr, and Edward Lazarus. *Third Parties in America: Citizen Response to Major Party Failure.* 2d ed. Princeton, N.J.: Princeton University Press, 1996.

Rutland, Robert A. *The Democrats: From Jefferson to Clinton.* Columbia: University of Missouri Press, 1995.

————. *The Republicans: From Lincoln to Bush.* Columbia: University of Missouri Press, 1996.

Sundquist, James L. *Dynamics of the Party System.* Washington, D.C.: Brookings Institution, 1973.

Wright, John R. *Interest Groups and Congress: Lobbying, Contributions, and Influence.* Boston: Allyn & Bacon, 1996.

The Presidency

Campbell, Colin. *The U.S. Presidency in Crisis: A Comparative Perspective.* New York: Oxford University Press, 1998.

Congressional Quarterly. *Powers of the Presidency.* 2d ed. Washington, D.C.: Author, 1997.

Cronin, Thomas E., and Michael A. Genovese. *The Paradoxes of the American Presidency.* New York: Oxford University Press, 1998.

Drachman, Edward R., Alan Shank, and Richard M. Pious. *Presidents and Foreign Policy: Countdown to Ten Controversial Decisions.* Albany: State University of New York Press, 1997.

Freidel, Frank B., and William Pencak. *The White House: The First Two Hundred Years.* Boston: Northeastern University Press, 1994.

Frendreis, John P., and Raymond Tatalovich. *The Modern Presidency and Economic Policy.* Itasca, Ill.: F.E. Peacock, 1994.

Hart, John. *The Presidential Branch: From Washington to Clinton.* 2d ed. Chatham, N.J.: Chatham House, 1995.

Hess, Stephen. *Presidents and the Presidency: Essays.* Washington, D.C.: Brookings Institution, 1996.

Jamieson, Kathleen H. *Packaging the Presidency: A History and Criticism of Presidential Campaign Advertising.* 3d ed. New York: Oxford University Press, 1996.

Jones, Charles O. *The Presidency in a Separated System.* Washington, D.C.: Brookings Institution, 1994.

Kiewe, Amos, ed. *The Modern Presidency and Crisis Rhetoric.* Westport, Conn.: Praeger, 1994.

Levy, Leonard W. and Louis Fisher, eds. *Encyclopedia of the American Presidency.* New York: Simon & Schuster, 1994.

Levy, Peter B. *Encyclopedia of the Reagan-Bush Years.* Westport, Conn.: Greenwood Press, 1996.

Lowi, Theodore. *The Personal President: Power Invested, Promise Unfulfilled.* Ithaca, N.Y.: Cornell University Press, 1985.

Martin, Fenton S., and Robert Goehlert. *How to Research the Presidency.* Washington, D.C.: Congressional Quarterly, 1996.

Michaels, Judith. *The President's Call: Executive Leadership from FDR to George Bush.* Pittsburgh, Pa.: University of Pittsburgh Press, 1997.

Morris, Richard S. *Behind the Oval Office: Winning the Presidency in the Nineties.* New York: Random House, 1997.

Nelson, Michael. *Guide to the Presidency*. 2d ed. Washington, D.C.: Congressional Quarterly, 1996.

_____. *The Presidency and the Political System*. 4th ed. Washington, D.C.: Congressional Quarterly Press, 1995.

Neustadt, Richard E. *Presidential Power and the Modern Presidents*. New York: Free Press, 1990.

Newman, Bruce I. *The Marketing of the President: Political Marketing as Campaign Strategy*. Thousand Oaks, Calif.: Sage Publications, 1994.

Nichols, David K. *The Myth of the Modern Presidency*. University Park: Pennsylvania State University Press, 1994.

Ragsdale, Lyn. *Vital Statistics on the Presidency: Washington to Clinton*. Washington, D.C.: Congressional Quarterly, 1996.

Smith, Craig A., and Kathy B. Smith. *The White House Speaks: Presidential Leadership as Persuasion*. Westport, Conn.: Praeger, 1994.

Tenpas, Kathryn D. *Presidents as Candidates: Inside the White House for the Presidential Campaign*. New York: Garland, 1997.

Thompson, Kenneth W., ed. *The Presidency and Foreign Policy*. Lanham, Md.: University Press of America, 1997.

_____. *Twenty Years of Papers on the Presidency*. Lanham, Md.: University Press of America, 1995.

Zernicke, Paul H. *Pitching the Presidency: How Presidents Depict the Office*. Westport, Conn.: Praeger, 1994.

Racial and Ethnic Groups

Aguilar-San Juan, Karin, ed. *The State of Asian America: Activism and Resistance in the 1990's*. Boston: South End Press, 1994.

Barker, Lucius J., and Mack H. Jones. *African Americans and the American Political System*. 3d ed. Englewood Cliffs, N.J.: Prentice Hall, 1994.

Chavez, Linda, and Gerald A. Reynolds. *Race and the Criminal Justice System: How Race Affects Jury Trials*. Washington, D.C.: Center for Equal Opportunity, 1996.

Cornell, Stephen E., and Douglass Hartmann. *Ethnicity and Race: Making Identities in a Changing World*. Thousand Oaks, Calif.: Pine Forge Press, 1998.

Curry, George E., and Cornel West, eds. *The Affirmative Action Debate*. Reading, Mass.: Addison-Wesley, 1996.

Deloria, Vine, Jr., and Clifford M. Lytle. *American Indians, American Justice*. Austin: University of Texas Press, 1983.

Estell, Kenneth, ed. *The African American Almanac*. Detroit: Gale Research, 1994.

Garcia, F. Chris. *Latinos and the Political System*. Notre Dame, Ind.: University of Notre Dame Press, 1988.

_____, ed. *Pursuing Power: Latinos and the Political System*. Notre Dame, Ind.: University of Notre Dame Press, 1997.

Grossman, Mark. *The ABC-Clio Companion to the Native American Rights Movement*. Santa Barbara, Calif.: ABC-Clio, 1996.

Johansen, Bruce E. *Native American Political Systems and the Evolution of Democracy: An Annotated Bibliography*. Westport, Conn: Greenwood Press, 1996.

Lowe, Lisa. *Immigrant Acts: On Asian American Cultural Politics*. Durham, N.C.: Duke University Press, 1996.

Lusane, Clarence. *No Easy Victories: Black Americans and the Vote*. New York: Franklin Watts, 1996.

Ng, Franklin, ed. *The Asian American Encyclopedia*. 6 vols. New York: Marshall Cavendish, 1996.

Nieman, Donald G. *Promises to Keep: African-Americans and the Constitutional Order, 1776 to the Present*. New York: Oxford University Press, 1991.

Nordquist, Joan, comp. *Latinos in the United States: Social, Economic, and Political Aspects—a Bibliography*. Santa Cruz, Calif.: Reference and Research Services, 1994.

Prucha, Francis P., ed. *Documents of United States Indian Policy.* 2d ed. Lincoln: University of Nebraska Press, 1990.

Schaefer, Richard T. *Racial and Ethnic Groups.* 6th ed. New York: HarperCollins, 1996.

Shapiro, Ian, and Will Kymlicka, eds. *Ethnicity and Group Rights.* New York: New York University Press, 1997.

Swain, Carol M. *Black Faces, Black Interests: The Representation of African Americans in Politics.* Cambridge, Mass.: Harvard University Press, 1993.

Takaki, Ronald, ed. *From Different Shores: Perspectives on Race and Ethnicity in America.* 2d ed. New York: Oxford University Press, 1994.

Thompson, William N. *Native American Issues: A Reference Handbook.* Santa Barbara, Calif.: ABC-Clio, 1996.

Van Deburg, William L., ed. *Modern Black Nationalism: From Marcus Garvey to Louis Farrakhan.* New York: New York University Press, 1997.

Wei, William. *The Asian American Movement.* Philadelphia: Temple University Press, 1993.

Weiss, Robert J. *"We Want Jobs": A History of Affirmative Action.* New York: Garland, 1997.

Wilkinson, Charles F. *American Indians, Time, and the Law: Native Societies in a Modern Constitutional Democracy.* New Haven, Conn.: Yale University Press, 1987.

Williams, Michael W., ed. *The African American Encyclopedia.* 8 vols. New York: Marshall Cavendish, 1993.

Wunder, John R. *Retained by the People: A History of American Indians and the Bill of Rights.* New York: Oxford University Press, 1994.

State and Local Government

Adrian, Charles R., and Michael R. Fine. *State and Local Politics.* Chicago: Nelson-Hall, 1991.

Aronson, J. Richard, and John L. Hilley. *Financing State and Local Governments.* 4th ed. Washington, D.C.: Brookings Institution, 1986.

Banfield, Edward C., and James Q. Wilson, *City Politics.* Cambridge, Mass.: Harvard University Press, 1963.

Berman, David, ed. *County Governments in an Era of Change.* Westport, Conn.: Greenwood Press, 1993.

Berry, Jeffrey M., Kent E. Portney, and Ken Thomson. *The Rebirth of Urban Democracy.* Washington, D.C.: Brookings Institution, 1993.

Christensen, Terry. *Local Politics: Governing at the Grassroots.* Belmont, Calif.: Wadsworth, 1995.

Dahl, Robert A. *Who Governs? Democracy and Power in an American City.* New Haven, Conn.: Yale University Press, 1966.

David, Stephen M., and Paul E. Peterson. *Urban Politics and Public Policy: The City in Crisis.* 2d ed. New York: Praeger, 1976.

DeGrove, John M., ed. *Balanced Growth: A Planning Guide for Local Government.* Washington, D.C.: International City Management Association, 1991.

Duncombe, Herbert Sydney. *Modern County Government.* Washington, D.C.: National Association of Counties, 1977.

Goetz, Edward G., and Susan E. Clarke, eds. *The New Localism: Comparative Urban Politics in a Global Era.* Newbury Park, Calif.: Sage Publications, 1993.

Grant, Daniel R., and Lloyd B. Omdahl. *State and Local Government in America.* 6th ed. Madison, Wis.: W. C. B. Brown & Benchmark, 1993.

Jeffery, Blake R., Tanis J. Salant, and Alan L. Boroshok. *County Government Structure: A State by State Report.* Washington, D.C.: National Association of Counties, 1989.

Johnson, Richard B. *Town Meeting Time: A Handbook of Parliamentary Law.* 2d ed. Malabar, Fla.: R. E. Krieger, 1984.

Judd, Dennis R., and Todd Swanstrom. *City Politics: Private Power and Public Policy.* New York: HarperCollins, 1994.

Menzel, Donald C. *The American County: Frontiers of Knowledge.* Tuscaloosa: University of Alabama Press, 1996.

Pagano, Michael A., and Ann O. Pagano. *Cityscapes and Capital: The Politics of Urban Development.* Baltimore: Johns Hopkins University Press, 1995.

Peterson, George E. *Big-City Politics, Governance, and Fiscal Constraints.* Washington, D.C.: Urban Institute Press, 1994.

Pohlmann, Marcus D. *Governing the Postindustrial City.* New York: Longman, 1993.

Savitch, H. V., and John Clayton Thomas, eds. *Big City Politics in Transition.* Newbury Park, Calif.: Sage Publications, 1991.

Shumsky, Neil L. *American Cities: A Collection of Essays.* New York: Garland, 1996.

Smith, Neil, and Peter Williams, eds. *Gentrification of the City.* Boston: Allen & Unwin, 1986.

Zimmerman, Joseph F. *The Massachusetts Town Meeting: A Tenacious Institution.* Albany: Graduate School of Public Affairs, State University of New York, 1967.

The Supreme Court

Abraham, Henry J. *The Judiciary: The Supreme Court in the Governmental Process.* 7th ed. Boston: Allyn & Bacon, 1987.

Baum, Lawrence. *The Supreme Court.* 5th ed. Washington, D.C.: Congressional Quarterly Press, 1995.

Biskupic, Joan, and Elder Witt. *Guide to the U.S. Supreme Court.* 3d ed. Washington, D.C.: Congressional Quarterly, 1997.

———. *The Supreme Court at Work.* 2d ed. Washington, D.C.: Congressional Quarterly, Inc., 1997.

Congressional Quarterly's Guide to the U.S. Supreme Court. 2d ed. Washington, D.C.: Congressional Quarterly Press, 1990.

Cooper, Phillip J., and Howard Ball. *The United States Supreme Court: From the Inside Out.* Upper Saddle River, N.J.: Prentice Hall, 1996.

Cushman, Clare. *The Supreme Court Justices: Illustrated Biographies, 1789-1995.* 2d ed. Washington, D.C.: Congressional Quarterly, 1995.

Eastland, Terry, ed. *Benchmarks: Great Constitutional Controversies in the Supreme Court.* Grand Rapids, Mich.: W. B. Eerdmans, 1995.

Epstein, Lee. *The Supreme Court Compendium: Data, Decisions, and Developments.* Washington, D.C.: Congressional Quarterly, 1994.

Franck, Matthew J. *Against the Imperial Judiciary: The Supreme Court vs. the Sovereignty of the People.* Lawrence: University Press of Kansas, 1996.

Greenberg, Ellen. *The Supreme Court Explained.* New York: W. W. Norton, 1997.

Hall, Kermit L., ed. *The Oxford Companion to the Supreme Court of the United States.* New York: Oxford University Press, 1992.

Latzer, Barry. *Death Penalty Cases: Leading U.S. Supreme Court Cases on Capital Punishment.* Boston: Butterworth-Heinemann, 1997.

McCloskey, Robert G., and Sanford Levinson. *The American Supreme Court.* 2d ed. Chicago: University of Chicago Press, 1994.

McGurn, Barrett. *America's Court: The Supreme Court and the People.* Golden, Colo.: Fulcrum, 1997.

McKeever, Robert J. *The United States Supreme Court: A Political and Legal Analysis.* New York: Manchester University Press, 1997.

Manfredi, Christopher P. *The Supreme Court and Juvenile Justice.* Lawrence: University Press of Kansas, 1998.

Meltsner, Michael. *Cruel and Unusual: The Supreme Court and Capital Punishment.* New York: Random House, 1973.

O'Brien, David M. *Storm Center: The Supreme Court in American Politics.* 4th ed. New York: W. W. Norton, 1996.

Paddock, Lisa, and Paul M. Barrett. *Facts About the Supreme Court of the United States.* New York: H. W. Wilson, 1996.

Schwartz, Bernard. *Decision: How the Supreme Court Decides Cases.* New York: Oxford University Press, 1996.

Tushnet, Mark V. *Making Constitutional Law: Thurgood Marshall and the Supreme Court, 1961-1991.* New York: Oxford University Press, 1997.

Urofsky, Melvin I., ed. *The Supreme Court Justices: A Biographical Dictionary.* New York: Garland, 1994.

Watson, George, and John A. Stookey. *Shaping America: The Politics of Supreme Court Appointments.* New York: HarperCollins, 1995.

Wilkins, David E. *American Indian Sovereignty and the U.S. Supreme Court: The Masking of Justice.* Austin: University of Texas Press, 1997.

Witt, Elder, ed. *The Supreme Court A to Z: A Ready Reference Encyclopedia.* Washington, D.C.: Congressional Quarterly Press, 1993.

Women

Abzug, Bella. *Gender Gap: Bella Abzug's Guide to Political Power for American Women.* Boston: Houghton Mifflin, 1984.

Barber, James D., and Barbara Kellerman, eds. *Women Leaders in American Politics.* Englewood Cliffs, N.J.: Prentice-Hall, 1986.

Burrell, Barbara C. *Public Opinion, the First Ladyship, and Hillary Rodham Clinton.* New York: Garland, 1997.

_____. *A Woman's Place Is in the House: Campaigning for Congress in the Feminist Era.* Ann Arbor: University of Michigan Press, 1994.

Carroll, Susan J. *Women as Candidates in American Politics.* Bloomington: Indiana University Press, 1985.

Cohen, Cathy J., Kathleen B. Jones, and Joan C. Tronto, eds. *Women Transforming Politics: An Alternative Reader.* New York: New York University Press, 1997.

Cox, Elizabeth. *Women in Modern American Politics: A Bibliography, 1900-1995.* Washington, D.C.: Congressional Quarterly, 1997.

Cullen-DuPont, Kathryn. *The Encyclopedia of Women's History in America.* New York: Facts on File, 1996.

DuBois, Ellen C., and Karen Kearns. *Votes for Women: A 75th Anniversary Album.* San Marino, Calif.: Huntington Library, 1995.

Duke, Lois L., ed. *Women in Politics—Outsiders or Insiders: A Collection of Readings.* 2d ed. Englewood Cliffs, N.J.: Prentice Hall, 1996.

Evans, Sara M. *Born for Liberty: A History of Women in America.* New York: Free Press, 1989.

Ferree, Myra M., and Patricia Y. Martin, eds. *Feminist Organizations: Harvest of the New Women's Movement.* Philadelphia: Temple University Press, 1995.

Flammang, Janet A. *Women's Political Voice: How Women Are Transforming the Practice and Study of Politics.* Philadelphia: Temple University Press, 1997.

Flexner, Eleanor, and Ellen F. Fitzpatrick. *Century of Struggle: The Woman's Rights Movement in the United States.* Rev. ed. Cambridge, Mass.: Belknap Press of Harvard University Press, 1996.

Foerstel, Karen, and Herbert N. Foerstel. *Climbing the Hill: Gender Conflict in Congress.* Westport, Conn.: Praeger, 1996.

Howard, Angela, and Sasha A. Tarrant, eds. *Reaction to the Modern Women's Movement, 1963 to the Present.* New York: Garland, 1997.

Ireland, Patricia. *What Women Want.* New York: E. P. Dutton, 1996.

Jeffreys-Jones, Rhodri. *Changing Differences: Women and the Shaping of American Foreign Policy, 1917-1994.* New Brunswick, N.J.: Rutgers University Press, 1995.

Keetley, Dawn E., and John C. Pettegrew, eds. *Public Women, Public Words: A Documentary History of American Feminism.* Madison, Wis.: Madison House, 1997.

Monroe, Judy. *The Nineteenth Amendment: Women's Right to Vote.* Springfield, N.J.: Enslow, 1998.

Moses, Claire G., and Heidi I. Hartmann, eds. *U.S. Women in Struggle: A Feminist Studies Anthology.* Urbana: University of Illinois Press, 1995.

Morin, Ann M. *Her Excellency: An Oral History of American Women Ambassadors.* New York: Twayne, 1995.

Neuman, Nancy M., ed. *A Voice of Our Own: Leading American Women Celebrate the Right to Vote.* San Francisco, Calif.: Jossey-Bass, 1996.

Ryan, Barbara. *The Women's Movement: Reference and Resources.* New York: G. K. Hall, 1996.

Schneir, Miriam, ed. *Feminism in Our Time: The Essential Writings, World War II to the Present.* New York: Vintage Books, 1994.

Stern, Sydney L. *Gloria Steinem: Her Passions, Politics, and Mystique.* Secaucus, N.J.: Carol, 1997.

Thomas, Sue. *How Women Legislate.* New York: Oxford University Press, 1994.

Thomas, Sue, and Clyde Wilcox. *Women and Elective Office: Past, Present, and Future.* New York: Oxford University Press, 1998.

Witt, Linda, Karen M. Paget, and Glenna Matthews. *Running as a Woman: Gender and Power in American Politics.* New York: Free Press, 1994.

Encyclopedia of American Government

List of Subjects by Category

CIVIL RIGHTS AND LIBERTIES
Affirmative Action
Bill of Rights
Birth Control
Busing
Censorship
Civil Disobedience
Civil Liberties
Civil Rights
Civil Rights Acts
Equal Protection of the Law
Feminism
Freedom of Assembly and Association
Freedom of Speech and Press
Gay Rights
Incorporation Doctrine
Nonviolent Resistance
Political Correctness
Privacy
Property Rights
Protest Movements
Religion
Reproductive Politics
Right to Bear Arms
Right to Die
Voting Rights

CRIMINAL JUSTICE
Capital Punishment
Crime
Criminal Justice System
Espionage
Grand Juries
Juvenile Justice
Law Enforcement
Police
Political Crime
Prisons and Jails
Probation
Punishment
Search and Seizure
State Police
Treason
Vigilantism

ECONOMIC ISSUES
Antitrust Law
Business and Government
Capitalism
Commerce Regulation
Consumerism
Federal Debt and Deficits
Freedom of Contract
Funding of Government
Grants-in-Aid
Iron Triangles
Labor Law
National Budgets
Social Security System
Tariffs
Taxation
Technology and Government
Welfare
Wills

FUNCTIONS OF GOVERNMENT
Accountability in Government
Administrative Procedures in Government
Agricultural Management
Civil Service
Communications Management
Disaster Relief
Education Management
Energy Management
Entitlements
Environmental Protection
Executive Functions
Federal Mandates
Health Care Management
Land Management
Legislative Functions
National Security
Public Utilities
Resource Management
Transportation Management

GOVERNMENT BODIES
Congress
Courts: Federal
Courts: State and Local
Drug Enforcement Administration

Electoral College
Federal Bureau of Investigation
Federal Trade Commission
Food and Drug Administration
Interior Department
Internal Revenue Service
Interstate Commerce Commission
Justice Department
Occupational Safety and Health Administration
Postal Service
Regulatory Agencies
Supreme Court
Treasury Department

HISTORY OF GOVERNMENT AND POLITICS
American Indians
American Revolution
Civil Rights Movement
Civil War Amendments
Declaration of Independence
Equal Rights Amendment
McCarthyism
Political Campaigns in U.S. History
Segregation
Slavery
Spoils System
Watergate
Woman Suffrage

INTERNATIONAL POLITICS
Ambassadors and Embassies
Foreign Relations
Immigration
International Law
Terrorism

LAW AND JURISPRUDENCE
Civil Law
Civil Procedure
Common Law
Constitution
Constitutional Law
Due Process of Law
Insurance Law
Judicial Review
Judicial System
Jurisprudence
Jury System

Law
Legal Ethics
Legal Systems
School Law
Telecommunications Law

LOCAL AND REGIONAL GOVERNMENT
City Government
County Government
Family and Government
Intergovernmental Relations
State Government
States' Rights
Town Meetings
Urban Renewal and Housing

MILITARY
Armed Forces
Conscientious Objection
G.I. Bill of Rights
Martial Law
Military Conscription
Military Justice
National Guard
Veterans' Rights
War Crimes

OFFICERS OF GOVERNMENT
Attorney General of the United States
District Attorneys
Elected vs. Appointed Offices
Presidency
Public Defenders
Public Prosecutors
Sheriffs

POLITICAL PHILOSOPHY
Checks and Balances
Citizenship
Conservatism
Democracy
Federalism
Justice
Left and Right
Liberalism
Natural Law
New Right
Political Science

Populism
Separation of Powers
Term Limits

POLITICS

Activist Politics
African American Politics
Asian American Politics
Citizen Movements
Democratic Party
Elections
Filibusters
Gender Politics
Grassroots Politics
Impeachment
Initiatives and Referendums
Interest Groups
Latino Politics
Lobbying

Machine Politics
Media
Nonpartisan Political Organizations
Political Action Committees
Political Campaign Law
Political Corruption
Political Ethics
Political Party Conventions
Political Platforms
Political Representation
Presidential Elections
Primary Elections
Public Opinion Polling
Republican Party
Two-Party System
Veto Power
Voting Behavior
Voting Processes
Women in Politics

INDEX

A page number or range in **boldface** type indicates a full article devoted to that topic.

AARP. *See* American Association of Retired Persons

ABA. *See* American Bar Association

Abolitionist movement, 650, 652, 654-655; and freedom of speech, 311; women in, 752-753

Abortion, 580, 616-619, 775; and Democratic Party, 544; and due process, 230; and feminism, 292, 294; nonviolent protests against, 500; and privacy, 580-581

Abortion laws, 617-619

Access contribution, 512

Accountability in government, **1-4**, 533, 775

Acheson, Dean, 462

Acid rain, 248, 254, 627

ACLU. *See* American Civil Liberties Union

Acquired immune deficiency syndrome (AIDS), 61

Activist politics, **4-8**, 775; and media, 5

ACU. *See* American Conservative Union

ADA. *See* Americans for Democratic Action

Adams, John, 80, 396, 518

Adams, John Quincy, 242-243; and 1824 election, 242, 595

Adjudication, 775

Administration, 775

Administrative law, 438, 775

Administrative Procedure Act (APA), 8-11

Administrative procedures in government, **8-11**

Adoption Assistance and Child Welfare Act (1980), 421

ADR. *See* Alternative dispute resolution

Adult education, and county government, 184

Adultery, criminalization, 195

Adversarial legal system, 116-117

AFDC. *See* Aid to Families with Dependent Children

Affirmative action, **11-16**, 139, 775; and Civil Rights movement, 139; and Democratic Party, 217; at University of California, 15

Affluent Society, The (Galbraith), 179

Afghanistan, Soviet invasion, 262, 266

African American politics, **16-21**

African Americans; and capital punishment, 71, 75; and churches, 644; and citizenship, 121-123, 145; and Democratic Party, 217; emigration out of the South, 145; and Espionage Act, 264; and Fifteenth Amendment, 147; and Fourteenth Amendment, 145; and lynching, 728; and Malcolm X, 590; and Million Man March, 95; and New Deal coalition, 733; and political correctness, 522; and political representation, 548; and Republican Party, 620; and segregation, 642-645; and slavery, 650, 652-655; and three-fifths rule, 173; voting behavior, 731; and voting rights, 131-132, 147, 737

Age, and voting behavior, 731

Aggravating circumstances, and capital punishment, 71

Agnew, Spiro T., 534

Agricultural Adjustment Act (1933), 152

Agricultural Adjustment Act (1938), 152

Agricultural management, **22-26**, 775; and grants-in-aid, 335

Agriculture, and environmental protection, 253

Agriculture Department, U.S., 23 (chart); creation, 299

Aid to Families with Dependent Children (AFDC), 272-273, 658, 747; and federal mandates, 283; and grants-in-aid, 336

AIDS. *See* Acquired immune deficiency syndrome

Air traffic control, 705

Airlines, government regulation, 611-612, 706-707

Alabama, University of, segregation, 132

Alabama and legal ethics, 445

Alaska, counties, 183

Alaska pipeline, 627

Albright, Madeleine, 28, 489

Alcatraz Island, American Indian occupation of, 31

Alcohol, taxes on, 322

Aleatory contract, 365

Alfred the Great, 153

Alien, 775

Alien and Sedition Acts (1798), 80, 311

Alinsky, Saul, 7

Allen, Debbie, 458

Alliance, 775

Ally, 775

Alternative dispute resolution (ADR), 118, 194

AMA. *See* American Medical Association

Ambassadors, 27, 775; and embassies, **26-29**

Amendments, constitutional, 172

American Association of Retired Persons (AARP), 369; and Social Security, 748

American Bar Association (ABA), and legal ethics, 445-446

American Civil Liberties Union (ACLU), 306, 368

American Conservative Union (ACU), 499

American Council on Education, and G.I. Bill of Rights, 332

American Federation of Labor (AFL), 423

American Indians, **29-35**; and Alcatraz occupation, 31; and civil rights, 135; and colonial expansion, 35; and religious freedom, 615; and voting rights, 738. *See also* Native Americans

American Legion, 392, 724; and G.I. Bill of Rights, 332

American Medical Association (AMA), 371; and health care, 392

American Nazi Party, 532

American Political Science Association, 549

American Revolution, 29, **35-38**, 775; and democracy, 212; and federal debts, 278; militias, 474; and natural rights, 492; nature, 207; and women's rights, 755

American Telephone and Telegraph (AT&T), 692; breakup, 41-42, 415, 611

American Woman Suffrage Association (AWSA), 754

Americans for Democratic Action (ADA), 499

Americans with Disabilities Act (1990), 284-285; and Civil Rights Act of 1991, 135

Amicus curiae brief, 677

Amish; and education, 637; and nonviolence, 500

Anarchism, 775

Anarchy, 775

Andersonville prison camp, 739

Anglo-American Law, 405

Antarctic whale sanctuary, 257

Anthony, Susan B., 753-754

Anti-Asian violence, 47-50

Antimiscegenation laws, 48, 579

Anti-Semitism, 80, 306

Antitrust law, **38-42**, 62, 151, 309, 775; enforcement, 275; and Federal Bureau of Investigation, 275; and Justice Department, 415; and telephones, 157

Antiwar protests, 500

APA. *See* Administrative Procedure Act

Appeal, 775

Appellate court, 775; federal, 192-193

Appellate process, 117-118, 402-403

Appropriation, 391, 775

Arafat, Yasser, 302

Arbitration, 775; and mediation, 118

Archer, Dennis H., 718

Argersinger v. Hamlin (1972), 592

Aristide, Jean-Bertrand, 46, 384

Aristotle, 404; and natural law, 491-492

Arizona, term limits, 694

Arkansas, term limits in, 694-695

Armed forces, U.S., 42-47, 775; antiterrorist units, 700; and martial law, 469; and military conscription, 474-476; and National Guard, 485-487; and presidency, 557

Armed Forces Reserve Act (1952), 486

Arms, right to keep and bear, 59

Arms control, 775; and national security, 489

Arms race, 775

Army, U.S., and court-martial, 480

Army/McCarthy hearings, 463-464

Arnold, Benedict, 709; as a synonym for treason, 296

Arraignment, 775

Arrears Pension Act (1879), 745

Arrest, 775

Art, and censorship, 83

Article 15, 480

Articles of Confederation, 169, 171, 211, 775; amendment process, 172; and government power, 645; and political representation, 546; state governments under, 278; and term limits, 694

Articles of War, 478

Asian American politics, **47-51**

Asians, and U.S. citizenship, 97

Assassination; and espionage, 263; Garfield, James, 141, 525-526; and gun control laws, 630; Kennedy, John F., 174; and Reagan, Ronald, 531; and terrorism, 698-699

Assault, 776

Assembly, right of, 32

Assembly and association, freedom of, 579

Assessors, county, 236

Asylum, political, 349

At-large election, 776

AT&T. *See* American Telephone and Telegraph

ATF. *See* Bureau of Alcohol, Tobacco, and Firearms

Athens, ancient, citizenship in, 96

Atomic bomb, 709

Atomic Energy Act (1946), and Federal Bureau of Investigation, 274

Attica state prison, 575

Attorney general of the United States, **51-53**, 206, 413, 415, 776; and attorneys, U.S., 597; and Civil Rights Act of 1964, 133

Attorneys, United States, 224, 597

Attorneys general, state, 597

Attucks, Crispus, 36

Auditors, county, 236

Augustus, John, 585

Authoritarianism, 776; and democracy, 212-213; and foreign policy, 303

Authority, 776

Automobile insurance, 366

Autonomy, 776

AWSA. *See* American Woman Suffrage Association

Baer, William, 286

Bail, 599; excessive, 55

Baker, Howard, 742

Bakke, Ralph, 14

Balance of power, 776

Balanced Budget and Emergency Deficit Control Act (1985), 684

Balanced budgets, 280-281

Ballot, 776

Bank, national, 158

Bank of the United States, Second, 725

Bank robbery, and Federal Bureau of Investigation, 274

Bank Secrecy Act (1970), 712-713

Banking fraud, 77

Bankruptcy, 191, 776; judges, U.S., 400; laws, 62

Banks, and Federal Deposit Insurance Corporation, 150

Barajas, Phyllis, 231

Bargaining, 776

Barron v. Baltimore, 56, 120; incorporation doctrine and, 358

Bartels, John R., 226

Battery, 776

"Battle Hymn of the Republic, The," 753

Bay of Pigs invasion, 266; and Central Intelligence Agency, 266; and Cuban Americans, 433

Behavioralism, 549

Bell, Daniel, 494

Bentsen, Lloyd, 442

Better Business Bureau, 77

BIA. *See* Bureau of Indian Affairs

Bicameralism, 776

Biden, Joseph, 441

Bill of Rights, U.S., **54-59**, 120, 628, 776; and American Indians, 32; and *Barron v. Baltimore*, 120; and capital punishment, 74; and common law, 154; and federalism, 288; and incorporation doctrine, 56-59, 81, 146, 227, 304, 357-360, 631; and military justice, 477; and Native Americans, 135; and natural law, 493-494; and religion, 614

Biodiversity Convention (1992), 490

Biological weapons, and terrorism, 699

Birth control, **59-62**, 616-619, 776; and due process, 230; and federalism, 290; and obscenity laws, 616; and privacy rights, 580; right to, 579

Birth control education, and Sanger, Margaret, 60

Birth Control League, 61

Black, Hugo, 359

Black codes, 145, 643

Black laws, 128

Black power movement, 137, 139

Blackmun, Harry, 580, 677

Blackstone, William, 80

Blaine, James G., 528

Blasphemy; and capital punishment, 71; and censorship, 80

Block grant, 282, 335-336, 776; and federal mandates, 283

Blount, William, 356

Bonaparte, Charles Joseph, 275

Bonds, 320, 776; government, 278; municipal, 320

Border Patrol, U.S., 350

Bork, Robert, 744

Bosnia, 489

Boston; busing in, 67; city government in, 702

Boston Massacre, 36

Boston Tea Party, 38, 339; and modern protests, 339

Bowers v. Hardwick (1986), 61, 326, 580; due process and, 230

Boycotts, 5 (chart), 107, 136, 500; consumer, 500; labor, 426;

Montgomery bus boycott, 341; secondary, 426

Bradley, Joseph P., 578

Bradley, Thomas, 20

Brady, James, 630

Brady Bill (1993), 459, 630

Branch Davidians cult, 277

Brandeis, Louis D., 577-578; and freedom of speech, 311

Brandenburg v. Ohio (1969), 306

Brandt, Willy, 489

British Empire, 107

Broadcast media, and censorship, 86

Broadcasting, government regulation, 609, 690-693

Brown, Arnold, 296

Brown, Jerry, and 1992 Democratic Party platform, 545

Brown, Willie L., Jr., 100

Brown v. Board of Education (1954), 18, 67, 124, 643, 675; and Fourteenth Amendment, 146

Bryan, William Jennings, 518, 554; and 1896 election, 565, 622; and populism, 554

Buchanan, James, 564, 620

Buckley v. Valeo (1976), 516-517

Budget, 776

Budget and Accounting Act (1921), 482, 683

Budget and Impoundment Control Act (1974), 268, 561

Budget deficit, 776; federal, and federal mandates, 285

Budgets, national, 278-281; and deficits, 683; and taxation, 681-684

Buffalo, government protection of, 254

Burden of proof. *See* Proof, burden of

Bureau of Alcohol, Tobacco, and Firearms (ATF), 206, 226, 711; and Branch Davidians, 277

Bureau of Competition, and Federal Trade Commission, 286

Bureau of Economics, and Federal Trade Commission, 286

Bureau of Indian Affairs (BIA), 375

Bureau of Internal Revenue, 381

Bureau of Investigation, creation of, 275. *See also* Federal Bureau of Investigation

Bureau of Justice Statistics, U.S., 199

Bureau of Mines, 376

Bureau of Narcotics and Dangerous Drugs, 225

Bureau of Outdoor Recreation, 376

Bureau of Prisons, federal, 416, 574

Bureau of Reclamation, 376

Bureau of the Census, 376; and Interior Department, 375

Bureaucracy, 776; and executive functions, 267; and iron triangles, 391

Bureaucrats, and lobbying, 392

Burger, Warren, 641, 678; and exclusionary rule, 640; and Watergate scandal, 744

Burglary, 777

Burke, Edmund, 167, 451

Burlington & Quincy Railroad Co. v. Chicago (1897), incorporation doctrine and, 358

Burnham, David, 2

Burr, Aaron; and election of 1800, 241; treason charges against, 710

Bush, George, 98, 161; and Americans with Disabilities Act, 284; and Biodiversity Convention, 490; cabinet, 442; and civil rights, 135; and environmental protection, 627; and Horton, Willie, 459; Iraqi assassination attempt on, 698; and North American Free Trade Agreement, 301; and social security, 748; and taxes, 684; and veto power, 726; and welfare liberalism, 454

Business, 777; and government, 62-66; and Republican Party, 622

Business and Professional Women's Clubs, and Equal Rights Amendment, 259

Busing, **66-70**, 777; in Boston, 67; in Cleveland, 68

Bylaw, 777

Cabinet, 777; federal, 267; U.S. president's, appointment of members, 235

Cable Communications Policy Act (1984), 691

Cable television, 691

Calhoun, John C., and filibusters, 296

California; affirmative action in, 16; gold rush, 728; Mexican Americans in, 431; property tax initiative, 363; Proposition 187, 362, 434; taxpayer revolts, 324; term limits, 694

Calley, William, 741

Cambodian immigrants, 50

Camp Hill state prison, 576

Campaign, 777

Campaign contributions, and ethics, 535

Canada, and Great Lakes, 257; legal system, 446-448

Canal transportation, 705

Capital crimes, and military justice, 480

Capital punishment, **71-76**, 192, 203, 777; and Clinton, Bill, 219; and military justice, 481; and Supreme Court, U.S., 607

Capitalism, **76-79**, 442, 777

Cardozo, Benjamin Nathan, and due process, 229

Carjacking, 200

Carmichael, Stokely, 136

Carnal Knowledge, 86

Carson, Rachel, 179

Carter, Jimmy, 496, 544; and attorney general, U.S., 53; and commerce regulation, 152; and Democratic party platform of 1980, 544; and regulatory agencies, 611; and social security, 748; and U.S. foreign relations, 303; and veterans, 722; and veto power, 726

Carter, Rosalyn, 726

Case law, relationship to common law, 154

Castro, Fidel, 433

Categorical grant, 282, 335

Caucus, 570, 777

Caucuses, party nominating, 237, 518, 540, 570-572

CCC. *See* Civilian Conservation Corps

Celler-Kefauver Anti-Merger Act (1950), 41, 152

Censorship, **79-87**, 777; of art, 83; and education, 82; of textbooks, 82, 85

Census, U.S., 47

Central Americans, 431, 434

Central Intelligence Agency (CIA), 265-266; and drug trade, 225; personnel system, 142; and terrorism, 698; and Watergate scandal, 528, 742, 744

Centrism, 442

Certificates of public convenience and necessity, 602-603

Certiorari, writ of, 118, 191, 676, 777

Chaplinsky v. New Hampshire (1942), 318

Chase, Samuel, impeachment of, 356

Chase, Stuart, 180

Chávez, César, 434, 500, 502

Checks and balances, **87-92**, 396-397, 777; political inertia caused by, 95; and separation of powers, 646-648; and state governments, 667; and Supreme Court, 675

Chemical weapons, and terrorism, 699

Cherokee, 29-30

Cherokee Nation v. Georgia (1831), 29, 675

Chicago; machine politics in, 467; segregation, 133

Chief executives, 777. *See also* Presidents; Mayors; Governors

Chief Justice of the United States, 190

Child abuse; and court proceedings, 420-421; and juvenile justice, 420

Child care, and feminism, 295

Child Labor Law (1916), 151

Children's Bureau, 251

Chile, and Central Intelligence Agency, 266

China, People's Republic of, and McCarthyism, 463

Chinese Exclusion Act, 48

Chinese immigrants, 47-49, 714

Chinese Six Companies, 48

Christian Coalition, 94

Christian Fundamentalists; and birth control, 61; and Equal Rights Amendment, 260

Christian Right, 167

Christopher, Warren, and terrorism, 701

Church of Jesus Christ of Latter-day Saints (Mormons);

and Equal Rights Amendment, 260; and First Amendment, 58

CIA. *See* Central Intelligence Agency

Cicero, and natural law, 492

CIO. *See* Congress of Industrial Organizations

Citizen, 777

Citizen movements, **92-96**, 777

Citizenship, **96-99**, 777; and African Americans, 121, 123; and Asians, 97; and Civil Rights Act of 1866, 128; and education, 637; and Fourteenth Amendment, 122-123, 143, 145; and Mexican Americans, 434; and Puerto Ricans, 434; and *Slaughterhouse Cases*, 146

City councils, 236

City government, 99-104; and machine politics, 467; and ward system, 101. *See also* Town meetings

City managers, 101, 237, 777

Civic education, 777

Civil disobedience, 7, **104-107**, 164, 777; and Gandhi, Mohandas, 107

"Civil Disobedience" (Thoreau), 500

Civil Division, Department of Justice, 416

Civil law, **107-109**, 777; and due process, 227; and martial law, 468

Civil liberties, **109-116**, 777; and citizenship, 98; and civil rights, 120; and incorporation doctrine, 357; and Sacco and Vanzetti, 110

Civil Liberties Act (1988), 50

Civil procedure, **116-119**, 777; and due process, 229

Civil rights, **120-126**, 777; and citizenship, 98; and Federal Bureau of Investigation, 274; in Haiti, 46; and House Committee on Un-American Activities, 264; and Justice Department, 415; and Supreme Court, U.S., 123-126

Civil Rights Act of 1866, 128-129, 145; and housing discrimination, 134

Civil Rights Act of 1875, 129

Civil Rights Act of 1957, 131-132

Civil Rights Act of 1960, 132

Civil Rights Act of 1964, 12, 19, 132-133; and Civil Rights Act of 1991, 135; and Equal Rights Amendment, 260

Civil Rights Act of 1968, 133-135; and Native Americans, 135

Civil Rights Act of 1991, 135; and Civil Rights Act of 1964, 135

Civil rights acts, **128-135**

Civil rights and citizenship, legislation affecting, 33 (chart)

Civil Rights cases (1883), 123, 129

Civil Rights Commission, U.S. *See* Commission on Civil Rights, U.S.

Civil rights laws, and filibusters, 296

Civil Rights movement, **135-140**, 215, 778; and activist politics, 7; and capital punishment, 75; and Civil Rights Act of 1964, 132; and Civil Rights Act of 1968, 133; and civil rights acts, 131-132; and Democratic Party, 217; and federalism, 290; and justice, 412; and Latinos, 435; and media, 5; nonviolent tactics, 500-501; and political change, 548; and voting rights, 737

Civil service, **140-143**, 778; and Internal Revenue Service, 378; and Justice Department employees, 413; and machine politics, 467; and political corruption, 525-526; and spoils system, 659; and veterans, 142, 722

Civil Service Act (1883), 515

Civil Service Commission, federal, 141, 526

Civil Service Reform Act (1978), 141, 526

Civil War, U.S., 620, 778; armed forces, 474; and federal government supremacy, 282, 672; impact, 143; and Lincoln, Abraham, 557; military conscription during, 474-475; and slavery, 650, 652, 654-655; and states' rights, 671-672; veterans, 721, 745; and war crimes, 739; and woman suffrage movement, 753

Civil War amendments, 57, **143-148**, 358, 778

Civil War veterans, 745

Civil wrongs, compared with crimes, 196

Civilian Conservation Corps (CCC), 217, 625, 747

Claims Court, U.S., 191

Clark, Marcia, 599

Class, 778

Class action, 119

Class conflict, 778

Clay, Henry, 568

Clayton Antitrust Act (1914), 39-41, 151

Clean Air Act (1963), 283

Clean Air Act (1990), 254

Clean Air Act amendments (1990), 627

Clean Water Act (1972), 283

"Clear and present danger" doctrine, 264

"Cleavage" theory, 543

Cleveland, Grover, and Interstate Commerce Commission, 388

Cleveland, Ohio, busing in, 68

Clinton, Bill, 327; and Brady Bill, 630; and business, 65; and cabinet, 236, 442; and conservatism, 168; and crime, 219; and crime bill, 88; and Democratic Party platform of 1992, 545; election of 1992, 243; and farm bill, 25; and Federal Bureau of Investigation, 275; and General Agreement on Tariffs and Trade, 680; and Haiti, 46; and health care, 392-393, 749; inauguration of, 561; in Korea, 45; line-item veto and, 727; and Middle East peace talks, 302; and national debt, 281; and National Education Association, 232; and national health insurance, 347; and National Security Council, 489; and Reno, Janet, 52-53; and sexual misconduct allegations, 224; and Shalala, Donna, 455; and state of union address, 647; and welfare liberalism, 454; and welfare programs, 218; and Whitewater affair, 536, 741; and women appointees, 760

Clinton, Chelsea, 561

Clinton, Hillary Rodham, 561, 758; and health care, 392; Health Care Task Force and, 330

Closed primary, 778

Cloture, 295-298, 778

Clyburn, Jim, 731

Coal mining, 248

Coalition, 778

Coast Guard, U.S., 383

Code of Professional Responsibility, 445

Cold War, 778; and espionage, 264; freedom of speech during, 313; and McCarthyism, 461; military conscription during, 475; political crimes during, 531; U.S. foreign policy during, 388

Colfax, Schuyler, and filibusters, 296

Collective bargaining, 426-427, 778

Collective security, 778

Colleges and universities, and political correctness, 523-524

Collier, John, 32

Colonialism, 778

Colorado, term limits, 694

Columbia University, political science school, 549

Combat, women in, 260

Commander in chief, 778

Commerce, 148; and international law, 382; interstate, 151

Commerce clause, 282, 284; and health care, 343; and law enforcement, 440

Commerce Department, U.S., 150

Commerce regulation, **148-152**, 778

Commission on Civil Rights, U.S., 49; and Civil Rights Act of 1960, 132; and Civil Rights Act of 1964, 133; creation, 131; first members, 131; powers, 131-132

Committee to Reelect the President (CREEP), 742

Committees of Correspondence, 36

Common Cause, 371, 497; and Equal Rights Amendment, 259

Common law, **153-154**, 438, 448, 778; and freedom of contract, 308-309; habeas corpus and, 468; and judges, 446-448; and legal ethics, 444; and legal systems, 446-448; and martial law, 469; and state supreme courts, 401

Common law, English, 153

Communications Act (1934), 690-691

Communications management, **154-158**

Communications Satellite Act (1962), 691

Communications Satellite Corporation (COMSAT), 691

Communism, 442, 778; and civil liberties, 111; and Republican Party, 623; and U.S. foreign policy, 388

Communist Party, U.S., 306, 314, 462; and Espionage Act, 264

Community Police Officers program, 441

Compensatory damages, 108

Compromise of 1787, 650

Compromise of 1850, 654

Computers; and government, 688-690; and privacy rights, 582

COMSAT. *See* Communications Satellite Corporation

Comstock, Anthony, 60, 81, 616

Comstock Act (1873), 616-617

Comstock Law (1873), 60, 81; and birth control, 290

Confederate States of America, creation, 655

Confederate war debt, and Fourteenth Amendment, 146

Confederation, Articles of. *See* Articles of Confederation

Conflict resolution, and law, 436

Congress, U.S., **158-163**, 778; and Attorney general, U.S., 51; and African American rights, 122; American Association of Retired Persons and, 369; Articles of Confederation, under the, 169; and borrowing, 320; and budget, 482; and campaign law, 515-517; and checks and balances, 88-89; and Constitution, 449, 451-452; and courts, 397; and Equal Rights Amendment, 259, 263; and Federal Bureau of Investigation, 275; and federal court system, 188, 399, 674; and freedom of speech, 309; and Interior Department, 375; and Interstate Commerce Commission, 388; and iron triangles, 391-393; and judicial

review, 675; and lobbying, 456, 458-459; and media, 471-474; and military conscription, 475; and national budgets, 681; and National Guard, 485; and political action committees, 514; and political corruption, 528-529; and political ethics, 535; and political representation, 548; powers, 449, 451; and presidency, 558, 561, 647-648, 682-683, 727; and presidential veto power, 724-727; and school desegregation, 66, 69; and silver standard, 554; and slave trade, 650; and Social Security, 655; and Supreme Court, 397; and taxation, 319; and telecommunications law, 692; televised hearings, 472-473; and television, 297; and term limits, 693-696; and Treasury Department, U.S., 710; and veterans, 722

Congress of Industrial Organizations (CIO), 423; and political action committee, 511

Congress of Racial Equality (CORE), 137

Congressional Budget and Impoundment Control Act (1974), 483, 683

Congressional elections of 1994, 168

Congressional legislative process, 163

Connecticut, town meetings in, 702

Connecticut Compromise, 173

Conscientious objection, **164-166**, 615, 778; and World War I, 475

Conscription. *See* Military conscription

Consensus, 778

Consent of the governed, 778

Conservatism, **166-169**, 778; and Goldwater, Barry, 494; and New Right, 494; and Republican Party, 623; and Right, the, 442; and Watergate scandal, 495

Conspiracy, 306

Constable, 649, 702

Constituency, 449, 779

Constitution, 779

Constitution, English, 153

Constitution, Soviet, 113, 115

Constitution, U.S., 113, 115, 153, **169-175**, 398-399, 672, 761-774; and abortion, 618-619; and apportionment clause, 319; and Articles of Confederation, 172; and balanced-budget amendment proposals, 281; and budgets, 278; and checks and balances, 87-90, 92; and citizenship, 96; and Civil War amendments, 143, 145-147; and commerce, 151-152; and Congress, 158, 160-162, 449, 451-452; and contract law, 76; and due process, 227-230; and education, 231; and electoral college, 240, 242; endurance, 174; and exports, 148; and federal court system, 187, 672; and federal mandates, 282-284; and federalism, 394; and Food and Drug Administration (FDA), 299; and freedom of contract, 308; habeas corpus and, 468; and impeachment, 354; and judicial review, 175-179, 394-397; and judicial system, 398-400, 402-403; and jury system, 406; and law enforcement, 440; and legal systems, 448; and local government, 184; and martial law, 469; and national budgets, 681-683; and natural law, 491, 493; and political parties, 497; and presidency, 557, 561; and presidential appointments, 660; and presidential elections, 562; and privacy rights, 577; and property rights, 586; and punishment, 606-607; ratification, 54; and separation of powers, 87, 394, 645; and slavery, 650; and taxation, 319; and term limits, 693-696; and treason, 709; and uniformity clause, 319; and veto power, 724-725; and voting rights, 736; and war power, 681; and woman suffrage, 757. *See also* Commerce clause; Due process clause; Equal protection clause; General welfare clause; Necessary and Proper clause; Privileges and immunities clause

Constitutional Convention, 171, 173, 178, 724-725; and electoral college, 241; and term limits, 693

Constitutional democracy, 779

Constitutional interpretation, 394-398; and judicial review, 394; and Supreme Court, 672, 675, 678

Constitutional law, **175-179**, 438, 779; and democracy, 213

Constitutionalism, 111, 113, 115, 779

Constitutions, state, 126, 640, 660, 663-664, 666-667; and amendment referendums, 360, 362-363; and American Revolution, 211; Confederate states, 146; and due process, 441; and education, 233; and government funding, 320; and impeachment, 354; and judicial review, 193-194, 402; and martial law, 469; and referendums, 239, 362; and term limits, 158, 693-695; and voting rights, 755-756

Consulates, 27, 779

Consuls, 27

Consumer fraud, 286

Consumer movement, and writers, 179, 181

Consumer protection; and Federal Trade Commission, 286; and Food and Drug Administration, 298-300

Consumerism, **179-183**, 779

Consumers' Research, 180

Consumers' Research Bulletin, 180

Continental Congress, 159; armed forces, 474; authority, 211; creation, 38, 169, 500; debts, 278; and Declaration of Independence, 209; and postal service, 555; and slavery, 650; and states, 211

Contraception. *See* Birth control

Contract, 148, 779

Contract, freedom of, 579

Contract law, 76-77; and insurance policies, 364-366

Contract with America, 168, 455

Coolidge, Calvin, 527

CORE. *See* Congress of Racial Equality

Coroners, county, 236

Corporation, 779

Corporations; and Fourteenth Amendment, 146; rights, 586

Corruption, police, 511

Cotton, and slavery, 650

Council of State Governments, 372

Council on Wage and Price Stability, 611

Counsel, right to; and due process, 228; and incorporation doctrine, 358

Counterespionage, 264

Counterfeit currency, 710

Counterfeiting, and Treasury Department, 274

Counterintelligence. *See* Counterespionage

County, 779

County commissioners, 185, 236

County government, **183-187**; and sheriffs, 648-650

County managers, 236

County supervisors, 185

County clerks, 236

Court of International Trade, U.S., 191

Courts, 779; and common law, 438; family, 271; impact on daily lives, 194; and juvenile justice, 417-419, 421-422

Courts, federal, **187-191**; and attorneys, U.S., 597; public distrust, 260

Courts, state, and judicial review, 395

Courts, state and local, **191-194**

Courts-martial, 480-481

Courts of Appeals, 190; federal, 190; U.S., 400

Covert action. *See* Espionage

Cox, Archibald, 356, 742-744

Cox, James D., 757

Cox Broadcasting Corporation v. Cohn (1975), 578

Crawford, William, 242

CREEP. *See* Committee to Reelect the President

Crime, **194-201**, 779; definitions, 194-195; and Democratic Party, 219; and drug trade, 225; nonviolent, 196-198; organized, 198-199; rates, 200; and Republican Party, 219; victimless, 199, 412; violent, 194, 196-199; white-collar, 197.

See also Political crime; Terrorism

Crime statistics, 199

Criminal Division, Department of Justice, 415

Criminal intent, 196

Criminal justice; and Federal Bureau of Investigation, 274; and Treasury Department, U.S., 710

Criminal justice system, **201-206**, 779; and capital punishment, 76; and punishment, 606. *See also* Police

Criminal law, 412; and due process, 227

Criminal procedure, 779; and due process, 229

Criminology, positivistic, 417

Cross-cutting requirement, 372

Cross-filing, 570

"Cross of Gold" speech, 565, 622

Cruel and unusual punishment. *See* Punishment, cruel and unusual

Cruikshank, United States v. (1876), 630

Crump, Ed, 465

Cruzan v. Director, Missouri Department of Health (1990), 582, 632; due process and, 230

C-SPAN, 472, 474

Cuba; and Bay of Pigs invasion, 266; communist revolution, 433

Cuban Americans, 431, 433-435

Cultural exchanges, and foreign relations, 303

Curley, James, 465

Customs Service, U.S., 711-712; and drug testing, 579; and drug trade

Cyclical deficit, 278

Daley, Richard J., 465, 467

Damages, 108

Danelaw, 153

Darden, Christopher, 436

Darrow, Clarence, 554

Davis, Angela, 373

Davis, Shelley, 2

DEA. *See* Drug Enforcement Administration

Dean, John, 742

Death penalty, 219

"Deathclock," 629

Debt ceiling, 278-279

Debt limit, 320

Declaration of Independence, **207-212**, 779; and civil liberties, 111; and Jefferson, Thomas, 211; and jury system, 406; and justice, 410; and natural law, 491, 493; and natural rights, 493; and political representation, 545; and principle of equality, 257; and religion, 613; and slavery, 650

"Declaration of Sentiments," 290

Declaratory Act (1766), 35

Decriminalization, 199

Defamation, and freedom of speech, 314

Defendant, 779

Deficit, 278

Deficit Reduction Act (1990), 281

Dehere Gun Fighters of America, 629

DeJonge v. Oregon (1937), 304

Delaney clause, 300

Delano, Frederick A., and G.I. Bill of Rights, 331

Demagogue, 780

Demilitarized Zone, 45

Democracy, **212-216**, 780; and martial law, 468; origins of word, 213

Democratic Party, **216-219**, 780; and civil rights, 217; convention of 1948, 542-543; convention of 1968, 218, 315, 540, 544; and crime, 219; factions within, 95; and National Farmers' Alliance, 553; political campaigns, 518-521, 540-541, 543-544, 564-566; presidents, 217; and Sierra Club, 499; and slavery, 654-655; supporters, 733; and welfare programs, 218

Democratic-Republican Party, 217, 396

Demos, 213

Dennis, United States v. (1950), 306

Denver, Colorado, and school busing, 68

Denver Broncos, 458

Deoxyribonucleic acid (DNA) testing, 510

Departments. *See under their names, such as Justice Department*

Dependent Pension Act (1890), 745

Deportation laws, 307

Deposition, 780

Depression. *See* Great Depression

Deregulation, 780

Deterrence, 780; and capital punishment, 73

Detroit, Michigan, 718; and school desegregation, 69

Dewey, Thomas, 596

Dickinson, John, 210

Dillon, John F., 102

Dillon's rule, 102, 183, 187, 780

Diplomacy, 27, 780; and international law, 384, 387

Diplomats, 27

Direct action, 780

Direct democracy, 780

Dirksen, Everett M., 736; and Civil Rights Act of 1964, 133

Disabilities, students with, 637

Disarmament, 780

Disaster relief, **219-223**, 780

Discrimination, 780; racial, and Civil Rights Act of 1964, 133

Disease control, 346

Disinformation, 263-264

Dissent, tolerance of, and civil liberties, 111

District attorneys, 107, 202, **223-225**, 236, 597, 780

District courts, federal, 189

District courts, U.S., 400

Diversion programs, 420

DNA. *See* Deoxyribonucleic acid

Domenici, Pete, 279

"Don't ask, don't tell," 327

Dorr's Rebellion, 470

Double jeopardy, 780; and incorporation doctrine, 359; and Seventh Amendment, 407

Douglas, Stephen A., and 1860 election, 620

Douglas, William O., 235, 579

Douglas v. California (1963), 592

Draft, military. *See* Military conscription

Draft lottery, 475

Draft registration, 262

Dred Scott v. Sandford (1857), 120-122, 145, 229; due process and, 229

Drug Enforcement Administration (DEA), 52, 206, **225-227**; and Justice Department, 416

Drug kingpin law, 75

Drug laws, and Federal Bureau of Investigation, 276

Drug testing, 579

Drug trade, 225

Drug traffic, and organized crime, 198

DRUGFIRE, 277

Drugs, decriminalization, 607

Dual federalism, 780

Due process clause, 57, 117, 123, 145, 631; and freedom of speech, 311

Due process of law, 61, **227-230**, 780; definitions, 227; and law enforcement, 440; and privacy rights, 579; procedural, 229-230; Slaughterhouse cases and, 123; substantive, 229-230, 289

Dukakis, Michael, 459, 571

Dulles, John Foster, 461

Earth Summit (1992), 490

Eastern Europe, and democracy, 213

Eastman, Joseph, 389

Education; and censorship, 82; and Civil Rights Act of 1964, 133; and democracy, 215; federal subsidies to, 233; and G.I. Bill of Rights, 331-333; and grants-in-aid, 335; and voting behavior, 731

Education, U.S. Office of, and Civil Rights Act of 1964, 133

Education Amendments (1972), 638

Education for All Handicapped Children Act (1975), 638

Education management, **231-234**, 780

EEOC. *See* Equal Employment Opportunity Commission

Egalitarianism, 780

Eighteenth Amendment, 199

Eighth Amendment, 55, 607; and capital punishment, 71, 74

Eisenhower, Dwight D., 131, 623; administration, 623; and McCarthy, Joseph M., 463; and National Guard, 486; and

Supreme Court, 675; and U-2 spy plane, 265

Elected vs. appointed offices, **234-237**

Election law violations, and Federal Bureau of Investigation, 274

Elections, **237-240**, 780; congressional, 162; nonpartisan, 101-102; primary, 237, 239; and public opinion polling, 594-597

Elections, at-large, and county government, 185

Elections, congressional, 158

Elections, recall. *See* Recall elections

Elector, 240

Electoral college, 173, **240-245**, 557, 780

Electoral vote, 240

Electorate, 735, 780

Electric utilities, 602-603

Electronic mail, 692

Electronic media, and political campaigns, 521

Elitism, 549, 780

Ellsberg, Daniel, 81

Ellsworth, Oliver, 399

Emancipation Proclamation, 143, 655; text of, 144

Embargo, 780; Middle East oil, 245-246

Embassies, 27, 781; and international law, 382

Eminent domain, 427, 781

Empirical theory, 549

Employment; and Civil Rights Act of 1964, 133; and veterans' preferences, 722

Employment discrimination; and Civil Rights Act of 1964, 133; and Civil Rights Act of 1991, 135; and Supreme Court, U.S., 135

Employment Division, Department of Human Resources of Oregon v. Smith (1990), 615

Empowerment, 781

Endangered species, 257

Energy, U.S. Department of, 248, 249 (chart), 250; Office of Energy Research, 248

Energy crises, 626

Energy management, **245-250**; and conservation, 248

Energy Policy Act (1992), 603

Enfranchise, 735

Entitlements, **250-253**, 781

Environment and Natural Resources Division, Department of Justice, 415

Environmental protection, **253-257**, 781; and energy production, 246, 248, 250; and Justice Department, 415; legislation, 624-627; and property rights, 587

Environmental Protection Agency (EPA), 152, 223, 254, 255 (chart), 283

EPA. *See* Environmental Protection Agency

Equal Employment Opportunity Act (1972), 723

Equal Employment Opportunity Commission (EEOC), 16; creation, 133

Equal employment opportunity guidelines, federal, 142

Equal Pay Act of 1963, and Equal Rights Amendment, 260

Equal protection clause, and Equal Rights Amendment, 260

Equal protection of the law, **257-259**, 781

Equal Rights Amendment (ERA), 258, **259-263**, 781; and feminism, 292; text of, 259

Equal rights and federalism, 290

Equality; and Christian beliefs, 613; and Constitution, U.S., 148; definitions, 258; and democracy, 215; of opportunity, 12, 781

Equality, principle of, 257-258; and Equal Rights Amendment, 259

Equality before the law, and Fourteenth Amendment, 143

Equality under law, 781

Equity, 108, 192

Equity law, 447

ERA. *See* Equal Rights Amendment

Erlichman, John, 742

Ervin, Sam, Jr., 742

Espionage, **263-267**, 781; and counterespionage, 264; and Federal Bureau of Investigation, 274; and political crime, 530

Espionage Act (1917), 80, 264, 311; and Rosenbergs, 265

Estates (political), 443

Ethics, 781; results-based, 533; rule-based, 533

Ethics in Government Act (1978); and lobbying, 460

Ethnic cleansing, and Bosnia, 349

Ethnicity, 781

E.U. *See* European Union

Eugenics, and birth control, 617

European Union (E.U.), 303

Euthanasia, 631, 633-634, 781

Evidence, 781

Evidence, rules of; and grand juries, 334

Excise tax, 148, 324

Exclusionary rule, 640, 781; privacy rights and, 578

Executive agreement, 781

Executive branch, 87, 781

Executive functions, **267-270**; and state government, 664-665, 667

Executive Order 11246, 12

Executive orders, 267-268, 781

Executive power, 87

Executive privilege, 743, 781

Exon, James, 279

Expert witness, 781

Extortion, and Federal Bureau of Investigation, 274

Extradition, 373; and foreign relations, 301

Exxon Valdez, 248

Factions, 496, 781

Fair Housing Act. *See* Civil Rights Act of 1968

Fair Labor Standards Act (1938), 152

Fair trade laws, 41

Fairness doctrine, 318, 691, 781; and Reagan, Ronald, 319

Faithless elector, 240

Fall, Albert B., 527

Falwell, Jerry, 93, 167, 495

Families and health care, 758

Family and government, **271-274**

Family and Medical Leave Act (1993), 271

Family planning. *See* Birth control

Fanny Hill (Cleland), 318

Farmers' Alliance, 498

Farmworkers, nonviolent protests, 500

Farrakhan, Louis, 95

"Favorite sons," 518, 539

FBI. *See* Federal Bureau of Investigation

FCC. *See* Federal Communications Commission

FDA. *See* Food and Drug Administration

FDIA. *See* Food, Drug, and Insecticide Administration

FDIC. *See* Federal Deposit Insurance Corporation

Federal, 372

Federal Aid Highway Act (1956), 430

Federal Aviation Administration (FAA), 707

Federal Bureau of Investigation (FBI), 52, 206, **274-278**; and Branch Davidians, 277; creation, 275; and crime statistics, 199; directors, 276; and drug trade, 225; and espionage, 264-265; and Justice Department, 416; name, 275; personnel system, 142; and police training, 511; special agent qualifications, 276; and Supreme Court nominations, 676; and terrorism, 698, 700; and Watergate scandal, 742, 744

Federal Communications Commission (FCC), 86, 155, 157, 690-691; creation, 690; and freedom of speech, 318

Federal Communications Commission v. Pacifica Foundation (1978), 319

Federal Corrupt Practices Act (1925), 515, 527-528

Federal criminal justice system, 204

Federal debt, growth, 320

Federal debt and deficits, **278-282**

Federal Deposit Insurance Corporation (FDIC), 150, 609

Federal Election Campaign Act (1971), 515, 528

Federal Election Campaign Act Amendments (1974), 516

Federal Election Commission, 517, 609

Federal Emergency Management Agency (FEMA), 219, 222

Federal Energy Regulatory Commission, 603

Federal Home Loan Bank Act (1932), 718

Federal Housing Administration (FHA), 718

Federal Insurance Contribution Act (FICA), 252

Federal mandates, **282-285**, 782

Federal preemption, 282

Federal Reserve, 782

Federal Reserve System (FRS), 710

Federal Savings and Loan Insurance Corporation (FSLIC), 611

Federal Security Agency, and Food and Drug Administration (FDA), 300

Federal Trade Commission (FTC), 39-40, 151, **285-287**; Bureau of Competition, 286; creation, 11; and Justice Department, 415

Federal Trade Commission Act (1914), 285

Federalism, **287-290**, 335, 782; and civil procedure, 119; and Constitution, 169, 173; and courts, 672; and grants-in-aid, 335, 338; and intergovernmental relations, 371-375; and judicial review, 395; and slavery, 650, 652, 654-655; and state governments, 662-663; and welfare, 745

Federalist Party, 396; and freedom of speech, 311; political campaigns, 517; and presidential elections, 563

Federalists, 782

Fee, 320

Feiner v. New York (1951), 304

Feinstein, Diane, 756

Felonies, 201; definitions, 605-606; and tax evasion, 382

Felony, 197-198, 782

Felony cases, and due process, 228

FEMA. *See* Federal Emergency Management Agency

Feminine Mystique, The (Friedan), 292, 294

Feminism, **290-295**, 617, 782; and birth control advocacy, 616-617, 619; and juvenile justice, 417; origins, 290; and political correctness, 523-524

Ferraro, Geraldine, 568

FHA. *See* Federal Housing Administration

Fifteenth Amendment, 17-18, 146-147; and African American voting rights, 130; and voting rights, 737

Fifth Amendment, 11, 32, 55, 57, 59; and capital punishment, 74; and due process, 175, 227; and Equal Rights Amendment, 259; and grand juries, 334; and incorporation doctrine, 358, 359; and jury system, 406; and privacy rights, 577, 579; procedural guarantees of, 418; and property rights, 229

"Fighting words," 318

Filibusters, 217, **295-298**, 782; and civil rights legislation, 133-134; roots of the word, 296

Filipino immigrants, 47, 49

Films, and censorship, 86

FINCEN. *See* Office of Financial Enforcement, and Office of Financial Crime Enforcement Network

Fingerprinting, 510

Firearms in the U.S. Mails Act (1927), 629

"Fireside chats," 566

First Amendment, 32, 54, 113 (chart), 304, 613; and American Indians, 34; and censorship, 80; and freedom of speech, 309, 313; and nonviolent protests, 500; and privacy rights, 577; and religion, 613-615; and right to protest, 588

First Estate, 443

First Ladies, roles of, 330

Fiscal policy, 782; federal, and Treasury Department, U.S., 710

Fiscal year, 782

Fish and Wildlife Service, U.S., 376

Fiske v. Kansas (1927), 311

Flag burning, 115, 317-318

Flag salute, 615

Florida; and capital punishment, 71, 74; and Cubans, 433; term limits, 694

Foley, Thomas S., 695

Food and Agricultural Organization (FAO), and United States, 387

Food and Drug Administration (FDA), **298-300**, 609; and health care, 346

Food and drug legislation, 179

Food, Drug, and Cosmetic Act (1938), 181, 299; (1958), 300; and Kefauver-Harris Amendment, 182

Food, Drug, and Insecticide Administration (FDIA), 299

Food stamps, 271, 782; and Aid to Families with Dependent Children, 747

Ford, Gerald; and attorney general, U.S., 53; and campaign law, 516; and Hatch Act, 526; and New Right, 495; and Nixon, Richard, 744; pardon of Richard Nixon, 357; and political campaign reform, 516; and regulatory agencies, 611; and veto power, 726

Foreign aid, 115

Foreign Commercial Service, 142

Foreign policy, 27, 782; and espionage, 263

Foreign relations, **300-304**

Foreign service, 27

Foreign Service, U.S., personnel system, 142

Forensic research, and Federal Bureau of Investigation, 277

Forest Service, U.S., 375

Formula grant, 782

Foster, Abby Kelley, 752

Founders, 782

Fourteenth Amendment, 17, 57, 59, 143, 145-146, 304, 782; and African Americans, 145; and capital punishment, 71; and Civil Rights Act of 1866, 129; and congressional powers, 129; and corporations, 146; and due process, 117, 123, 145, 176, 227, 229, 418, 631; and equal protection of law, 257; and Equal Rights Amendment, 259; and federalism, 288-289; and freedom of speech, 311; and incorporation doctrine, 357; and Native Americans, 135; and principle of equality, 257; and privacy rights, 577, 579-580; and right to trial by jury, 407; and segregation, 643; and

Supreme Court, U.S., 123; and voting rights, 737

Fourth Amendment, 11, 55; and privacy rights, 577-578; and search and seizure, 639-642

Framers, 240, 782

Franchise, 148, 735, 782

Franklin, Benjamin, and postal service, 555

Fraud, 782

Free Soil Party, and slavery, 654

Free speech, 782; and censorship, 80; and Espionage Act, 264; and flag burning, 317

Free trade, 782

Freedom, 782

Freedom of assembly and association, **304-308**, 782; and democracy, 213; and incorporation doctrine, 358

Freedom of contract, **308-309**; and due process, 230

Freedom of Information Act (1966), 2

Freedom of religion, and incorporation doctrine, 357

Freedom of speech; and campaign law, 516; and democracy, 213; and incorporation doctrine, 357-358; and Internet, 692; and military justice, 478; and political correctness, 522; and schools, 637

Freedom of speech and press, **309-319**, 783

Freedom of the press, and incorporation doctrine, 357-358

Freedom Riders, 137

Freeh, Louis J., 226, 275

Freemen, 702

Frémont, John Charles, 564; and 1856 election, 620

French and Indian War, 35

French Revolution; and democracy, 212; and natural rights, 492; and popular sovereignty, 624

Friedan, Betty, 292, 294

Friedman, Lewis, 689

FRS. *See* Federal Reserve System

FSLIC. *See* Federal Savings and Loan Insurance Corporation

FTC. *See* Federal Trade Commission

Fugitive slave laws, 650

Full employment, 783

Functional finance, 278

Funding of government, **319-324**; and grants-in-aid, 335; and tariffs, 680

Furman v. Georgia (1972), 71

Gabler, Mel and Norma, 82

Galbraith, John Kenneth, 179

Gallup, George, 595

Gambling, 148, 196, 198-199; and government funding, 324; legalized, 199

Gandhi, Mohandas, 7, 107; and nonviolent resistance, 500

Gangs; Asian, 51; juvenile, 421

Gann, Paul, 363

GAO. *See* General Accounting Office

Garfield, James; assassination, 141, 525-526

Garvey, Marcus, 93

Gas chamber, 73

GATT. *See* General Agreement on Tariffs and Trade

Gault, in re (1967), 417, 418, 419

Gay rights, **325-327**; and Democratic Party, 544

Gender; politics, **327-331**; and voting behavior, 731

General Accounting Office (GAO), and national budgets, 683

General Agreement on Tariffs and Trade (GATT), 680-681, 783; and United States, 387

General Allotment Act (1887), 32

General court, 702

General election, 783

General Land Office, 375

General law county, 183

General Motors, and Nader, Ralph, 182

General Postal Union, 556

General revenue sharing, 335, 783

General Revision Act (1891), 375

General welfare clause, 172; and national budgets, 681, 683

Geneva Conventions, 740

Geological Survey, 375

George III, 38, 354

Georgia, and capital punishment, 71

Germany, and jurisprudence, 405

G.I. Bill of Rights (1944), 49, **331-334**, 723, 747, 783

Gideon, Earl, 592

Gideon v. Wainwright (1963), 592; due process and, 228

"Gilded Age," 622

Gingrich, Newt, 168; and welfare liberalism, 455

Ginsburg, Ruth Bader, 675, 677

Gitlow v. New York (1925), 57, 146, 311; due process and, 228; incorporation doctrine and, 358

Glickman, Dan, 25

Global Climate Protection Act (1987), 627

Global warming, 254

Goering, Hermann, 740

Goetz, Bernhard, 729

Gold rush, California, 728

Gold standard, 554

Goldwater, Barry, and 1964 election, 494, 567, 623

Good Government associations, 498

Good time, 606

GOP, 783

Gore, Al, 88, 226, 489, 571, 630

Government, 783

Government funding. *See* Funding of government

Governors, state, 664; appointment powers, 233, 235; and executive functions, 233, 235, 267, 269, 335, 665; and grants-in-aid, 337; and National Guard, 485; and veto power, 667; women as, 760

Gramm, Phil, 94, 685

Gramm-Rudman-Hollings Deficit Reduction Act (1985), 280-281, 684

Grand juries, 202, **334**, 783; and incorporation doctrine, 357-358; and public prosecutors, 599; and secrecy, 334

Granger laws, 151

Grant, Ulysses S., 671; and civil rights acts, 129; and 1868 election, 622; line-item veto and, 726

Grants-in-aid, 282, **335-338**, 372, 783; and intergovernmental relations, 374

Grantsmanship, 372

Grassroots action, 783

Grassroots politics, **338-342**

Gray, L. Patrick, III, 275

Gray Panthers, 370

Great Britain; and constitutional law, 448; law enforcement, 441; legal system, 446, 448; Parliament, 354; political parties, 714-715

Great Depression, 40; commerce regulation during, 152; and housing, 717; and Interstate Commerce Commission, 389; and liberalism, 453; and national budgets, 278, 280; and resource management, 625; and rural electrification program, 245; and Social Security System, 655; and urban renewal, 717; and welfare, 746

Great Lakes, and environmental protection, 254

Great Society, 218, 251, 282, 747, 783; and consumer movement, 181; and federal mandates, 283

Greece, ancient, citizenship in, 97

Green, Edith, and Equal Rights Amendment, 259

Green v. County School Board of New Kent County (1968), 68

Greenhouse effect, 248

Greenpeace, 368

Greenspan, Alan, 711

Gregg v. Georgia (1976), 71

Griffiths, Martha, and Equal Rights Amendment, 259

Grimké, Angelina and Sarah, 752

Griswold, Estelle, 61

Griswold, Roger, 160

Griswold v. Connecticut (1965), 61, 579; due process and, 230; incorporation doctrine and, 289

Gross domestic product (GDP), 783

Guam, 375

Guardian Angels, 729

Guided discretion statutes, and capital punishment, 71

Guiteau, Charles, 525

Gulf of Tonkin Resolution (1964), 558

Gun control, 627-631, 783

Gun Control Act (1968), 459, 630

Gun laws, 219

Habeas corpus, 469, 783; martial law and, 468

Hague, Frank, 465

Hague Convention (1907), 739

Hague v. Congress of Industrial Organizations (1939), 304

Haig, Alexander, 700

Haiti; U.S. occupation, 46, 384; and United States, 46

Haldeman, Bob, 742

Hall, Leonard, 566

Hamilton, Alexander, 278, 682; and Congress, 451; and Madison, James, 716; and national bank, 172

Hammer, Armand, 303

Harding, Warren, 527, 676

Harrington, Michael, 218

Harrison, Benjamin, 243

Harrison, William Henry, 177, 518-519; and 1840 election, 519, 563

Hart-Celler Act (1965), 353

Hatch Act (1939), 526

Hate crimes, 318; and homosexuals, 326

Hate speech, 318

Hawaiian state politics, 49

Hayden, Tom, 315

Hayes, Rutherford B., 243

Hays, Will, 527

Health and Human Services Department, U.S., 345; and Food and Drug Administration (FDA), 298, 300; and Medicare and Medicaid, 345

Health care; and families, 758; and grants-in-aid, 335; and Johnson, Lyndon B., 218; and veterans, 724

Health Care Financing Administration, 346

Health care management, **343-347**; and issue networks, 392

Health Education and Welfare, Department of, and Food and Drug Administration (FDA), 300

Health Security Plan, and Clinton, Bill, 347

Hemlock Society, 633

Henry, Patrick, 36

Hepburn Act (1906), and Interstate Commerce Commission, 389

Hernandez, Aileen, 368

Hess, Rudolf, 740

Hidden Persuaders, The (Packard), 179

"High crimes and misdemeanors," 357

Higher education, and women's studies, 292

Hijacking, airline, and terrorism, 699

Hill, Anita, 3

Hill, Rowland, 556

Hispanic Americans. *See* Latinos

Hiss, Alger, 265

Historical jurisprudence, 404

Hmong immigrants, 50

Hobbes, Thomas, and natural law, 492

Hollywood Ten, 462

Holmes, Oliver Wendell, Jr., 310; and freedom of speech, 311

Holocaust, and immigration, U.S., 353

Home rule, 183, 783

Home rule statutes, 703

Homestead Act (1862), 375, 429, 745

Homesteading, 430

Homosexuality; criminalization, 195; and due process, 230; and political correctness, 523; and privacy rights, 580

Hoover, Herbert; and housing, 717; and Roosevelt, Franklin D., 280

Hoover, J. Edgar, 274-276, 416

Horizontal equity, 320

Horton, Willie, 459

House Committee on Un-American Activities (HUAC), 315-316, 462; and espionage, 264; and Hiss, Alger, 265; and McCarthyism, 265

House Judiciary Committee; and impeachment, 354, 356-357; and Nixon, Richard, 744

House of Commons, British, 298

House of Representatives, U.S., 158, 160-163, 783; Banking Committee, 536; composition, 158; election of members, 173, 451, 646; and Equal Rights Amendment, 259; and filibusters, 295; Immigration Committee, 307; and

impeachment, 354-355, 357; leadership, 162; legislative functions, 449; and political action committees, 513-514; and presidency, 557; and presidential elections, 241; Rules Committee, 9; and term limits, 693; women in, 760

Housing, 717-720; projects, 717

Housing Act (1949), 718

Housing Act (1954), 719

Housing and Urban Development, U.S. Department of, (HUD); and Civil Rights Act of 1968, 134; creation, 720

Housing discrimination, 133; and Civil Rights Act of 1866, 134; and Civil Rights Act of 1968, 133-134

Howe, Julia Ward, 753

HUAC. *See* House Committee on Un-American Activities

HUD. *See* Housing and Urban Development, U.S. Department of

Hughes, Charles Evans, 398

Hull, Cordell, 681

Human Events, 494

Human rights, 120, 491 (chart), 783; and international law, 387; and political crime, 530; and United States, 387; and Universal Declaration of Human Rights, 387

Humphrey, Hubert H., 736; and 1968 election, 572

Humphry, Derek, 633

Hunt, E. Howard, 742

Hurtado v. California (1884), 289

Hussein, Saddam, 385; and terrorism, 698

Hutchinson, Ann, 613

Hydrogen bomb, 709

ICC. *See* Interstate Commerce Commission

ICJ. *See* International Court of Justice

Ideology, 783

IGR. *See* Intergovernmental relations

Illegal aliens, 350

Illinois, and Equal Rights Amendment, 262

IMF. *See* International Monetary Fund

Immigrants, illegal, and public education, 637

Immigration, **348-354**, 783; Asian, 47-48; Cuban, 433; Latino, 431; and machine politics, 465, 467; Mexican, 431; Puerto Rican, 432

Immigration Act of 1917, 48

Immigration Act of 1924, 48

Immigration and Nationality Act (1952), 353

Immigration and Naturalization Service (INS), 53, 206; and drug trade, 225; and Justice Department, 416

Immigration Reform and Control Act, 354

Impeachment, **354-357**, 784; and British Parliament, 354; and federal judges, 190; and Nixon, Richard, 356-357, 744; and president, U.S., 89; and separation of powers, 647

Imperialism, 784

Implementation, 784

Impoundment, 784

Income level, and voting behavior, 731

Income tax, 280; and Constitution, U.S., 319-320; corporate and personal, 322; federal, 680; and federal mandates, 283; and government funding, 324; and Internal Revenue Service, 378-379, 381-382; reform, 324; and Sixteenth Amendment, 320, 379; and Supreme Court, U.S., 380

Incorporation doctrine, 146, 227-229, **357-360**, 784; and Bill of Rights, 57-59; unincorporated rights and, 358

Incumbent, 512, 784

Independence, American, 38

India, 107

Indian Bill of Rights. *See* Civil Rights Act of 1875

Indian Civil Rights Act, 34, 135

Indian Gaming Act (1989), 35

Indian immigrants, 47-48

Indian Office, 375

Indian Reorganization Act (1935), 30, 32

Indian reservations, and Federal Bureau of Investigation, 274

Indian Territory, 430, 649

Indiana, and Equal Rights Amendment, 260

Indictment, 784; and grand juries, 334

Individualism, 784; and protection of civil liberties, 109

Individuals with Disabilities Education Act (1990), 638

Industrial policy, 784

Industrial Revolution, and resource management, 624

Information superhighway, 784

Infrastructure, 784

Initiative, 784

Initiatives, 363, 694, 784; direct, 360; and grassroots politics, 340; indirect, 360; and referendums, 239, **360-364**

Injunctions, 108, 784

Innocence, presumption of, and jury system, 407

INS. *See* Immigration and Naturalization Service

Insurance law, **364-367**

Intelligence. *See* Espionage

Intercollegiate Society of Individualists, 494

Interest groups, **367-371**, 391, 496, 784; and iron triangles, 391-393; nonpartisan, 496-499

Intergovernmental relations (IGR), **371-375**, 784

Interior Department, **375-378**

Internal Revenue Bureau, 378

Internal Revenue Code, 381

Internal Revenue Service (IRS), **378-382**, 710-711; audits by, 381-382; charges of abusive practices, 2; and computer technology, 686; and Justice Department, 416; and Watergate scandal, 528

Internal Security Act (1950), 314

International City Management Association, 372

International Court of Justice (ICJ), 386-387

International Criminal Police Organization. *See* Interpol

International law, **382-388**, 438, 784; and foreign relations, 301

International Monetary Fund (IMF), and United States, 387

International organization, 784

Internet, 784; government regulation, 692

Interpol; and Justice Department, 416; and terrorism, 700

Interposition, 670, 784

Interstate commerce, 152; and insurance policies, 364; and public utilities, 601-603

Interstate Commerce Act (1887), 388, 707

Interstate Commerce Commission (ICC), 151, **388-391**, 609; creation, 11; and trucking industry, 705

Intestacy, 749

Intolerable Acts, 38

Involuntary servitude, and military conscription, 475

Iran; revolution of 1979, 246; and seizure of American hostages, 385; and terrorism, 699

Iran-Contra scandal, 741

Iraq, and terrorism, 698

Iron triangles, 63, 66, 269, **391-393**, 784

IRS. *See* Internal Revenue Service

Islamic militants, bombings, 701

Israel, and Yom Kippur War, 245

Issue network, 391-392

Jackson, Andrew, 725; and American Indians, 30; and Democratic Party, 217; and election of 1824, 242, 563, 595; and freedom of press, 311; and spoils system, 140, 659; and Supreme Court, 675; and veto power, 725; and War of 1812, 469

Jackson, Jesse, and political correctness, 522

Jacksonian democracy, 659

Jacksonian era, and machine politics, 465, 467

Jamaican immigrants, 93

Janklow, Bill, 665

Japan, agricultural subsidies, 22

Japanese Americans, 97; and Civil Liberties Act, 50; World War II internment, 50, 92, 112, 411

Japanese immigrants, 47-49

Jarvis, Howard, 363

Jaworski, Leon, 744

Jefferson, Thomas, 80; administration, 659; and

American Indians, 29; and Declaration of Independence, 209-211; and Democratic Party, 216; and election of 1800, 241, 563; and freedom of speech, 311; and *Marbury v. Madison*, 396; and national bank, 160, 172; and religion, 614; and states' rights, 670

Jehovah's Witnesses, 615, 637; and conscientious objection, 164

Jenkins v. Georgia (1974), 86

Jesus Christ, and nonviolence, 500

"Jim Crow" laws, 643, 784

Johnson, Andrew; and civil rights acts, 128; impeachment of, 355-356

Johnson, Lady Bird, 174

Johnson, Lyndon B.; and campaign law, 515; and civil rights, 131, 217; and Civil Rights Act of 1964, 132; and civil rights acts, 132; and Congress, 296; and Daley, Richard J., 467; and election of 1964, 567; and Great Society, 251, 453; and housing, 720; and housing discrimination, 133; and Kennedy, Robert F., 413; liberal legislation of, 454; and Special Advisory Commission on Civil Disorders, 268; succession to the presidency, 174; and urban riots, 139; and veto power, 726; and Vietnam War, 558; and Voting Rights Act, 736; and Wallace, George, 487; and war on poverty, 218; and welfare, 747; and workplace safety, 504

Johnson v. Zerbst (1938), 592

Jones Act (1917), 432

Judges; and common law, 446-448; impeachment of, 356; tenure, 115

Judges, federal; appointment, 235; and impeachment, 90

Judges, local and state, 193; election, 236

Judgment, 784

Judicial activism, and Supreme Court, 678

Judicial branch, 87, 784

Judicial federalism, 398

Judicial power, 87

Judicial review, 87, 175-179, **394-398**, 784; and *Marbury v. Madison*, 396; and presidency, 558; and Supreme Court, 674

"Judicial revolution," 230

Judicial system, **398-403**, 784; and presidency, 744

Judiciaries, state, 665-666

Judiciary, and checks and balances, 89

Judiciary Act (1789), 51, 398-399, 674-675; and *Marbury v. Madison*, 396

Jungle, The (Sinclair), 299

Juries; and appellate courts, 192; and common law, 154; incorporation doctrine and, 358

Jurisdiction, 785

Jurisprudence, **403-406**, 785

Jury, 785

Jury, trial by, 203; and military justice, 478; U.S. Constitution on, 406-407

Jury system, 117, **406-410**; and Civil Rights Act of 1875, 129; and common law, 448

Justice, **410-413**, 785; civil, 412; and Civil Rights movement, 412; criminal, 410-412; definitions, 410, 436; and punishment, 604; retributive, 606-607; social, 412

Justice, social, and feminism, 295

Justice Department, 206, **413-417**; and attorney general, U.S., 51; and attorneys, U.S., 597; Bureau of Prisons, 416, 574; Civil Rights Division, 131, 415; Criminal Division, 415; and Drug Enforcement Administration, 225, 416; Environment and Natural Resources Division, 415; and Federal Bureau of Investigation, 274-275, 416; Immigration and Naturalization Service, 416; and Interpol, 416; National Central Bureau, 416; Office of Justice Programs, 417; and Supreme Court, 676; U.S. Marshals Service, 416

Justice of the peace, 649

Justice system; and adversarial system, 591, 600; and jury system, 406

Juvenile delinquency, 418-419

Juvenile justice, **417-422**; and *In re Gault*, 418

Juvenile Justice and Delinquency Prevention Act (1974), 418, 420

Kansas, state government of, 323

Kansas-Nebraska Bill, 620

Katz v. United States (1967), 579

Kaufman, Irving, 708

Keating, Charles H., Jr., 78

Kefauver-Harris Amendment, 182

Kelley, Clarence, 275

Kelly Act (1925), 706

Kennedy, Anthony, 677

Kennedy, Edward, 89, 344; and 1980 Democratic Party platform, 544

Kennedy, Jacqueline, 174

Kennedy, John F.; assassination of, 174; and Bay of Pigs invasion, 266; and campaign law, 515; and civil rights, 132, 217; and civil rights acts, 132; and Civil Rights movement, 590; and Daley, Richard J., 467; debates with Richard Nixon, 567; and election of 1960, 243, 521, 567, 572; and Kennedy, Robert, 53, 413; and New Frontier, 453; and nuclear test ban, 488; and veto power, 726

Kennedy, Robert F., 52, 413

Kennedy-Nixon debates, 498, 521, 566

Kentucky, and woman suffrage, 757

Kevorkian, Jack, 633

Keyes v. Denver School District No. 1 (1973), 67

Keynes, John Maynard, 280

Kidnapping; and Federal Bureau of Investigation, 274; and terrorism, 699

King, Martin Luther, Jr., 18-19, 132, 136; Chicago campaign, 133; "I Have a Dream Speech," 19, 412; and Montgomery bus boycott, 136, 341; and nonviolent resistance, 500; and Southern Christian Leadership Conference, 136-137

Kiowa, 32

Kleindienst, Richard, 742

Korea, Bill Clinton in, 45

Korean Americans, 48

Korean immigrants, 47-49

Korean War; and commerce regulation, 152; conscientious objection and, 164; and McCarthyism, 463; seizure of steel mills during, 395; and Truman, Harry S, 558; and United Nations, 387; veterans, 724

Ku Klux Klan, 126, 129, 239, 443, 532; and Right, the, 443

Ku Klux Klan Acts, 129

Kuhn, Maggie, 370

Kuwait, Iraqi invasion, 385

Labor, U.S. Department of, and Occupational Safety and Health Administration, 504

Labor, U.S. secretary of, 425

Labor law, **423-427**

Labor-Management Relations Act. *See* Taft-Hartley Act

Labor movement, nonviolent tactics, 500

Labor unions, 66; and federal law, 152; and feminists, 290; and House Committee on Un-American Activities, 264; and political action committees, 513

Laissez-faire, 785

Land and Conservation Fund, 376

Land grants, 250

Land management, **427-431**

Landon, Alf, and 1936 election, 595

Landrum-Griffin Act (1959), 424, 427

Langer, William, 297

Laotian immigrants, 50

Latino politics, **431-435**

Latinos; and electoral politics, 546; and voting behavior, 731; and voting rights, 738

Law, **435-439**, 785; purpose, 436; theories, 403-406. *See also* Natural law

Law enforcement, **439-442**; agencies, 785; and drug testing, 579; and grants-in-aid, 335; and political crime, 530. *See also* Police

Law Enforcement Executive Development Seminar, 276

Leadership, 785

League of Nations, 387

League of Women Voters (LWV), 497-498; and Equal Rights Amendment, 259

Left, the, 442-443, 785; and political correctness, 524

Left and Right, **442-444**

Legal ethics, **444-446**

Legal systems, **446-448**

Legal tender, 77

Legislative branch of government, 87, 785

Legislative functions, **448-453**

Legislative oversight, 1, 785

Legislative power, 87

Legislative veto, 785

Legislatures, state; bicameralism, 664; and initiatives, 360-362

Legislatures and democracy, 212

Legitimacy, 785

Lesbian, 785

Lesbianism, and feminism, 294

"Letter from a Birmingham Jail" (King), 137

Lever Food Control Act (1917), 151

Levitt, Arthur, 611

Lewis, Gib, 365

Libel, 577; and freedom of speech, 314

Liberalism, **453-456**, 785; backlashes against, 8; and Left, the, 442

Liberty bonds, 278

Liberty Party, and slavery, 654

Libya, and terrorism, 698, 700

Liddy, G. Gordon, 742

Lien, 785

Lieutenant governors, state, 665

Limited government, 785; concept, 91

Lincoln, Abraham, 621; and Civil War, 474, 558, 655; and conscientious objection, 164; and election of 1860, 564, 620; and Emancipation Proclamation, 143, 655; and *habeas corpus*, 558; and military conscription, 474

Lincoln-Douglas debates, 519, 620

Lincoln Memorial, 19, 138, 376

Line-item veto, 667, 683, 726-727, 785; meaning of, 724

Line Item Veto Act (1997), 727

Lipset, Seymour Martin, 494

Liquidated damages, 108

Literacy tests, 132, 785; and civil rights acts, 133

Literary Digest, 595

Litigation, 785; and insurance companies, 366-367

Little Rock, Arkansas, 486

Lobbying, 391, **456-460**, 785; and grassroots politics, 338; and interest groups, 369; and iron triangles, 392; and woman suffrage movement, 754; and women's movement, 758

"Lochner age," 579

Lochner v. New York (1905), 579

Locke, John, 91; and democracy, 212; and natural law, 492; and property rights, 587

Lone Wolf v. Hitchcock (1903), 32

Long, Huey, 465, 552

Los Angeles; city council elections, 48; Korean population, 48

Los Angeles County, Board of supervisors, 186

Lotteries, 199; state, and government funding, 324

Louis XVI, 443

Louisiana; counties, 183; segregation, 123; Slaughterhouse cases in, 123

Louisville, Kentucky, urban renewal, 717

Loving v. Virginia (1967), 579

Luther v. Borden (1849), 470

LWV. *See* League of Women Voters

Lynch, Charles, 728

Lynchings, and vigilantism, 728

Lyon, Mathew, 160

McCaffery, Seamus, 193

McCarran-Ferguson Act (1945), 364

McCarran-Walter Act (1952), 97

McCarthy, Joseph R., 461, 464

McCarthyism, **461-465**, 785

McCord, James, 742

McCormack, John, 736

McCorvey, Norma, 618-619

McGovern, George, 742

Machiavelli, Niccolò, 492

Machine politics, 101, **465-468**, 785; defined, 465; San Francisco, 728

Machinist Non-Partisan Political League, 499

McKinley, William, and 1896 election, 565, 622

McLarty, Thomas, 536

McVeigh, Timothy James, 701

Madison, James, 410; and Bill of Rights, 54; and Congress, 449, 452; and due process, 227; and justice, 410; and *Marbury v. Madison*, 396; and pluralism, 547; and political parties, 716; and separation of powers, 90-91, 645; and states' rights, 670

Magistrate judges, U.S., 400

Magna Carta, 153; and due process, 227; and government funding, 319

Magnet schools, 69

Maine; elections, 242; term limits, 694; town meetings in, 702

Major Crimes Act (1885), 32

Majority leader, 786

Majority party, 713, 786

Malcolm X, 590

Mandates, federal. *See* Federal mandates

Mandatory arrest laws, 786

Mandatory sentencing laws, 786

Mann, Horace, 231

Mansfield, Mike, and filibusters, 297

Manslaughter, 786

Manual of Courts Martial (MCM), 478

Mapp v. Ohio (1961), 61, 640; due process and, 228

Marbury, William, 396

Marbury v. Madison (1803), 88, 396, 674; judicial review and, 394

March on Washington (1963), 137-138

Market economy, 786

Marriage, and privacy rights, 579

Marshall, John, 29, 56, 395, 674; and Burr, Aaron, treason trial, 710; and judicial review, 395; and *Marbury v. Madison*, 396

Marshall, Thurgood, 18, 675; and *Brown v. Board of Education*, 643

Marshals Service, U.S., 416

Martial law, **468-470**, 786; *habeas corpus* and, 468

Marx, Karl, 586; and property rights, 587

Marxism, 786; and business, 66

Maryland, and Agnew, Spiro T., 534

Mass media, 786

Massachusetts; government of, 269; primary elections, 570; representative bodies in, 703; state police, 668; and taxpayer revolts, 324; town meetings in, 702

Massachusetts Colony, 613

Maternal and Child Health Block Grant, 759

Mayflower Compact, 701

Mayors, 99-101, 237, 786; and executive functions, 267-268, 335; and grants-in-aid, 337

MCM. *See* Manual of Courts Martial

Meany, George, 423

Meat Inspection Act, 179

Media, **470-474**, 786; and activist politics, 5; definitions of, 473; and government, 688; and political correctness, 524; and politics, 514; and public opinion polling, 594, 596; and public prosecutors, 599; and Republican Party, 623; and Roosevelt, Franklin D., 566

Media, news; and freedom of speech, 315; and Watergate scandal, 225

Mediation, 786

Medicaid, 152, 218, 345, 747, 786; and federal mandates, 283

Medical treatment, right to refuse, 230

Medicare, 152, 218, 345, 657, 747, 786; American Association of Retired Persons and, 369

Melting pot, 786

Mennonites, 164

Mental disabilities, and capital punishment, 74

"Mercy killing," 631

Meredith, James, 137

Merit systems, 140-142, 786

Merit Systems Protection Board, 141

Merrill, Steve, 662

Merryman, ex parte, 469-470

Mexican-American War, 164, 431; and Thoreau, Henry David, 500

Mexican Americans, 431-432, 434-435

Mexico; economic conditions, 432; and emigration, 350

Meyer v. Nebraska (1923), 579

Michigan, term limits, 694

Microsoft Corporation, 42

Migratory Bird Treaty (1916), 387

Migratory Bird Treaty Act (1918), 387

Military Appeals, Court of, 191

Military conscription, **474-476**, 786; and conscientious objectors, 164; and Equal Rights Amendment, 259-260; and World War I, 311

Military justice, **477-481**

Military police, 478

Militias, 687, 786; and American Revolution, 474; and martial law, 469; and military conscription, 474

Mill, John Stuart, 304

Miller, United States v. (1939), 631

Miller-Tydings Act, 41

Miller v. California (1973), 85, 318

Miller v. Texas (1894), 630

Milligan, ex parte, 470

Milliken v. Bradley (1974), 69

Million Man March, 95

Milton, John, *Areopagitica*, 80

Minerals Management Service, 377

Minimum standard, 282

Minimum wage laws, 152; and due process, 230

Minority party, 713

Miranda rights, 786

Misdemeanors, 197-198, 200-201, 786; definitions, 605

Mississippi; University of, 137; voter residency requirement, 735

Mississippi River, transportation on, 705

Missouri, term limits in, 694

Missouri Compromise line, 652, 654

Missouri Compromise of 1820, 120, 650

Missouri v. Holland (1920); international law and, 387

Mitchell, Clarence, 134

Mitchell, John, 53, 357, 742

Mobilization, 786

Model Rules of Professional Responsibility, 446

Modern Age, 494

Molina, Gloria, 186

Mondale, Walter, and 1984 election, 568

Money laundering, 711

Money supply, national, 278

Monopolies, 39, 787; and oligopolies, 77

Monroe, James, 563; and 1820 election, 241

Monroe Doctrine, 787

Montana, term limits in, 694

Montesquieu, Baron de; and democracy, 212; and separation of powers, 645

Montgomery, Alabama; bus boycott, 136, 341; march on, 137

Moral Majority, 8, 495

Morality, 787

Morgan, Arthur, 625

Mormons. *See* Church of Jesus Christ of Latter-day Saints

Morrill Land Grant Act (1862), 429

Mosaic law, 153

Moseley-Braun, Carol, 21

Mothers Against Drunk Driving, 342

Motor Carrier Act (1935), 390

Motor Voter Bill (1993), 498

"Motor Voter" registration, 735

Mott, Lucretia, 290-291, 752

Muir, John, 256

Mulroney, Brian, 301

Multiculturalism, 522, 787

Multinational corporation, 787

Municipal corporation, 183

Murder, 787

My Lai massacre, 741

NAACP. *See* National Association for the Advancement of Colored People

Nader, Ralph, 179, 182

NAFTA. *See* North American Free Trade Agreement

Nast, Thomas, 466, 714

Nation of Islam, 95, 590

National American Woman Suffrage Association (NAWSA), 754

National Archives, 207

National Association for the Advancement of Colored People (NAACP), 18, 368; and *Brown v. Board of Education*, 643; and Civil Rights Act of 1968, 134; and Communist Party, 307; creation, 136; and Fourteenth Amendment, 146

National Association for the Advancement of Colored People Legal Defense and Education Fund, 18

National Association for the Advancement of Colored People v. Alabama (1958), 579

National Association of County Officials, 372

National bank, and Hamilton, Alexander, 172

National Broadcasting Company (NBC), 690

National budgets, **482-485**

National Central Bureau, U.S., 416

National Conference of Commissioners on Uniform State Laws (1968), 418

National Conference of State Legislatures, 372

National Congress of American Indians, 134

National Crime Victimization Survey, 199

National debt, 278, 787

National Defense Act (1916), 485-486

National Education Association (NEA), 232; and Equal Rights Amendment, 259

National Executive Institute, 276

National Farmers' Alliance, 553, 555

National Firearms Act and Federal Firearms Act (1934), 629

National Governors' Association, 372

National Guard, **485-487**, 628, 787

National health insurance, 346, 787

National Industrial Recovery Act, 558

National Labor Relations Act (1935), 152, 423, 425, 500

National Labor Relations Board (NLRB), 152, 424-427

National League of Cities, 372

National liberation movement, 787

National Municipal League (NML), 101, 498

National Organization for Women (NOW), 368; creation, 292; and Equal Rights Amendment, 259

National Origins Act, 353

National park system, 376; and Roosevelt, Theodore, 622

National parks, 376, 626

National Review, 494

National Rifle Association (NRA), 371, 628; lobbying, 459-460

National security, **487-490**, 787; and Federal Bureau of Investigation, 274-275; and privacy rights, 582

National Security Council, 489

National Woman Suffrage Association (NWSA), 754

National Woman's Party, 754

National Women's Conference, 294

Nationalism, 787

Native American Church, 34, 616

Native Americans. *See* American Indians

Nativism, 787

NATO. *See* North Atlantic Treaty Organization

Natural disasters; and environmental protection, 253; martial law during, 468; and National Guard, 487

Natural law, 29, 404, **490-494**, 787; and Declaration of Independence, 210; and jurisprudence, 403-404; and Thomas Aquinas, 403-404

Natural monopoly, 148, 601

Natural rights, 787

Naturalization, 787

Navajo, 30

NAWSA. *See* National American Woman Suffrage Association

Nazi Party, American, 306

Nazis, and espionage, 264

NBC. *See* National Broadcasting Company

NEA. *See* National Education Association

Near v. Minnesota (1931), 80, 315

Nebraska; elections, 242; term limits, 694; unicameral legislature, 664

Necessary and proper clause, 158, 172, 282, 284

Nevada, gambling in, 199

New Deal, 152, 217, 282, 746, 787; coalition, 520, 733; and consumer movement, 180; and federal mandates, 283; and machine politics, 468; and regulatory agencies, 609; and Republican Party, 623; and Social Security, 655; and Supreme Court, U.S., 397; and welfare, 746-747

New England; city government in, 702; home rule statutes in, 703; town meetings in, 701-703

New Hampshire; primary elections, 570; state government, 662

New Jersey, and woman suffrage, 757

New Left, 442, 787

New Right, 167, 442, **494-496**, 787

New York City; police, 506; and Puerto Rican immigration, 432; and Tweed, William "Boss," 465

New York State Assembly, 450

New York State capitol building, 661

New York Times, The, 596

New York Times Co. v. Sullivan (1964), 314

New York Times Co. v. United States (1971), 81, 315

News broadcasting, public confidence in (chart), 472

Nichols, Terry Lynn, 701

"Night watch" system, 506

Nineteen Eighty-four (Orwell), 114, 437

Nineteenth Amendment, 93, 259, 737, 750, 754, 757; and jury system, 408

Ninth Amendment, 55; and privacy rights, 577

Nixon, Richard; and American Indians, 34; attempted impeachment, 356-357, 744; and Congress, 296; debates with John F. Kennedy, 567; and Drug Enforcement Administration, 225; and election of 1960, 243, 521, 567, 623; and election of 1968, 243, 567; and election of 1972, 495, 516, 741-742; and Equal Rights Amendment, 259; and exclusionary rule, 640; and

Federal Bureau of Investigation, 275; and general revenue sharing, 337; and government spending, 268; and military conscription, 166; and Mitchell, John, 53; and national budget, 683; and Occupational Safety and Health Administration, 504; and political crime, 532; and regulatory agencies, 611; resignation, 744; and revenue sharing, 337; and Social Security, 748; and Supreme Court, U.S., 561, 640; and veto power, 726; and Watergate scandal, 527, 741-745

Nixon administration, and abuses of power, 141

NLRB. *See* National Labor Relations Board

NML. *See* National Municipal League

Nonpartisan, 787

Nonpartisan Political League, 498

Nonpartisan political organizations, **496-500**

Nonpartisan primary, 787

Nonpartisan slating groups, 496

Nonproliferation, 787

Nonviolence, and civil disobedience, 104-105, 107

Nonviolent direct action, 787

Nonviolent resistance, **500-503**

"Normalcy," 622

Norman Conquest of England, 649

Normative theory, 549

Norris, Frank, 179

North American Free Trade Agreement (NAFTA), 9, 681, 787; and Bush, George, 301; and immigration, 350

North Atlantic Treaty Organization (NATO), 44, 302, 787

North Dakota, term limits in, 694

Noto v. United States (1961), 306

NOW. *See* National Organization for Women

NRA. *See* National Rifle Association

Nuclear energy, 626

Nuclear test ban, 488

Nuclear weapons and terrorism, 699

Nullification, 671

Nuremberg principle, 530, 741

Nuremberg trials, 740

NWSA. *See* National Woman Suffrage Association

OAS. *See* Organization of American States

OASDI. *See* Old Age, Survivors, and Disability Insurance

OAU. *See* Organization for African Unity

Obscenity, 61; and pornography, 81-82, 84-86; and Social Security, 318

Obscenity laws, 60-61; and birth control, 616

Occupational Safety and Health Act (1970), 504

Occupational Safety and Health Administration (OSHA), 152, **504-505**

Ocean Dumping Act (1988), 627

O'Connor, Sandra Day, 675, 677-678

ODALE. *See* Office of Drug Abuse Law Enforcement

Office of Consumer and Business Education, and Federal Trade Commission, 286

Office of Drug Abuse Law Enforcement (ODALE), 225

Office of Education, U.S., 332

Office of Financial Enforcement, and Office of Financial Crime Enforcement Network (FINCEN), 712

Office of Justice Programs (OJP), and Justice Department, 417

Office of Management and Budget (OMB), 611

Office of National Narcotics Intelligence (ONNI), 225

Office of Personnel Management, 141, 526

Office of Saline Water, 376

Office of Strategic Services (OSS), 264

Office of Surface Mineral Reclamation and Enforcement, 377

Ohio, term limits in, 694

Oil imports, 245-246

Oil pipelines, government regulation, 705-706

OJP. *See* Office of Justice Programs

Oklahoma, term limits in, 694

Oklahoma City federal building bombing, 697, 701

Old Age, Survivors, and Disability Insurance (OASDI), 657

Old Testament, and punishment, 606

Olney, Richard, 415

OMB. *See* Office of Management and Budget

Omnibus Crime Control and Safe Streets Act (1968), 670

On Liberty (Mill), 304

One-party rule, 788

Oneida Community, 614

ONNI. *See* Office of National Narcotics Intelligence

OPEC. *See* Organization of Petroleum Exporting Countries

Open primary, 788

Oppenheimer, J. Robert, 709

Order, 788

Oregon; and compulsory education, 637; term limits, 694

Organization for African Unity (OAU), 303

Organization of American States (OAS), 303

Organization of Petroleum Exporting Countries (OPEC), 245

Original intent, 788

Orphan Drug Act (1983), 300

Orwell, George, 114, 437

Osborn Committee, 332

OSHA. *See* Occupational Safety and Health Administration

OSS. *See* Office of Strategic Services

Ozone depletion, 254

PAC. *See* Political action committees

Pacifism, 788; and conscientious objection, 164

Pacifists, and Espionage Act, 264

Packard, Vance, 179, 181

Palko v. Connecticut (1937), 57; incorporation doctrine and, 359

Pardon, 582-583; presidential, 357, 744

Paris Adult Theatre v. Slaton (1973), 85

Paris Postal Conference of 1863, 556

Parks, Rosa, 136, 341, 510

Parliamentary procedure, and filibusters, 295

Parliamentary systems, 449; and separation of powers, 648

Parole, 577, 582

Parole boards, 235

Participatory democracy, and town meetings, 701-704

Parties. *See* Political parties

Partisan politics, 788

Partnership for Health Act (1966), 336

Party whip, 713, 788

Patent law, 62

Patent Office, U.S., 375; creation, 299

Patents; and agriculture, 299; and federal court system, 190

Patient Self-Determination Act (1991), 633

Patriotism, 788

Patronage, 788

Patterson, Haywood, 228

Paul, Alice, 105

PC. *See* Political correctness

Pearl Harbor; bombing, 469; Japanese attack, 112, 469

Peck, Gregory, 401

Pendergast, Tom, 465

Pendleton, Clarence, 16

Pendleton Civil Service Act (1883), 141, 525

Pennsylvania, state police, 669

Pension Office, 375

Pentagon papers, 81

People's Party, 553-554

Perot, H. Ross, 93; and grassroots politics, 342

Persian Gulf War, 246, 477; and federal budget, 281

Personal freedoms, definitions, 109

Peters, Brock, 401

Petit Jury, 407

Petition of Right (1628), and due process, 227

Petitioning, 788

Petitions, 360; and voter initiatives, 360

Peyote, 616

Pickering, John, impeachment of, 356

Pilgrims, 701

Pitt, William, 35

Planned Parenthood Federation of America, 617

Planned Parenthood League of Connecticut, 61

Plato, and natural law, 491-492

Plea, 788

Plea bargaining, 224, 594, 788; and public prosecutors, 599-600

Pledge of Allegiance, 637

Plessy, Homer, 123

Plessy v. Ferguson (1896), 92, 123, 146, 257, 643, 675

Plural society, 788

Pluralism, 549, 788; and interest groups, 367

Plurality, 240, 788

Plyler v. Doe (1982), 637

Plymouth Colony, 624

PMC. *See* Post War Manpower Conference

Pocket veto, 161, 725

Poindexter, Joseph, 469

Police, 201, **506-511**, 788; and corruption, 439; and county government, 184; and discretion in making arrests, 229; origins of the word, 507; and privacy rights, 578; and public prosecutors, 599; and search and seizure, 639-642

Police brutality, 511

Police power, 788; definition, 282

Policing, community-oriented, 201, 506

Polis, 507

Political action committees (PACs), 367, 391-392, 496, 499, **511-515**, 788; connected, 512; and iron triangles, 392; nonconnected, 512

Political activists, and military justice, 478

Political asylum, and immigration, 349

Political boss, 788

Political campaign law, **515-517**

Political campaigning; and electoral college, 243; and ethics, 534; and political action committees, 511-514, 517, 535; and public prosecutors, 597

Political campaigns; and philosophy behind the electoral college, 241; in U.S. history, **517-521**; and voting

behavior, 733; and voting processes, 734

Political correctness, **521-525**, 788

Political corruption, **525-530**; and machine politics, 465, 467-468

Political crime, **530-533**

Political ethics, **533-537**

Political machine, 788. *See also* Machine politics

Political parties, 496, 542, 788; opposition, 713. *See also* Two-party system *and individual party names*

Political party convention delegates, and primary elections, 566, 570-572

Political party conventions, 237, 518, **537-542**, 572; and party platforms, 542-545; and television, 538-541

Political philosophy, 788

Political platforms, **542-545**, 789

Political representation, **545-548**

Political science, **548-551**, 789; definitions, 549

Political system, 789

Politics, 789; origins of the word, 507

Polk, James Knox, 564

Poll taxes, 789; and Twenty-fourth Amendment, 147, 737

Polling. *See* Public opinion polling

Pollution, 789; and environmental protection, 253, 284-285

Poor People's March on Washington, 251

Population, U.S.; African Americans, 431; Latinos, 431, 433-435

Population control, and abortion, 618

Population Fund, 490

Populism, 340, **551-555**, 789; and Ku Klux Klan, 443

Populist movement, failure, 94

Pornography, and birth control education, 60

Positive law, and jurisprudence, 404

Positivism, 789

Post War Manpower Conference (PMC), and G.I. Bill of Rights, 332

Postal laws, and birth control, 60

Postal service, **555-557**; and air carriers, 706

Postal Service, U.S. (USPS), 556

Postbehavioralism, 549

Power, 789

Preponderance of the evidence, 108

Presentment clause, and veto power, 724

Presidency, **557-562**, 789; and attorneys, U.S., 597; and checks and balances, 90; and Congress, U.S., 87-88, 161, 163, 561, 647-648, 682-683, 727; and Food and Drug Administration (FDA), 300; and impeachment, 354-357; and Internal Revenue Service, 378; and international organizations, 387; and Interstate Commerce Commission, 388; and judicial review, 88, 395; and judicial system, 744; and Justice Department, 413; and martial law, 469; and media, 472-473; and National Guard, 485, 487; and National Industrial Recovery Act, 558; and National Labor Relations Board (NLRB), 424; and powers of appointment, 234-235; and regulatory agencies, 611; and Senate, U.S., 647; and separation of powers, 87-90, 92, 645-648; and succession, 174, 177; and Supreme Court, U.S., 558, 561, 646, 674-676; and term limits, 693-694, 696; and veto power, 88, 449, 724-727; and Washington, George, 646; and Watergate scandal, 741-745

President, U.S., and executive power, 267-269

Presidential candidates, and party platforms, 544

Presidential Election Campaign Fund, 515

Presidential election of 1800, 241-242, 517, 563

Presidential election of 1820, 241, 563

Presidential election of 1824, 242, 563, 595

Presidential election of 1840, 517, 519, 563

Presidential election of 1844, 568

Presidential election of 1856, 564, 620

Presidential election of 1860, 564, 567, 620, 671

Presidential election of 1868, 622

Presidential election of 1876, 565

Presidential election of 1892, 520

Presidential election of 1896, 554, 565, 622

Presidential election of 1912, 565

Presidential election of 1932, 280

Presidential election of 1936, 595

Presidential election of 1948, 595-596

Presidential election of 1960, 243, 572; and media, 521

Presidential election of 1964, 494, 567

Presidential election of 1968, 494-495, 567, 572

Presidential election of 1972, 495, 540, 741

Presidential election of 1980, 168, 496

Presidential election of 1984, 568

Presidential election of 1988, 168, 571-572

Presidential election of 1992, 168, 454

Presidential elections, **562-569**; and electoral college, 243-244; and primaries, 570-572

Presidential system, 449, 789

Presidents; Democratic, 217; Republican, 622

Presser v. Illinois (1886), 630

Price discrimination, 148

Primary elections, 540, **569-572**, 789; all-white, 147; blanket, 570; closed, 570; direct, 570; nonpartisan, 570; open, 570; and presidential elections, 565; runoff, 570

Prior restraint, 80-81, 304; and freedom of speech, 311, 315

Prisons and jails, **572-577**

Privacy, **577-582**, 789

Privacy, right to, and birth control, 59, 61

Privacy Act (1974), 2, 582

"Private law," 107, 777

Privatization, 789

Privileges and immunities clause, 58; and due process, 227; and Fourteenth Amendment, 145; and Slaughterhouse cases, 146

Probate, 749

Probation, **582-585**, 606, 789; definition, 583

Procedural due process. *See* Due process of law, procedural

Procedural rights, 55

"Pro-choice" movements, 617, 789

Proclamation of 1763, 35

Progressive Movement, 151, 340, 625, 789; and legislatures, 449; and populism, 555

Progressive tax, 789

Progressivism; and consumer movement, 179; and nonpartisan elections, 497

Prohibition, 148; repeal of, 199

Proof, burden of, 107-108, 224; and due process, 229

Propaganda, 789; and disinformation, 263

Property rights, 62, **585-587**, 789; and Fifth Amendment, 229; and military justice, 478

Property taxes, 322, 324; and taxpayer revolts, 324

Proposition 13 (California), 166, 363

Proposition 187 (California), 352

Proposition 209 (California), 16

Propositions, ballot, 360

Prosecutor, 789; public, 201-202

Prostitution, 148, 198-199; and Federal Bureau of Investigation, 274

Protectionism, 789

Protest movements, **587-591**, 790

Provost marshals, 478

Proxy voting, and political party conventions, 540

Public administration, 790

Public Citizen, 182

Public defenders, **591-594**, 790

Public good, 790

Public Health Service, 346

Public interest, 790; group, 367

Public Law 280, 32, 34

Public opinion and media, 471-472, 474

Public opinion polling, **594-597**, 790; and political candidates, 514; and term limits, 693; and voting behavior, 732

Public policy, 790

Public prosecutors, 107, **597-600**, 790; and grand juries, 599

Public services, and fees, 320

Public utilities, **600-604**, 790; and county government, 184; government regulation, 150

Public Utilities Regulatory Policy Act (1978), 603

Public Works Administration, 747

Puerto Ricans, 431-434; and citizenship, 432; in New York City, 432

Puerto Rico, 375

Punishment, **604-608**; corporal, 605; cruel and unusual, 74, 607, 779; and military justice, 481

Punitive damages, 108, 605

Pure Food and Drug Act, 151, 180, 299

Qadhafi, Muammar, and terrorism, 698

Quakers, 164, 614; and nonviolence, 500

Quasi-municipal corporation, 183

Quayle, Dan, 541

Queen v. Hicklin (1868), 318

Quinlan, Karen, 632

Quorum, 790

Rabin, Yitzhak, 302

Race; and political correctness, 522-523; and voting behavior, 731

Racial discrimination, and jury system, 408

Racial minorities, and Equal Rights Amendment, 262

Racism, 790

Racketeering, and Federal Bureau of Investigation, 274

Radical Republicans. *See* Republicans, Radical

Radicalism, 790

Radicals, 790

Radio; and censorship, 86; and government, 474; and political campaigning, 521. *See also* Broadcasting

Railroad Retirement Act (1937), 655

Railroads; government regulation, 151, 603, 610, 704-705; and Interstate Commerce Commission, 389, 391; and populism, 553

Railway Land Grant Act (1850), 430

Randolph, Edmund, 51

Rape, 790; and abortion, 617

Rape victims, and privacy, 578

Rationalism, 790

Rationing, and World War II, 152

Reagan, Ronald, 166; and affirmative action, 16; and assassination attempt, 531, 630; and Civil Liberties Act, 50; and conservatism, 167; and Democratic obstructionism, 297; disaster relief and, 222; and election of 1968, 494; and election of 1980, 496; and environmental legislation, 627; and fairness doctrine, 319; and media, the, 157; and national budget, 683-684; and New Right, 496; and regulatory agencies, 611; and school busing, 69; and social security, 748; and Supreme Court, U.S., 89; and terrorism, 700; and welfare liberalism, 454

Realpolitik, and national security, 487, 489-490

Reapportionment, 104

Recall elections, 360, 363, 790; and grassroots politics, 340

Reconstruction, 129, 655

Reconstruction era, political scandals during, 140

Red Cross, 740

Redeeming social importance, 82

Redistributive policies, 790

Referendums, 239, 360-363, 790; and grassroots politics, 340

Reform, 790

Reformation, Protestant, 153

Refugee Act (1980), 354

Refugees, 50, 349

Regime, 790

Regressive tax, 790

Regulation, 790

Regulatory agencies, **609-612**, 790; economic reasons for, 609; and health care, 343-346; political reasons for, 610. *See also individual agencies*

Regulatory Analysis and Review Group, 611

Rehabilitation Act (1973), 637

Rehabilitation and punishment, 606

Rehnquist, William H., 188, 561, 677; confirmation as chief justice, 89

Relativism, 790

Religion, **612-616**

Religion, Native American, and Civil Rights Act of 1968, 135

Religious Right, 167

Removal of American Indians, 29-30

Reno, Janet, 52-53, 226, 441, 630

Representation, 791

Representative democracy, 791; and citizenship, 98

Reproductive politics, **616-620**

Reproductive rights, and due process, 230

Republic, 791

Republican-Democratic Party, 563

Republican government, 449

Republican Party, 166, **620-624**, 791; and abortion, 619; creation, 217, 564, 620; and crime, 219; and Equal Rights Amendment, 262; and farmers, 498; and federal mandates, 285; and New Right, 168; political campaigns, 513, 519, 543-544; presidents, 622; rise to power, 672; and Roosevelt, Franklin D., 696; supporters, 733; and Watergate scandal, 495

Republicans, Radical, 620

Reserved powers, 791

Resolution Trust Corporation, 611

Resource Conservation and Recovery Act (1976), 223

Resource management, **624-627**

Restraining order, 791; and freedom of speech, 315

Restraint of trade, 38

Reuther, Walter, 423

Revenue Act (1971), 515, 528

Revenue sharing, and federal mandates, 283

Revenues, 320

Reverse discrimination, 13-15

Revolution, 791

Revolutionary government, 791

Reynolds v. Simms (1964), 258

Reynolds v. United States (1879), 614

Rhode Island; martial law in, 470; town meetings in, 702

Richards, Ann, 365

Richardson, Elliot, 742

Richmond Newspapers, Inc. v. Virginia (1980), 316

Right, the, 442-443, 791; and political correctness, 524; and Republican Party, 624

Right to bear arms, **627-631**, 791

Right to die, **631-636**, 791

"Right to life" movement, 617, 618, 791

Right-to-work laws, 791

Rights, 791

Rights of the accused, 791

Riots; antidraft, 475; and martial law, 469

Riots, urban; and civil rights acts, 133; and Civil Rights movement, 139

Robbery, 791

Robert T. Stafford Disaster Relief and Emergency Assistance Act (1988), 222

Roberts v. City of Boston (1850), 644

Robertson, Pat, 93, 167

Robertson v. Baldwin (1897), 630

Robeson, Paul, 314

Robinson Patman Act, 40

Rockefeller, John D., 38

Roe v. Wade (1973), 580, 618-619; due process and, 230; federalism and, 289; feminist movement and, 292

Roman Catholic Church; and abortion, 618-619; and birth control, 617-618; and conscientious objection, 164; and Latinos, 431; schools, 234

Roman Catholicism, and political candidacy, 572

Roman Catholics; and birth control, 61; and Equal Rights Amendment, 260

Roman empire, 724; citizenship, 96

Roman law, 446, 448

Roosevelt, Eleanor, 625

Roosevelt, Franklin D., 566; administration, 217; and banks, 558; and budget deficits, 280; and consumer protection, 299; and "court packing" plan, 176, 398; and election of 1932, 280, 566; and election of 1936, 595; and federal mandates, 283; and G.I. Bill of Rights, 331-332; and housing, 717; and Justice Department, 415; and martial law, 469; and media, 566; and

New Deal, 217, 453, 520; and polio, 559; and presidency, 557; and presidential power, 562; and Republican Party, 623; and social justice, 412; and Supreme Court, U.S., 58, 176, 397; and Tennessee Valley Authority, 625; and Twenty-second Amendment, 696; and veto power, 726; and welfare, 745-746

Roosevelt, Theodore, 39; administration, 622; and antitrust law, 39, 275; and environmental protection, 256; and Interstate Commerce Commission, 389

Rosenberg, Julius and Ethel, 265, 532, 708

Roth v. United States (1957), 82, 318

Rousseau, Jean-Jacques, 492; and natural law, 493

Ruckelshaus, William, 744

Rule making, 791

Rule of law, 791

Rule 22, 295; and cloture, 296-297

Russia, and nuclear terrorism, 699

Sable Communications v. Federal Communications Commission (1989), 319

Sabotage, and Federal Bureau of Investigation, 274

Sacco, Nicola, 110

Sales taxes, 322, 324; gasoline, 430

Salinas De Gortari, Carlos, 301

Samoa, 375

San Francisco, 100, 103; vigilantism in, 728

San Quentin penitentiary, 73

Sanger, Margaret, 60, 290, 616-617

"Saturday night massacre," 744

Satyagraha, 107

Savings and loan institutions; bailout, 281; government regulation, 611

Saxbe, William, 744

Scalia, Antonin, 677

Schaub, William C., 424

Schenck v. United States (1919), 264

Schlafly, Phyllis, and Equal Rights Amendment, 262

Schlink, Frederick J., 180

School board, 791

School desegregation, 66-70

School law, **637-639**

School prayer, 638, 791

School segregation, 126, 643; and *Brown v. Board of Education*, 124-126; and Civil Rights Act of 1960, 132; and Civil Rights Act of 1964, 133

Schools, public, 231, 233-234

Schriebman, Robert, 2

Schroeder, Pat, 441

Schwarzkopf, Norman, 477

SCLC. *See* Southern Christian Leadership Conference

Scott, Dred, 120-121. See also *Dred Scott v. Sandford*

Scottsboro Boys case, and due process, 228

Search and seizure, **639-642**, 791; unreasonable, 228

SEC. *See* Securities and Exchange Commission

Secession, 671, 791; southern states, 672

Second Amendment, 55, 59, 628; incorporation doctrine and, 358

Second Estate, 443

Secrecy, and grand juries, 334

Secret Service, U.S., 206, 711; and Federal Bureau of Investigation, 275

Sectionalism, and party politics, 654

Secular humanism, 85

Securities and Exchange Commission (SEC), U.S., 269, 609, 611

Security, national, 487, 489-490

Security fraud, 78

Sedition Act (1798), 160, 311

Sedition Act (1917), 80

Sedition Act (1918), 311

Seeger, Pete, 316

Segregation, **642-645**, 791; and Civil Rights Act of 1875, 129; and Civil Rights Act of 1964, 133; and Civil Rights movement, 137; de jure and de facto, 67-68, 642; Montgomery bus boycott and, 341; nonviolent protests against, 500; in northern states, 133; and southern Democrats, 217

Segregation, school. *See* School segregation

Seidman, William, 711

Selective Service Act (1917), 475-476

Selective Service Act (1940), 331

Self-determination, 792

Senate, 792

Senate, U.S., 158, 160-163; Banking Committee, 711; Budget Committee, 279; and civil rights legislation, 127; and cloture, 296-297; composition, 158; election of members, 173, 646; and Federal Bureau of Investigation directors, 274; and filibusters, 295-298; Finance Committee, 2; and impeachment, 355; and Internal Revenue Service, 378; and Interstate Commerce Commission, 388; Judiciary Committee, 3, 89; and Justice Department, 413; legislative functions, 449; majority leader, 295; and National Labor Relations Board (NLRB), 424; and political action committees, 513-514; and presidency, 647; and Rule 22, 296; and Supreme Court, 674, 676; women in, 760

Senate Judiciary Committee, 676

Senates, state, 664

Seneca Falls Convention, 290, 548, 753, 792

Senior Executive Service, 141

Sentencing, 203; and public prosecutors, 600

Separate but equal doctrine, 123, 125, 146, 257, 643, 792; and *Plessy v. Ferguson*, 123

Separation of powers, 287, **645-648**, 792; and civil liberties, 112; and iron triangles, 269; and political parties, 715; and state governments, 663-664, 667

Servicemen's Readjustment Act (1944), 331. *See also* G.I. Bill of Rights

Sessions, William, 275

Settlement, 792

Seventeenth Amendment, 158

Seventh Amendment, 55, 59; incorporation doctrine and, 358; and right to trial by jury, 407

Seventh-day Adventists, 615

Sexual harassment, 3; and workplace, 293

Shalala, Donna, 442, 455

Sharswood, George, 444

Shays's Rebellion, 169

Sheriffs, 236, **648-650**, 792; origin of term, 649

Sherman Antitrust Act (1890), 39, 151, 285; enforcement, 285; and Justice Department, 415

Sierra Club, 368, 499

Sikhs, 49

Silent Spring (Carson), 179

Silver standard, 554

Simpson, O. J., 202, 436, 599

Sinclair, Upton, 179, 299

Single-member district, 792

Sirica, John, 742

Sister city programs, 303

Sit-ins, and Civil Rights movement, 137

Sixteenth Amendment, 379; and funding of government, 320; and income tax, 320

Sixth Amendment, 55, 59; and incorporation doctrine, 228, 358; and public defenders, 592; and right to speedy trials, 194; and right to trial by jury, 407; and Supreme Court, U.S., 592

Skinner v. Oklahoma (1942), 579

Skokie, Illinois, American Nazi Party and, 306

Skyjacking, and terrorism, 699

Slander, freedom of speech and, 314

Slating organizations, 498-499

Slaughterhouse cases (1873), 123, 146, 257; due process and, 227

Slave rebellions, 654

Slavery, **650-655**, 792; abolition, 655; and Civil War, 650; and *Dred Scott v. Sandford*, 120; and Kansas-Nebraska bill, 620; and Missouri Compromise, 120; and political parties, 217; and Republican Party, 620; and segregation, 642; and states' rights, 671; and Thirteenth Amendment, 143, 145; and U.S. Constitution, 173

Smith, Joseph, assassination, 58

Smith v. Allwright, 147

Smoot-Hawley Tariff Act (1930), 681

SNCC. *See* Student Nonviolent Coordinating Committee

Snowbarger, Vince, 323

Social Security Act (1935), 655-656, 658; and Medicare and Medicaid, 345

Social Security system, 251-252, **655-659**, 792; American Association of Retired Persons and, 369; challenges to, 749; entitlements, 747-748; payroll taxes, 322

Socialism, 442

Socialization, 792

Solicitor general of the United States, 52

Solomon, Gerald, 9

Souter, David, 677

South Africa, 107

South Americans, 431

South Dakota; state government, 665; term limits, 694

Southeastern Promotions, Ltd. v. Conrad (1975), 86

Southern Christian Leadership Conference (SCLC), creation, 136

Sovereignty, 287, 792; American Indian, 32; and national security, 490

Soviet Union, 47; and Afghanistan invasion, 262; and anti-U.S. espionage, 264; breakup of, 44, 699; and McCarthyism, 463; military, 43

Spanish-American War, 432; veterans, 722

Special Advisory Commission on Civil Disorders, 268

Special districts, 237

Special legislative courts, federal, 191

Special prosecutors, 224

Speech and press, freedom of, **312**

Spies. *See* Espionage

Spoils system, 140-141, **659-660**, 792; and machine politics, 465; and patronage, 525; and political corruption, 525

Springer v. United States (1881), 378

SSI. *See* Supplemental Security Income

Stalin, Joseph, 43, 47

Stamp Act (1765), 35, 500

Standard Oil Company, 38

Standards of proof, 107-108; and juveniles, 419

Stanton, Edwin, 355

Stanton, Elizabeth Cady, 290, 752, 754

Stare decisis, 154, 401, 438, 446-447, 678, 792

Starr, Kenneth, 224

State, definition of, 792

State bar associations, and legal ethics, 445-446

State constitutions. *See* Constitutions, state

State courts, 400-401

State Department, U.S., 27; and McCarthyism, 462

State departments of corrections, 574

State government, **660-667**; checks and balances, 667; and compulsory education, 637; and counties, 184; and federalism, 662-663; funding, 324; and public utilities, 601, 603-604; and unemployment insurance, 657

State governors, and martial law, 469-470

State laws, and judicial review, 395

State legislatures, and equal protection of the law, 258

State police, **667-670**, 792

State senates, and filibusters, 298

State's attorneys, 223

States' rights, **670-672**, 792; and southern Democrats, 217

States' Rights ("Dixiecrat") Party, 542, 672

Statesmanship, 792

Statue of Liberty, 348, 352

Status offense, 420

Status politics, and New Right, 494

Statute of limitations, 792

Statutory law, 438

Stereotypes; gender, 327; sexual, 293

Sterilization, and privacy rights, 579

Stevens, John Paul, 677

Stevens, Thaddeus, 620

Stewart, Potter, 85

Stock market crash, 389

Stone, Harlan Fiske, 275, 416

Stone, Lucy, 752-754

Stonewall Inn riots, 326

Strategic Arms Limitation Talks (SALT), 792

Straw polls. *See* Public opinion polling

Strip mining, 248

Stromberg v. California (1931), incorporation doctrine and, 358

Structural deficit, 278

Student Nonviolent Coordinating Committee (SNCC), 137

Subgovernment, 391

Subpoena, 792; power, 334

Substantive due process, 580. *See* Due process of law, substantive

Suffrage movement, 792

Suffragette, 793

Suffragists, and gender definitions, 330

Sugar Act, 35

Suicide, 632-633; criminalization, 631; and Kevorkian, Jack, 633; physician-assisted, 633-634

Sunset law, 1, 793

Sunshine law, 1, 157, 793

Superpowers, 793

Supplemental Security Income (SSI), 658; American Association of Retired Persons and, 369

Supply-side economics, 793

Supremacy clause, 287, 793; and judicial review, 395

Supreme Court, U.S., 191, **672-679**, 793; and abortion, 618-619; and African American citizenship, 120; and African Americans, 146; American Indians, 29, 32, 34; and appellate process, 118, 290; and Bill of Rights, 55, 57-59; and birth control, 617-618; building, 405; and campaign law, 516; and capital punishment, 71-72, 74-75, 607; and checks and balances, 88, 675; and city charters, 102; and civil liberties, 115; and civil rights, 123-126, 135, 306; and Civil Rights Act of 1866, 134; and Civil Rights Act of 1875, 123; and Civil Rights cases, 129; "clear and present danger" doctrine and, 264; and communications management, 157; and Communist Party, 306-307; and compulsory education, 637; and Congress,

160-162, 397; and conscientious objection, 164; and Constitution, U.S., 399; and due process, 227-230, 440; and employment discrimination, 135; and espionage, 264; and federal court system, 187, 190; and federal mandates, 284; and flag burning, 317; and Fourteenth Amendment, 123; and freedom of assembly and association, 304, 306-307; and freedom of speech, 264, 310-311, 313-319; and grand juries, 334; and gun control, 628-631; and income tax, 380; and incorporation doctrine, 289, 357-360; and insurance law, 364; and international law, 387; and Interstate Commerce Commission, 389; and judicial review, 175-179, 394-398, 400; jurisdiction, 674; and juvenile justice, 417, 418, 419; and Ku Klux Klan Acts, 129; and labor law, 151-152; and law enforcement, 440-441; and legal ethics, 446; and martial law, 470; and Montgomery bus boycott, 136, 341; and National Industrial Recovery Act, 558; and New Deal legislation, 397; and obscenity, 81-82, 84-86; and patronage system, 526; powers, 125; and presidency, 396, 558, 561, 646; and principle of equality, 257; and privacy rights, 577-580, 582; and reapportionment, 104, 258; and religious freedom, 613-616; and right to die, 632-633; and Roosevelt, Franklin D., 176, 397; and school desegregation, 66-69; and school segregation, 643; and search and seizure, 640-642; and Second Amendment, 628; and segregation, 643; size, 397; solicitor general and, 52; and term limits, 695; and veterans' preferences, 723; and Watergate scandal, 744

Supreme Court justices, selection, 675

Supreme courts, state, 192-193, 401

Swann v. Charlotte–Mecklenburg Board of Education (1971), 67

Sweatt v. Painter (1950), 257

Taft, Robert, 595

Taft, William Howard, 397, 676

Taft-Hartley Act (1947), 152, 424

Talmadge, Norman, 127

Tammany Hall, 465, 525

Taney, Roger, 229

Taos Pueblo, 34

Tariff policy, 62

Tariffs, 650, **680-681**, 793; and foreign policy, 303; protectionist, 671; rates, 681

Tax, income. *See* Income tax

Tax audits, and political crime, 356

Tax base, 320

Tax courts, and income tax, 382

Tax Reform Act (1986), 162-163

Taxation, **681-685**, 793; consumption, 322; and county government, 184; and fairness, 319, 322-324; and government funding, 319-320, 322-324; and government revenue, 278; and insurance industry, 364; and Internal Revenue Service, 378-379, 381-382, 710-712; and justice, 79; and Justice Department, 416; and police force funding, 506; and political representation, 546; and Social Security, 656-657

Taxes; and abatements, 322; Articles of Confederation, under the, 169; and Congress, 160; consumption, 322; and neutrality, 322; payroll, 655; progressive, 319-320, 324; proportional, 323; regressive, 320, 323; and responsiveness to economic changes, 324

Taxpayer revolts, 8

Teapot Dome scandal, 515, 526-527

Technology and government, **685-690**

Tecumseh, 563

Telecommunications law, **690-693**; and freedom of speech, 318

Telecommunications satellites, 691

Telephone, government regulation, 690, 692

Television, 538; and censorship, 86; and Congress, 297; and government, 470, 472-474; government regulation, 690-693; and political campaigns, 459, 567; and political party conventions,

538-541; and Watergate hearings, 742. *See also* Broadcasting

Television news, public confidence in (chart), 472

Ten Commandments, compared to party platforms, 544

Ten Most Wanted list, and Federal Bureau of Investigation, 276

Tennessee Valley Authority (TVA), 625

Tenth Amendment, 55, 282; and civil rights, 120; and commerce regulation, 151; and education, 231; and states' rights, 670

Tenure of Office Act, 355

Term limits, 158, **693-696**, 793; retroactive, 694

Termination of American Indian Tribes, 32

Territories, U.S., administration, 375

Terrorism, 530, 532, 591, **696-701**, 793; and counterespionage, 264; definitions, 697

Testimony, 793

Texas; and capital punishment, 71, 75; martial law in, 470; Mexican Americans in, 431

Texas Rangers, 668

Texas v. Johnson (1989), 317

Thalidomide, 181

Third Amendment, 55, 59; incorporation doctrine and, 358; and privacy rights, 577

Third Estate, 443

Third party, 793; movements, 243, 245, 553, 713-714

Thirteenth Amendment, 17, 128, 143, 145, 655; and military conscription, 475; and Supreme Court, U.S., 475

Thomas, Clarence, 16, 675, 677; confirmation hearings, 3

Thomas Aquinas, and natural law, 403-404, 492

Thoreau, Henry David, 106, 164; influence on Mohandas Gandhi, 107; and nonviolent resistance, 500

Three-fifths rule, and Constitution, U.S., 17

Three Mile Island nuclear power plant, 626

Thurmond, Strom, 127; and filibuster, 297

Time, Inc. v. Hill (1967), 577

Tinker v. Des Moines Independent Community School District (1969), 317, 637

Title VII, Civil Rights Act of 1964, 12, 133

Title IX, 638

To Kill a Mockingbird (1962), 401

Tobacco, taxes on, 322

Tolson, Clyde, 275

Torts, 604, 793

Totalitarian governments, 43

Town meetings, 100, **701-704**, 793; and democracy, 213

Toys R Us, 286

Trade policy, and foreign relations, 303

Trade relations, 303

Traffic court, 192

Traffic law, 666

Traitor, defined, 709

Transportation Act (1920), 389

Transportation management, **704-708**; and grants-in-aid, 335; and Interstate Commerce Commission, 388-389; and land management, 430

Treason, 532, **708-710**, 793; and Constitution, U.S., 171, 709; definitions, 709-710; and Federal Bureau of Investigation, 274; and impeachment, 354

Treasurers, county, 236

Treasury, secretary of, 710, 713

Treasury Department, U.S., **710-713**; and Congress, U.S., 710; and Internal Revenue Service, 378-379, 381-382

Treaties, international, and Supreme Court, U.S., 387

Treaties and international law, 382-385, 387

Treaty, 793

Trial, 793; by jury, 55

Trials, and civil procedure, 116-119

Triangle Shirtwaist Company fire, 505

Tribal courts, 32

Trucking, government regulation, 705

Truman, Harry S, 595; and American Indians, 134; and Bureau of Land Management, 376; election of 1948, 243, 596;

and Fair Deal, 453; and Korean War, 558; seizure of steels mills by, 395

Trust, 793

Turner, George, impeachment of, 356

Turner, Nat, 654

TVA. *See* Tennessee Valley Authority

Tweed, William "Boss," 465-467, 525

Twelfth Amendment, 240, 243; and election of 1800, 241; and electoral college, 240

Twenty-first Amendment, 199

Twenty-second Amendment, 557, 694, 696

Twenty-third Amendment; and electoral college, 240

Twenty-fourth Amendment, 737; and poll taxes, 147

Twenty-sixth Amendment, 738

Two-party system, **713-716**, 793; and nonpartisan political organizations, 499; and party platforms, 542; and voter turnout, 239

Tydings Committee, 462

Tyler, John, 177

Tyson, Laura, 455

U-2 spy plane, 265

UCMJ. *See* Uniform Code of Military Justice

UCR. *See* Uniform Crime Reports

UFW. *See* United Farm Workers

Unabomber, 701

Unalienable Rights, 209

Unanimous consent, 295

Unemployment, 152; compensation, 657; and recessions, 280

Unemployment insurance, 272; and Social Security, 655, 657-658

Unfunded mandate, 282

Unicameral legislature, 793

Uniform Code of Military Justice (UCMJ), 478, 480

Uniform Crime Reports (UCR), 199-200

Uniform Juvenile Court Act, 418

Uniform laws, and juvenile justice, 418

Uniform Probate Code, 749

Unincorporated area, 183

Unit rule, 240; and electoral college, 240, 242-244; and political party conventions, 540

Unitary government, 287, 374

United Farm Workers (UFW), 434

United Nations, 303, 386, 793; and civil liberties, 115; General Assembly, 385; and International Court of Justice, 386; and international law, 385-387; and Korean War, 387; and peacekeeping, 388; Population Fund, 490; Security Council, 385, 388; and terrorism, 700; and United States, 387

United Nations Charter, and United States military, 387

United States Conference of Mayors, 372

United States v. . . . See *key name of court case*

United We Stand, 93, 342

Universal Declaration of Human Rights, 387, 530, 793

Universal Negro Improvement Association, 93

Universal Postal Union (UPU), 556

Universal suffrage, 735, 793

Unruh, Jesse, 484

Unsafe at Any Speed (Nader), 179, 182

UPU. *See* Universal Postal Union

Urban population, U.S., history, 102

Urban renewal and housing, **717-720**

Urbanization. *See* Police

V-chip, 692

VA. *See* Veterans Administration

Van Buren, Martin, and 1840 election, 517, 519

Vanzetti, Bartolomeo, 110

Venable, Abraham, 296

Venereal disease, 61

Verdict, 794

Vermont, town meetings in, 702-703

Vertical equity, 320

Veterans, 794; and Equal Rights Amendment, 262; iron triangles and, 392; and preferences, 142; and World War I, 331; and World War II, 331, 333

Veterans Administration (VA); health care, 724; and housing, 718

Veterans' Affairs, Department, 392; creation, 724

Veterans Appeals, Court of, 191

Veterans of Foreign Wars (VFW), 392, 724

Veterans Preference Act (1944), 722

Veterans' rights, **721-724**

Veto, gubernatorial, and voter initiatives, 361

Veto, line-item. *See* Line-item veto

Veto power, 87-90, 91 (chart), 92, 173, **724-728**, 794; and Johnson, Andrew, 355; and presidency, 161, 449; and Roosevelt, Franklin D., 557; and state governors, 667; and Washington, George, 557

VFW. *See* Veterans of Foreign Wars

VICAP. *See* Violent Criminal Apprehension Program

Vice presidency, and succession to the presidency, 174

Vice president, U.S.; and Congress, 162; nomination, 540-542, 562; and Senate, 296

Vietnam Era Veterans' Readjustment Assistance Act (1974), 723

Vietnam Memorial, 721

Vietnam War; and Asian immigration, 47; and Civil Rights movement, 139; and conscientious objection, 164; and Democratic Party, 544; and Johnson, Lyndon B., 558; military conscription during, 476; protests against, 500, 637; and terrorism, 698; veterans, 723; and war crimes, 741

Vigilantism, **728-729**, 794; definitions, 728

Violence, drug-related, 51

Violent Criminal Apprehension Program (VICAP), and Federal Bureau of Investigation, 276

Virgin Islands, 375

Visa policies, and foreign relations, 301

Vocational Rehabilitation Administration, 251

Voice of America, and McCarthy, Joseph M., 463

Voir dire, 409

Vote, right to, 146-147

Voter initiatives. *See* Initiatives

Voter registration, 239, 735

Voting age, 735

Voting behavior, **730-733**; women, 759

Voting processes, **734-735**

Voting rights, **735-738**; and African Americans, 132, 239; and Civil Rights Act of 1957, 131-132; and Civil Rights Act of 1964, 133; and civil rights acts, 131; and democracy, 213; and women, 239, 750-754

Voting Rights Act of 1965, 147, 738; and jury system, 409

Voting Rights Act of 1970, 735

Waco, Texas, and Branch Davidians, 277

Wade, Ben, 620

Wage discrimination, 293

Wagner Act. *See* National Labor Relations Act (NLRA)

Wallace, George, 132, 487; and election of 1968, 495

War; and armed forces, 43-44, 47; and conscientious objection, 164, 166; and espionage, 264; and foreign relations, 301-302; free speech during, 264; and national budgets, 278-279; power to declare, 158; protests against, 104; and treason, 709

War crimes, **739-741**, 794; and political crime, 530

War of 1812; federal policies during, 671; martial law during, 469

War on Poverty, 218, 252, 341; and grassroots politics, 341

War Powers Resolution of 1973, 561

War Revenue Act (1919), 629

Ward system, 101

Wardens, prison, 574

Warren, Charles, 577

Warren, Earl, 82, 123, 146, 676; and incorporation doctrine, 289; and segregation, 643

Warsaw Pact, 44

Wartime; and martial law, 468; military justice during, 478

Washington, George, 241, 646; and attorney general, U.S., 51; first administration, 175; and presidency, 557; and term limits, 693; and veto power, 725

Washington State, term limits in, 694-695

Water Quality and Solid Waste Disposal Act (1965), 376

Watergate scandal, 53, 226, 356-357, 495, 516, 527-529, 532, **741-745**, 794; and Gray, L. Patrick, III, 275; and media attention, 225

Watt, James, 611

Waxman, Henry, 344

Webster, William, 275

Weeks v. United States (1914), 640

Welch, James N., 463

Weld, William, 269

Welfare, **745-749**; and Clinton, Bill, 218; and Social Security, 655, 658

Welfare liberalism, 453

Welfare state, 167, 794; and Republican Party, 168

Whalen v. Roe (1977), 582

Whig Party; political campaigns, 517-519, 563; and Republican Party, 620; and slavery, 654

Whistle-blower, 1, 794

White flight, 69

White House tapes, 356

Whitewater affair, 536

Whitewater scandal, 741

WIC. *See* Women, Infants, and Children Program

Wickersham, George, 275

Wilder, Douglas, 20

Wildlife; and environmental protection, 257; refuges, 376

Wiley, Harvey, 299

Wilkie, Wendell, 623

Willard, Frances, 758

Wills, **749-750**, 794

Wilson, Pete, 759

Wilson, Woodrow, 550, 558, 622; election of 1912, 243; election of 1916, 243; and filibuster Senators, 296; and political science, 549

Wiretapping, illegal, 356

Wirz, Henri, 739

Wisconsin v. Mitchell (1993), 318

Wisconsin v. Yoder (1972), 637

Witness, 794

Wolf v. Colorado (1949), due process and, 228

Woman suffrage, 214, 238, **750-754**, 794; and democracy, 215; movement, 105, 547; and Progressive movement, 498

Woman's Rights Convention, 753

Women; and military conscription, 476; and political representation, 548

Women clergy, and Equal Rights Amendment, 260

Women in politics, 327, 329-331, **754-760**; First Ladies and, 330

Women, Infants, and Children Program (WIC), 759

Women's Bill of Rights (1967), 292

Women's rights; and equal protection of the law, 258; and veterans' preferences, 723

Women's studies, and feminism, 292

Worcester v. Georgia (1832), 29

Works Progress Administration (WPA), 217, 747

World Anti-Slavery Convention, 752

World Bank, and United States, 387

World Court. *See* International Court of Justice

World Trade Center bombing, 700-701

World War I; and commerce regulation, 151; and consumer movement, 180; and Espionage Act, 264; espionage during, 80; and Federal Bureau of Investigation, 275; freedom of speech during, 311; and income tax, 379; military conscription during, 475; and national debt, 279; U.S. entry into, 296, 558; veterans, 331, 722; and woman suffrage movement, 754

World War II; and commerce regulation, 152; and consumer movement, 181; Demobilization after, 331-332; and espionage, 264; and federal immigration laws, 353; freedom of speech during, 313; and Germany, 47; and income tax, 379; Japanese American internment during, 92; martial law during, 469; and national

debt, 279; Office of Strategic Services during, 266; Supreme Court, U.S., during, 58; veterans, 331, 333, 724; and war crimes, 530, 740
WPA. *See* Works Progress Administration
Wright, Fanny, 752

Wright, Jim, 544
Wyoming, term limits in, 694-695
Wyoming Territory, woman suffrage in, 214, 737, 754

Yates v. United States (1957), 314
"Year of the woman," 760

Yom Kippur War, 245
Yosemite Valley, 256
Young Americans for Freedom, 494

Zero-sum, 794
Zoning, 427-428; laws, 587